THE MYSTIC MANAGER

THE MYSTIC MANAGER

▼

John P. Cicero, PhD

iUniverse, Inc.
Bloomington

The Mystic Manager

iUniverse books may be ordered through booksellers or by contacting:

iUniverse
1663 Liberty Drive
Bloomington, IN 47403
www.iuniverse.com
1-800-Authors (1-800-288-4677)

ISBN: 978-1-4401-7248-9 (sc)
ISBN: 978-1-4401-7249-6 (ebk)

Printed in the United States of America

iUniverse rev. date: 05/31/2011

DEDICATION

This book is dedicated to my son, Michael. More than anyone else I have met, he follows the Mystic Management principles not because he read this manuscript but because that is who he is.

It is also dedicated to my wife and editor, Christina. She forced me to produce something beyond anything I could have managed on my own. And our marriage survived her relentless scrutiny. My only regret is I had to give up at least fifty ellipses and settle for mere commas and periods.

PREFACE

The Mystic Manager is a vision on many levels. Its stated goal is to offer a unique approach to the development of positive corporate culture. Its higher purpose, however, is to create change in the world of business and help prevent us from destroying our planet through shortsightedness and greed.

I teach in the business department at the local community college. I have made it a personal mission to heighten my students' awareness of how greed and a basic lack of ethics is pointing us to global and irreversible disaster in just a few lifetimes from now. After our classroom discussions, however, I am always left with the big elephant in the room. How can one possibly generate enough positive change to stop such a massive machine of vested interests moving toward imminent destruction? How can one change the dynamics of an economic system that by its very nature leads to the elimination of every species on Earth including man?

I woke up from a nap the other day with a great epiphany. If one were to convert *The Mystic Manager* into pure thought and allow it to leak into the collective global consciousness, maybe it could, by its very existence, be a tipping point for positive change. And I believe it's doing that, quietly and peacefully. The true intent of this book is beyond language and beyond the simply rational. It is a gift of spirit intended to raise awareness and instill a sense of urgency to do the right thing. As its author I am simply the book's messenger.

John P. Cicero
October 16, 2010

CONTENTS

PART III

UNION

PART I

THE PRINCIPLES OF MYSTIC MANAGEMENT

Chapter 1

▼

THE GOVERNOR'S CLUB

Jack dashed from the elevator, ran outside, hailed a cab and hoped he'd be on time for once. He was meeting Sam, his former college roommate, for lunch. The restaurant was the kind of place CEOs and college professors frequented and sometimes normal folk. It was typical: walnut panels, coffered ceiling, thick carpet, and little vases with the flower of the day trying to survive until the dinner hour when it would be replaced with the evening flower and squat oil lamp. The city could have been anywhere from New York to Seattle or maybe even Rome to Istanbul. It really doesn't matter. Now, the conversation Jack is about to have with his buddy and fellow CEO, Sam, now that matters.

Jack entered the foyer of the restaurant with casual confidence, like he hadn't rushed to get there almost on time. Sam, on-time-Sam, attention-to-detail-Sam, and almost-never-wrong-Sam was sitting at their usual table eyeing his drink like he had just come down from upstairs to see if his guest had arrived yet.

"Hey, Jack! I took the liberty of drinking your martini, ordered you another and put in for today's special, some kind of swordfish garnished and blackened, a parsley sprig, six potatoes all in a row, seaweed garnished with chopped rosemary, and a partridge in a pear tree."

3

"In other words, a bacon blue cheese burger with steak fries and a gin and tonic on the side."

"How did you know? You have become clairvoyant, a seer, perhaps a shaman?"

"Not yet but that's kind of what I wanted to talk to you about, Sam. Since you claim to be all-knowing perhaps you could help this mere mortal sift the truth from the baloney. I've heard some interesting things of late. I, actually we, have been invited to participate in an extraordinary management seminar. It's only $10,000 for four hours."

Sam almost choked on his drink and blurted out, "$10,000 for a half day, are you nuts and whadda you mean *we*?"

"Nuts, maybe, but here's the skinny. It seems there are these two guys running around proposing a whole new management theory. From what I hear it's a self-actualizing experience, one of those make-you-feel-tingly-all-over insights."

"I doubt if it's a whole new management theory, and as far as feeling tingly all over, I seriously doubt if a management seminar would do it."

"You're such a slime."

"And proud of it. Seems those professorial types keep changing the names of things and feeding us the same old same old and for a lot less than $2,500 an hour I might add! You know the drill: *quality circles* in 1960, *total quality management* in 1990, and today it's *managing the white space*. Same old same old. And this one is so different, how?"

"I never said they were professorial types ... but are you ready for a laugh? Their new theory is called Mystic Management."

"Oh, well then, we had better get right on it! I definitely want to be an early adopter. Maybe I'll even put a dry ice pond in my office to enhance that ethereal effect when I'm trying to woo some client into a several million dollar deal. Perhaps a new age quartet in the background and, what the hell, let's do the whole thing naked! I can understand you coming to me for advice over the years because I am smarter than you, but, Jack, you should be able to figure this one out for yourself, don't you think? Now, what did you really want to talk about?"

"That's one thing I have always loved about you, Sam, your open-mindedness. You never go off just because something sounds stupid."

"Oh my God, you're serious. You want to discuss our attending a seminar on Mystic Management at a mere $10,000 for half a day. Is lunch provided or is that extra? I know, the seminar is in beautiful New Zealand at a secluded resort and airfare is included. I've got it, you get a leather briefcase with a crystal ball inside that plugs into the USB port of your laptop and predicts ... well, everything! I know, free phone sex to take your mind off the fact that your business is failing because you are an idiot for spending untold thousands on useless seminars!"

"My initial reaction exactly, except for that last part. I am a devoted husband and father; I choose suicide instead of phone sex."

"Bad choice, but typical of you. Now, what's this really about?"

"A Mystic Management seminar coming up next Thursday morning at the Governor's Club."

"Okay, I'll eat my bacon blue cheese burger and you talk."

"Well, it all started with this simple flyer that came across my desk the other day. Usually the junk mail is screened out, but, somehow this one made it to my in-basket. All it said was *Mystic Management – Want To Know More? Go to MysticManagement.com*. As the flyer headed for the trash, I found myself typing in the URL just for the heck of it. I was in the mood for a good laugh.

"Before I could peruse the site the phone rang. It was Susan Marks. You remember Susan; she was the one even smarter than you. Well, Susan starts talking about this management seminar she attended last week and how she's a changed woman. I immediately explained how it was too late; I was happily married. She said that thing she used to tell you, you know about the last woman on Earth stranded on a desert island? Anyway, she told me to shut up and listen; this was serious. She proceeded to tick off a list of attendees. Very impressive; sounded like a *Fortune 500* lunch club. Not everybody was a CEO, but everybody who attended held a position of responsibility in a heads-up company. There were only a couple of names I didn't recognize. Trust me, the list was impressive. So then she starts to tell me the seminar was entitled *Mystic Management: A Call for Prophets Not Profits*."

"Isn't that a bit of an oxymoron at $10,000 a half day?"

"You promised to eat and be quiet. By the way, lunch with the presenters is included. To be honest my initial reaction wasn't much more positive than yours. I told her I thought her brain had fused and was just an inert lump of carbon lodged between her ears. I also told her I thought there would be significant replacements in the *Fortune 500* this coming year, no doubt as a result of Mystic Management fallout. I could see the headlines: "Mystic managers evaporate and are replaced by cyborgs." She again told me to shut up and listen.

"So she ticked off the list of participants for the second time, only more slowly so I couldn't miss how impressive the list really was. She wanted to know if I thought it possible that they were all nuts or that just maybe something important was happening. Okay, fifteen or so of the smartest execs I know of probably didn't experience instant group insanity. But $10,000 for four hours still had me at a distance. How's your cheeseburger?"

"Wondrous; you still have the hots for her, don't you?"

"Please, just listen and stop with the smartass remarks. So, Susan with the perfect breasts ..."

"Especially in that black suit thing designed by the transsexual from Clarmont."

"Will you stop it, this is serious. How's your cheeseburger? Oh, I already asked that."

"All right Jack, spill it."

"Well, Susan, like I was saying, said she was a changed woman and as a direct result of this four-hour seminar. She said the Mystic Management seminar was a bargain at twice the price. That would make it $5,000 per hour! So, Sam, Susan is a bright woman, actually the brightest exec we know. You have to admit that. And she's in the company of fourteen other bright execs. And she swears they all feel exactly the way she does. She said she would be happy to send me a paper on *The Principles of Mystic Management;* and while she thought the principles themselves would probably appeal to an enlightened fellow like myself, she did not think I would find them either unique or worth $10,000 just seeing them on paper. She absolutely insisted that sitting in the seminar with Phillip and Christian Hansen, the father and son team who came up with the principles, changes your life. Something happens; something connects.

"Susan said she would personally give me $10,000 if I didn't think four hours with the Hansens was a transformational, life altering experience. And she fondly spoke of you and made the same offer."

"You're serious."

"Absolutely."

"Fine, next Thursday then at the Governor's Club. Your cheeseburger is getting cold."

Chapter 2

▼

REFLECTIONS ON MYSTIC MANAGEMENT

Today Koy Sosa is interviewing Phillip and Christian Hansen, the dynamic father and son duo who are capturing the global management scene with a new management paradigm called Mystic Management. When she first heard the term "Mystic Management" she thought it a bit hokey; actually, inappropriate if the Hansens wanted to be taken seriously. However, as unlikely as it may seem, CEOs all over the world are listening and corporations are taking decisive and positive action based on the Hansens' high-minded ideals and Mystic Management principles.

"Let me see, I've got a newsclip on Mystic Management somewhere in this mess. Ah, here it is."

At the Hyatt Hotel in Irvine, California, one hundred corporate chief executive officers from more than twenty countries gathered today to begin a three-day workshop on Mystic Management. This is the second in a series of seminars and workshops; the first was a brief half-day seminar where the CEOs met in small groups at various locations around the country and around the world. While the introductory seminars have been offered to small groups for approximately the past year, today's follow-up workshop is a much larger forum where the execs can share their experiences following their initial exposure to the

Principles of Mystic Management. The workshop leaders are noted psychologist Phillip Hansen and his son Christian Hansen, CEO of Used Water Works, Inc., the company making environmental history in Death Valley, California.

The workshop is not about productivity, continuous quality, customer service, technology, coping with change, or increased profits. The workshop is about community building, humanizing the corporate environment, self-esteem, sustainability, and a vision of "prophets not profits." The workshop revolves around the six tenets of what the Hansens call "Mystic Management." There are six basic principles: Collaborative Creativity, Ego Empowerment, Gentle Generosity, Karmic Kindness, Inclusive Integrity, and Systems Sensitivity.

With so many high-powered CEOs listening we may be on the verge of a new blueprint for business and world economics based on compassion instead of dollars. Expect to hear a lot more from this dynamic father-and-son duo.

Koy shouted to herself, "Yes, you'll be hearing a lot more from them and from me, Koy Sosa, star reporter!" She giggled in childlike excitement. Her bright red dress danced around her slim waist and ebony calves as she bounded out of her apartment toward the elevator. She was meeting the Hansens in exactly twenty minutes for a very early breakfast. After breakfast she is invited to accompany them to the Governor's Club for a half-day seminar with fifteen or so local top execs.

"Dynamic duo is right," she thought. "Four CEO seminars last month, seven lectures this month, that big to-do in Irvine, and today, inviting me to a breakfast interview and a $10,000 seminar – me, Koy Sosa, unknown reporter. And lunch at The Governor's Club after the seminar, life is good. I knew sleeping with Sam Simpson would pay off some day; now Sam and Jack, there's a pair. I haven't seen Sam in ages; I don't think I'll ever get over that 'boy' and when he's ready I'll be there to reel him in. Of course, that may not be in this lifetime. Anyway, it was really nice of him to set this up for me. I can't believe that after Sam signed up for the seminar, he gave Phillip Hansen a call asking if he would be interested in a little free publicity, that he knew a really dynamite reporter. Evidently Phillip thought that was a grand idea and, so, I'm on my way. I'm so excited I could just bust!"

Koy arrived at the restaurant exactly on time and had no trouble spotting Phillip and Christian. "They look just like they described themselves," Koy said to herself. "Well, of course they look like themselves. God, I must be nervous." She approached the two men, hand extended, "Hi, I'm Koy Sosa. It's truly a pleasure to meet you."

"You come highly recommended and we're delighted."

They had barely exchanged amenities and Koy got right to work. "I brought this newsclip about your seminar in Irvine last month. While it mentions the six tenets of Mystic Management, it doesn't tell me anything about them. Perhaps defining the principles would be a good starting place?"

Both men nodded in agreement, genuinely tickled by her enthusiasm. They took an instant liking to her.

Koy, armed with her steno pad, suggested, "I guess starting with the first principle of Mystic Management, Collaborative Creativity, makes sense. What, exactly, do you mean by Collaborative Creativity?"

Phillip began, "I'm glad you're planning to attend the seminar this morning. I think you'll probably get more detail than you bargained for. But I agree that basic definitions over breakfast are a good starting place. We're smiling because we have good feelings about you; your positive attitude says it all. You can be sure that we'll give you all the time and information you need to feel totally comfortable with Mystic Management. However, you might want to slow down and relax just a tad."

Koy smiled back confessing, "This is my first interview of this type. I've spent my whole career, all ten years of it, reporting financial statistics. I am a wreck. Thanks for trying to make me feel more comfortable. You know, I'm not such a dunce that I haven't read up on Mystic Management before getting here. What I'm looking for, though, is the principles in your own words, personally, from you to me. I've got the facts; I can probably quote you more statistics on Mystic Management than you'd want to hear. For example, how many seminars there have been, who the participants were, where they were from, the companies represented, and so on and so on. I really want to hear it from you.

Maybe I can give Mystic Management a new twist, something really special, something really personal."

Christian leaned forward and said, "There is absolutely no doubt you will make it special and we appreciate that. So, Dad, in a sentence, what is Collaborative Creativity?"

Phillip responded without hesitation. "I see it as the ability to listen to and to respect all ideas, remaining open and trying to use at least one new idea in some form in every decision scenario. It is placing value on creativity for its own sake."

"That's two sentences," said Christian.

"And I like both of them," responded Koy. "How about a couple more, only this time on Ego Empowerment."

"That's my personal favorite," said Christian. "Ego Empowerment allows people to achieve goals without beating it out of them. I tell you where I'm trying to go and let you figure out how to best get there. It's a fundamental team concept. The trick is to let go of the parenting attitude, the 'I know how to do it best' attitude, the 'mine is the only way' attitude, and probably a hundred other counterproductive attitudes. This one takes a big chunk of positive self-esteem to pull off.

"Interestingly enough this is a principle that women are innately better at. By nature or certainly by socialization women are more process oriented. They really believe it's 'how you play the game that counts.' Of course, when I say 'they' I mean that big group in the middle of the bell curve. There are always exceptions. For example, Dad and I are very good at this one and you've probably noticed that we're both men."

"You're really cheating," said Koy. "That's at least half a dozen sentences."

"He's like that," chimed in Phillip.

"So, who's going to take a crack at Gentle Generosity, and under two pages please," Koy enthusiastically interjected.

"I've got this one in a nutshell," said Phillip. "It's going the extra step to encourage; it's being compassionate. Compassion is a cornerstone of Mystic Management. Without compassion the rest doesn't matter."

"I can appreciate that," said Koy. "And, Karmic Kindness?"

Christian and Phillip put arms on each other's shoulders and orated in unison, "What goes around comes around, and kindness is the better way; compassion, compassion, compassion."

"You've got my vote," laughed Koy. "Okay, two more to go. We can do it. Who's going to field Inclusive Integrity?"

"Two words," said Phillip, "value diversity."

"And before you ask," volunteered Christian, "Systems Sensitivity suggests that all of the principles are related to each other and become an integral part of the organizations within which they are practiced. Fundamental to producing global change, the impact of those principles extends beyond the corporate climate and into the environments those organizations touch, both individually and collectively. How's that for a mouthful?"

"Thank you," said Koy. "Now I can spend the rest of my day trying to figure out what, exactly, that means and hopefully giving some journalistic life to the Mystic Management principles, and maybe even in terms the average manager can understand. You guys are bit much at breakfast."

The waiter sheepishly stood by, trying to break into the conversation. "Would anyone care for anything else?"

Koy put one finger up and smiled, holding the waiter off a moment longer. "One last thing, how did you come up with Mystic Management; how was it born?" Koy looked at the waiter and said, "I'm just rude, you were asking if we wanted anything else. Nothing for me, thanks."

There was a simultaneous, "No thank you, I'm stuffed," from Phillip and Christian.

Koy said to the waiter, "I'll take the check, please. Then, turning back to Phillip and Christian, "So, where was I? Oh, yes, one last thing before we head out, how did you come up with Mystic Management? How was it born?"

With a definitely mischievous gleam in his eye Phillip said softly, "It's not how Mystic Management was born; not how, but where." Christian nodded in agreement and added his own mischievous smile.

Before Koy could pursue the "where" issue, Phillip and Christian had slipped out of the booth and were almost out the door, waving over their shoulders.

"Thanks for breakfast, we'll see you in a few at the Governor's Club," hollered Phillip.

She paid the check, mumbling to herself, "What's the big mystery? I would think one place is as good as another for an idea to be born."

As she turned to leave, the sun shone through the window, its rays momentarily catching a pink-tinted glass vase next to the cash register, turning the restaurant's interior a beautiful pink. Koy was startled by a brief otherworld sensation and shook herself as if out of a sleep as she walked toward the door and headed for the Club, kind of wondering why the Hansens hadn't waited for her. About then she heard some guy yelling from the back of a taxi, "Hey, beautiful, want to share a cab?" It took her a second to realize that it was Sam. For just another second she entertained the idea that the Hansens knew Sam would be pulling up to whisk her away.

"Sam! How cool of you. I just finished breakfast with the Hansens. If the rest of the morning is half as impressive, well, I don't know where this could go. Being with those two men has a special quality about it."

"Oh my, and I was kind of hoping ... "

"Will you stop; you know my heart belongs to you, Sam. It always will, even though I left you for that two-year assignment overseas. But I think those Hansen fellows have captured something else and when I figure out what it is I'll write it down and you can read my story. And, by the way, I don't know how you convinced Phillip to include me in today's seminar but I will be forever grateful."

"Ah, now we are getting somewhere."

"So, how's Jack?"

"Insane, I think, and to protect him I agreed to come along today. I still think he's nuts and I'm more so for going along with this $10,000 seminar thing."

"Actually, Sam, I think you're going to get your money's worth. I have a very good feeling about this."

"We'll see. I will let you know what I think over lunch. Well, we're here; let's find out what the dynamic duo has to say."

In spite of his propensity for being late, Jack was already there when Sam and Koy walked in. "Sam, Koy! Good to see you guys, especially you, Koy. Did Sam tell you he thinks I'm nuts for agreeing to this seminar thing with the Hansens?"

"I think 'nuts' was his exact word. God, Jack, it's been forever. How's the family?"

"Fantastic actually. I am trying to be a role model for Sam but it's not working. He is still afraid of getting 'hooked' as he calls it. Perhaps you can work him over a little and try to convince him that intimacy is only as bad as you make it."

"Only as bad as you make it? Now what's that supposed to mean? Your poor wife. Actually, poor is not a good choice of words. I saw that she settled that medical fraud case for about $20 million."

"Yeah, that was quite something. She is a constant source of amazement: good-looking, smart, and thinks Sam here needs to grow up."

"Wow, she is smart."

"Okay, you two, I, Sam Simpson, promise to turn over a new leaf starting today, actually tonight. Koy, will you have an intimate dinner with me and then sex at my place?"

"You're so disgusting, but I would consider having that intimate dinner without sex. And then we could see where it goes from there."

"Yeah, hopefully not you going overseas like last time."

"God, some things never change," said Jack as he meandered toward the seminar room.

Koy found the seminar mesmerizing. Sam and Jack had no interest in asking Susan Marks to reimbursement them, as she had offered to do if they didn't think it was worth the price. They both found it everything she claimed and worth every penny; a bargain at twice the price. The three were so inspired they each declared a need to go their separate ways after lunch to let the morning simmer. They had to let the seminar settle throughout their beings: mind, body, and soul. Something had happened; something had connected.

It turned out that both Phillip and Christian were top-notch speakers. Each presented scenarios exemplifying the six principles of Mystic Management. Father and son played off each other brilliantly, mixing roles of professor, straight man, executive, and counselor as if blending the perfect mental meal. The conceptual plate was tasty and intellectually filling. Koy stuffed both her head and her steno pad with the Hansens' delicacies. Sitting alone in her apartment later that day, she began trying to put the seminar experience into words suitable for newsprint.

About that same time Phillip and Christian's plane lifted into the sky for the ride to their next seminar destination.

"Well Dad, do you think we gave Koy what she was looking for today?"

"She got a lot more than she bargained for," was Phillip's immediate response. "When she begins to transcribe her notes she'll discover there are a lot of feelings and perceptions that are going to be hard to put into words. Her experience as a statistical business reporter is about to be challenged. Whatever she comes up with will have to be grounded more in faith than fact. I wish I could be a fly on the wall as she tries to make perfect sense out of our managerial artscape. Somehow she'll do it though, I sensed that from the moment we met her."

"I couldn't agree more," added Christian.

Father and son gave each other a gentle high five and settled into the task of plane-riding.

* * * * *

Arms waving in the air and black hair trying to jump over her ears, Koy exclaimed, "I can't believe it! I listened to this Mystic Management stuff just this morning. It made perfect sense at the time. Now, as I look at my notes and scan my memory, I'm not so sure what's fact and what's wishful thinking. Making logical sense out of all this is useless. It sounds too theoretical, too pie-in-the-sky, too ivory-tower even for the ivory tower. I think I need to sit back, have a cup of tea and try to capture the essence of what was said, and to get back in touch with what I was feeling in that seminar room. Boy, something was going on in that room, something way beyond the words. The Hansens elicited an unbounded trust from me, total belief in what they were saying. And I know that it was the same for all of the participants; hell, Sam did not make one wisecrack and Jack didn't doze off once! There's no rational way to account for what went on. I mean, I have a real penchant for the facts, the numbers. I am a show-me reporter. They showed me all right; I'm just not sure what it was they showed me."

Koy spent the next several hours going over her notes, again and again. She spent the next several days putting to paper what she had heard and, more importantly, what she had felt. Her article on Mystic Management came out as a special report about two weeks after her encounter with Phillip and Christian. It was immediately picked up by the Associated Press and found its way into every major newspaper in the country as did Koy Sosa, star reporter.

* * * * *

REFLECTIONS ON MYSTIC MANAGEMENT
(unabridged draft)
by
Koy Sosa

It had the appearance of a normal day for this reporter as I headed to an early breakfast meeting with Phillip and Christian Hansen, proponents of a management theory they call Mystic Management. I sensed almost immediately upon meeting Phillip and Christian that the day would be anything but normal. After our breakfast conversation I attended a four-hour seminar entitled, *Mystic Management: A Call for Prophets, Not Profits.* By the end I sensed the whole business world might soon be anything but normal. Phillip, noted psychologist and author, and his son Christian, CEO of Used Water Works, are advocates for a management philosophy that can only be dreamed of in this competitive and ever-changing global business environment. It would be fair to say that a spirituality underlies Mystic Management. It is compassionate, a quality sorely lacking in what most of us have experienced as "business." The Hansens are uncompromising in their ideals, asking, "Should we hold generally accepted business practices as sacred and become further immersed in the post-*Future Shock* clutter or should we hold high ideals as sacred in the hope of rising out of the clutter?" Their high ideals revolve around the six Principles of Mystic Management: (1) Collaborative Creativity, (2) Ego Empowerment, (3) Gentle Generosity, (4) Karmic Kindness, (5) Inclusive Integrity, and (6) Systems Sensitivity.

Fifteen paying top executives and I, guest of the Hansens, attended the seminar at the Governor's Club; a seminar that, by the way, cost $10,000 for four hours! Right away, you know something's going on. The people on the list of attendees give away absolutely nothing and certainly not $10,000 just to hear the same old same old.

Phillip opened the seminar with a discussion of his perceptions of the real world. Sensing his audience's skepticism, he wanted to set the stage for the Principles of Mystic Management: principles that fit into the real world of global business principles that can and should be applied to every business enterprise.

In Phillip's own words, "No matter where I have been or what work I have been engaged in, someone has always been quick to point out that the real world is someplace else. If you think back, you have probably had a similar experience. Consider this: I have over forty years of varied work experience. However, according to many, none of those experiences qualify as real-world encounters. I have been a college professor and administrator; a middle manager for a *Fortune 500* company; a consultant to business, education, and government; a sole proprietor; an artist; a psychologist; and today a seminar co-leader advocating something called Mystic Management. If none of my experiences qualify as real-world, I can't even imagine how challenging the real world must be and how brave the souls must be who claim to have traversed its hard-knocks topography.

"As a younger man, when the opinions of others influenced me more, I left a very comfortable faculty position specifically to gain some experience in that real world that everybody was talking about. Thirsting for reality and significance, I entered the corporate milieu. I thought that I might better serve my students with some real-world experience behind me. I could justify temporarily giving up what I loved, teaching, in order to someday go back to the classroom minus the stigma of never having worked in the real world.

"I wasn't on that new corporate job a week before someone made it very clear that the real world was in a different part of the corporation! It definitely was not where I was. It was in some other department, some other function in some other building.

"It's fascinating how people are always pointing out where the real world is. And, of course, it's never where you are; or at least it has never been where I am, especially now as 'The Father of Mystic Management.' I wonder if other 'fathers' had this kind of trouble? Charles Babbage, 'The Father of the Computer,' or, perhaps, Frederick Taylor, 'The Father of Scientific Management,' or Elton Mayo, 'The Father of the Human Relations Movement,' or Christian here, my son, the father of his two lovely daughters, Bridget and Samantha.

"In any event, the real world is always someplace else, someplace where others are or have purportedly been. At the very least, they know intimately someone who's in the real world right now, as we speak. If you're in training, the real action is in sales. If you're in sales, the real action is in some other company. And if you're in sales in that other company, then the action is someplace else altogether, and I know a guy who ....

"The implication is always that the real world, a place where I never seem to be, is somehow harder;

tougher; more demanding, dangerous, elite; faster; showier; more exciting, more dramatic, and clearly out of my reach. And, of course, when I was younger the real world was even more elusive. Just ask my son Christian here.

"The result is uncomfortable at best. Our identity and self-esteem suffer in this quest for the elusive real world. The desire to belong, to be a part of some defined special community, the desire to be relevant, distorts our view of our present individual reality. Our world collapses into cloudy confusion. In this confusion much time and energy are spent trying to rid ourselves of the inner 'shoulds' and 'I'm not good enoughs.' In this quest for inner growth we often become detached from our own reality, whatever that reality is (i.e. college student, teacher, administrator, manager, artist, psychologist, or Mystic Management proponent).

"Indeed, our individual present moments, the only real world we have, slip right past us and we watch; we watch as if spectators at our own lives.

"This is a game for which the price of admission is too high. I would profess that wherever you are is real enough. After over forty years of working in jobs deemed non-real-world by others, I still can't tell the difference in realness between the stresses of tomorrow's mid-term examination, tomorrow's neurotic patient, tomorrow's art show, tomorrow's planning report, tomorrow's cash flow, or for that matter today's lecture on Mystic Management which I was thinking about yesterday.

"You are the 'they' I refer to. As CEOs you can, I am sure, claim title to the real world. We can be sure that you are in the real world. You can also be assured that I am in the real world. In fact, by virtue of your spending $10,000 to be here this morning, it is possible that I am in the real world and you have been deluded. This could be the Enron of management seminars. Regardless, as it has been so aptly pointed out, 'Wherever you go, there you are.' And here we are; you're here, I'm here, Christian is here, and the Principles of Mystic Management are here. We are all real and will be even more real by noon today. I promise."

Phillip moved immediately to the first Principle of Mystic Management, Collaborative Creativity. He worked in a bit of reverse psychology stating, "While creativity may be good for the arts, it's definitely bad for business. I'm sure we agree that the last thing anybody wants is creative assembly line workers or robots as the case may be. I suspect each product would be a little different, a few would work as planned, now and then one would work exceptionally well, and many would fail altogether. This would be all too wishy-washy for achieving effective and efficient resource management. Random excellence is not a sought after commodity. And of course this makes perfect sense. Who'd risk it? Somehow, though, the assembly line mentality has come to define the totality of the workplace, making it unbendingly consistent, within specification, controllable, predictable, and uninvitingly inhuman and mechanistic. Machines need not be creative and the assembly lines building those machines need not be creative either. On the other hand, that first assembly line was immensely creative, based on the idea of interchangeability of parts, another immensely creative idea. And together those innovations changed the course of industrialization."

In my own words, this reporter sees Collaborative Creativity, the first tenet of Mystic Management, not as resistant to mechanization and robotics, but resistant to the mechanization of the human spirit and the treating of people as robots. Unless our plan is to totally remove the human element from the workplace, we might want to turn our attention toward dealing with people as the vibrant, creative, and unique beings that we are. Collaborative Creativity respects the creative genius, the creative spirit and refuses to squash it in the name of consistency or profit or any other productivity axiom. And this creativity is collaborative, team-built.

Again in Phillip's words, "I'm not suggesting we haven't accomplished great things as a society. Wasn't putting three men on the moon and bringing them back a wonderfully creative idea, wasn't it magnificent? The idea officially took shape with the conception of the Apollo Program and informal discussions around a table in early 1959. The idea officially came to fruition ten years later with the first extraterrestrial landing, a landing on Earth's moon in July of 1969! Not long after that, the stack of paperwork supporting a manned space mission stood taller than the Saturn V Rocket used for that first moon landing. This is the typical way of organizations. Ideas begin and grow as scattered creative germs and ultimately evolve into carefully documented diseases. It's the natural order of things to move from simple to complex. One strain of the organizational disease is bureaucracy. We've all been exposed to bureaucracy and most of us don't like the symptoms. Like most cures, the vaccine must be formulated from the original germ. In this case bureaucracy must be infected with the germ of an idea, a creative germ. Collaborative Creativity is that germ and is fueled by the energy flaring out from the human aura as individuals create. To create is to allow passage into the next dimension of doing business. To create is to breathe new life into the going concern."

Pressed for more detail, Phillip and Christian shared their view of Collaborative Creativity as a new business ethic. Like Plato on Ethics, the Hansens on Collaborative Creativity would prefer creativity for its own sake, because it is right action. They will, however, in the name of practicality settle for an organization embracing creativity because it will ultimately strengthen the bottom line. Regardless of the motive the pursuit of creativity should become a new dimension of corporate social responsibility.

To close the discussion of Collaborative Creativity, Christian cited his company, Used Water Works, as an example of the collaboratively creative process. The company is in the water recycling business and their logo is a complex of water pipes with the words "Used Water *WORKS* for Mankind" cleverly worked into the design. The company name and logo were outcomes of a collaborative effort, a brainstorming session involving employees at all levels within the organization. The key was cooperation and the recognition and consideration of all ideas. Collaborative Creativity does not happen in a vacuum.

This reporter is not oblivious to the serious practical objections to the notion of Collaborative Creativity, and for that matter, to all of the Mystic tenets. High ideals appear to have high price tags. However, the Hansens showed that anything less than high ideals would be more expensive in the long run. There is no future and no profit in shortsightedness.

The essence of the second Principle of Mystic Management, Ego Empowerment, deals with how one might manage a collaboratively creative organization. One cannot effectively manage creativity from a position of authority. "I am the boss and you will be creative." I don't think so. A more workable approach is, "We are a team, this is our goal, let's find a way to reach that goal."

Ego Empowerment demands keeping one's ego in check in order to empower others. Christian opened this section of the lecture with the following statement, "Ego Empowerment is the oxymoron in the new paradigm of collaborative management *weltanschauung*." It was wonderful. He looked intently at his audience and then at his father who simply shrugged and threw up his hands.

Phillip moved to the front of the stage and pretend-whispered to the participants, "I should have known better than to bring my son with me, he has an MBA you know. What he's trying to say is that even though Ego Empowerment is a bit of a contradiction in terms, it fits the model of quality or team management. And *weltanschauung*, well, you'll have to ask him. Surely in a publish-or-parish environment, poor Christian would perish; actually he might perish right here, right here in the real world."

"Now that's unfair," quipped Christian. "*Weltanschauung* gives us a global flavor and, besides, it fits right in. It does, after all, mean a comprehensive philosophy of the world and mystical contemplation."

"That certainly clears it up. We should have named our new paradigm Weltanschauung Management. It seems to me we are having enough trouble with the word *mystic*. Nonetheless you can be credited with using the words *empowerment, oxymoron, paradigm, collaborative,* and, of course *weltanschauung* all in a single sentence. Very impressive."

"You know, that's not very ego empowering."

By this time the participants were chuckling and getting the idea. How often are we put down simply because what we've come up with seems different, kind of silly? How often on the other hand does someone take the time to help reshape our silliness into something dynamic and powerful? Empowering others is tricky business. As Christian so aptly put it, "You have to be willing to accept, appreciate, reshape, and recreate; and all with no expectation of personal gain."

This reporter recognizes the apple pie sound of this. Moreover, it is hard to argue against empowering others without being perceived as a troll. I think that's why many CEOs have gone along with empowerment as a part of a quality management strategy only to wake up in the middle of the night in a cold sweat at the thought of actually allowing their employees to make critical decisions. Often CEOs become leery of too much delegation. To alleviate their concern, they minimize delegation, push the organization structure into a steep pyramid, and adhere to only those parts of quality management that deal with continuous improvement and customer service. They simply revoke empowerment, the employee enhancing part of a quality organization culture. It's that proverbial "throwing out the baby with the bath water." Without employee empowerment as the cornerstone, there's nothing new in quality management. Well, that's not exactly true, there is statistical process control, benchmarking, reengineering, managing the white space, ISO 12000, and the Malcomb Baldridge Award. These are formal constructs that can be added to the strategic plan to benchmark progress. Empowerment remains the challenge that company executives simply can't handle. Empowerment demands something bigger than big business, and so the next Mystic Management Principle, Gentle Generosity, takes shape.

According to Phillip, "Empowerment is something we do; it's an action verb. Gentle Generosity is something we are; it's a personal quality. It's the quality that allows us to empower *and* feel comfortable with that decision. It's freeing up our own insecurities while at the same time going the extra step to encourage others. It's compassionate."

While Gentle Generosity looks like a very desirable trait, Christian asks the interesting question, "Who would more likely be associated with a Gentle Generosity, Attila the Hun or Winnie the Pooh? And as President/CEO of your company, with whom would you rather be compared, Attila or Pooh? The Hun is a fighter, warrior, and conqueror. Pooh Bear is fat, yellow, and occasionally gets his head stuck in a honey jar. Which image would be most likely to enhance the bottom line and maintain the confidence of your Board of Directors and your stockholders? We all know that nice people finish last; being liked is unimportant. Good executives need to be self-strokers with no need for reinforcement or encouragement from outside themselves. And herein lies a problem: self-stroking causes hierarchical schizophrenia, a disease of organizational position. As one moves up the organizational ladder he or she should seek council only from those at a higher organizational level. When one finally reaches the top one may seek advice only from oneself. Hence the adage: "It's lonely at the top." Oh yes, and here is where the schizophrenia sets in; one is forced to interact with oneself with regard to all sides of an issue. This clearly demands more than one personality. Hierarchical schizophrenia is the number one killer of Collaborative Creativity and crippler of Ego Empowerment. A Gentle Generosity in spite of its Pooh image is the only known cure."

Listening to Christian advise an audience made up primarily of CEOs to give up Attila the Warrior for Winnie the Pooh was quite something. It was truly a call to high ideals. Simply put, teamwork and collaboration are not warrior tools, they are the sum and substance of process orientation, encompassing not only the ability but also the need to interact with other individuals at all levels of the organization. Gentle Generosity is a win-win strategy that impacts the bottom line in a positive way and can, therefore, draw confidence from boards, stockholders, and other company stakeholders. The trait itself, to have Gentle Generosity, starts to move into the spiritual realm of Mystic Management and foretells its next principle, Karmic Kindness.

So far in the discussion, Mystic Management espouses creativity practically gone wild, dangerously empowering others to maintain that creativity, and, of all things, calling upon Winnie the Pooh as our role model. How is it that a group of high powered executives at the Governor's Club, spending $10,000 for a half-day seminar, have not stormed the podium and strangled Phillip and Christian on the spot for business blasphemy? How is it that they are paying attention to what is being said and sensing it's right action? This reporter was there, and what was happening at the Governor's Club on a Thursday morning was perplexing. Christian's explanation was couched in something he referred to as "a hole in reality."

After a particularly pointed series of questions about the first three principles and how they're "nice, but," Christian threw his hands up and yelled, "Stop! Allow me to frame the concepts we are talking about in a totally different context, a context that may allow you to get your experiences and intellects out of the way. Let me tell you a story.

"There are three significant types of holes in the universe: black holes that absorb everything; white holes that absorb nothing; and holes in reality, which I will explain. One typical Friday is when I first suspected that holes in reality actually existed. Some days are just strange in their happenings and I remember this one clearly.

"First thing that fateful Friday morning my wife dropped the glass coffeepot on the ceramic tile kitchen floor where it shattered into countless pieces. Upon arriving at work a bit later, the first fellow I spoke with related that he had barely bumped the glass shower doors enclosing his tub and they fell out of their tracks cracking into countless pieces upon the bathroom floor. When I arrived at the secretary's desk, I overheard her explaining how a stone had hit her car's windshield on the way to work, leaving countless pieces of glass literally hanging from the rubber moldings. The sliding glass door in another gentleman's study had apparently exploded for no reason at all He said it was as if the door were hit by an invisible bullet; there was simply a loud bang! The door splintered from the center out, leaving countless pieces of the safety glass in the frame like a glass puzzle. All day it seemed as though people everywhere were breaking drinking glasses, dropping dishes, knocking over knickknacks and, in every imaginable way, ridding the Earth of many objects made of glass. Why?

"I think this phenomenon has to do with physical reality being an illusion. This is not an idea original with me. For example, statements from renowned physicists suggest that the next level of physics will be achieved through meditation. Some preliminary proof rests in the fact that no atomic particle, the very building block of physical reality, had ever been discovered until after someone suggested that it was there.

"And so we come to the idea of holes in reality. On a given Friday an inordinate amount of glass is breaking for no apparent reason. There is more glass broken than sheer probability can account for. If physical reality is nothing more than illusion and if physics might advance through meditation, might not meditation be the key to all that broken glass? After all, meditation is doing for the cosmos today what the CB radio did for the freeways of America in the late 1970s. *Om* is the *breaker 19* of the meditative world.

"Anyway, back to the hole in reality. Assume that the cosmic mind is always awake, always pulsating. The vibration is always there. Have you ever wondered why? I think the force behind this constant vibration has to do with monks and I think monks have to do with the hole in reality.

"Have you ever stopped to think about how anachronistic monks who meditate behind cloistered walls really are? In a high tech world, what is their purpose? For that matter, what has their purpose ever been? I think I know. I think that chanting, meditating monks keep us connected to the Cosmic Consciousness. I think chanting, meditating monks generate the minimum acceptable levels of vibration necessary to create and maintain the illusion of physical reality.

"On a Friday morning, one of the monks must have fallen asleep while meditating. Perhaps, just perhaps, that particular monk was in charge of glass-reality. And then, just like that, poof, all that broken glass. A hole in reality."

"On this Thursday morning at the Governor's Club, the monk in charge of the traditional principles of management has fallen asleep and, just like that, poof, all those classic principles of management, gone. A hole in reality. The Principles of Mystic Management fill that hole in reality and you will just have to deal with it best you can until lunch. And your $10,000 checks are on the back table. You can pick them up on your way out if you have any doubts about what we are proposing and its promise of a sustained future."

Without so much as a breath between words, Christian immediately launched into the fourth principle of Mystic Management. "Karmic Kindness is the antithesis of the *no pain, no gain* philosophy. What goes around comes around and kindness is the better way. There is a wonderful bumper sticker out there that says "Mean People Suck." So do mean managers. Then there's the bumper sticker that takes it a step further "Commit Random Acts of Kindness." Sometimes I think we should stop reading management books and simply check out bumper stickers. My contribution to the world of bumper stickers deals with paradigm shifts, "Shift Happens." And Mystic Management is that shift.

My reporter-self compelled me to look up the definitions of both karmic and kindness. "Karmic" from the Hindu or Buddhist refers to the total effect of one's conduct during the successive phases of his or her existence. Karma has to do with destiny and having to come back and do it right should we mess it up while we're here this time. Then there is kindness. "Kind" takes up almost a whole page in my dictionary. To be kind is to be friendly, generous, warm-hearted in nature, sympathetic, understanding, charitable, humane, considerate, forbearing, tolerant, generous, giving, agreeable, beneficial, and natural, and, of course, compassionate. Now there is a powerful word, I had no idea.

Christian and Phillip stood close to each other and spoke in unison, "Karmic Kindness is the soul of the corporation. Each job you hold is a lifetime and each act of kindness in each of those jobs takes you closer to your destiny. And your destiny, whether you choose to attend to it or not, is community building and sustainability; it is equality and oneness with all those around you; it is love." The two men focused on their audience and stood silent for a full three minutes. They said nothing with their voices. The audience rejoiced in the silence and also said nothing with their voices.

It was the most intense audience participation I have ever experienced and yet not a word was exchanged. I could not fathom how they did it. The two men, father and son, standing together proposing love as a principle of management was mesmerizing and, on the surface, totally ridiculous. There was far more going on than met the eye. The lecture hall took on an otherworldly aura. The sun-filtered light coming through the trees and through the tinted glass of the seminar room windows turned the entire scene a subtle but definite pink. I have struggled for two weeks with how to write this segment without appearing ridiculous myself. The bottom line is that I've finally concluded that it is unimportant how ridiculous I might seem. What's important is the message, and I have communicated it the best way I know how. Each of us perceives our reality somewhat differently. And it is in these differences that we come to the fifth tenet of Mystic Management, Inclusive Integrity.

Christian took the lead here, "Inclusive Integrity acknowledges differences; it is diversity personified, a celebration of diversity, and this celebration is not always a natural tendency. Typically, the more like us another is on the surface, the more likely we are to accept him or her. It's the "I'm okay, I'm okay" philosophy. The less difference between us the better. This behavior leads to the establishment of exclusive organizations. For example, there are Irish, Catholics, and, of course Irish-Catholics. There are Italians, Americans, and Italian-Americans. Once I even heard about a club of Irish-Catholic-Americans. Let's see, African-American, Hispanic, and I think it's Hispanic not from Spain or Puerto Rico or Mexico but only from South America. Then of course there's Jewish, but if they're from Israel or New York City, well, they're different. And there's Hansen, not to be confused with Hanson, son of Hans. This has all the trappings of a market segmentation strategy. We might as well be discussing Chevrolet, Pontiac, Oldsmobile, Buick, and Cadillac; or Wrangler, Levis, and Calvin Klein, or maybe even Scott and whatever the quilted one is. We can't possibly be talking about human beings. Then again, if I'm a Buick and you're a Buick, that's good. If I'm a Buick and you're either a Chevrolet or a Cadillac, that's bad. We're all GM but we look different and we handle differently. The fact that all three can get us from San Diego to Seattle via the interstate is irrelevant."

Christian continued without falling through thin ice as he skated upon and around his audience's values. He did manage to make his point; he concluded by citing the all too common examples of employee performance being evaluated on how closely the job resembled the way the supervisor would do it, rather than on whether or not the objectives were met. His closing comment on Inclusive Integrity was, "To accept diversity is not enough and to value it is only a beginning."

The final tenet of Mystic Management is Systems Sensitivity. This is the synergy and synchronicity of it all. This tenet is the glue, the matrix, the connectedness of any one thing to all things. It's the feedback loop, the reinforcer.

This reporter left the half-day $10,000 seminar with a different view of what might be possible for corporate America. This reporter left Phillip and Christian Hansen's talk with a different feeling about business, a distinctly non-statistical, untested, spiritually motivated, and hopeful future, a compassionate future. Not one participant picked up his or her check on the way out. Shift happens.

CHAPTER 3

▼

THE ROCK SHOP PROSPECTOR

There were times when Phillip Hansen found himself quite amusing. He was not always the serious professional running all over the globe with his son Christian, giving seminars and workshops on Mystic Management. This was one of those times. It was early May, about 6:30 p.m., and already dark. With the lights on and the drapes open Phillip could see his reflection in the study window of that old Waterford, Virginia, house. The specter-like figure in the window was about five-eight (five-eight and one-half to be exact), and more thin than fat (except around the sixtyish waist, sixty years that is). Phillip was not exactly handsome, but not too bad either, nor graying too much. All in all he was a pretty average looking fellow. Suddenly, it was as if he had caught the giggles from his window-pane-divided reflection, and he just stood there laughing out loud along with the image in the window. He couldn't help himself as he thought about how horribly civilized he was and unaccustomed to such outbursts.

On this particular May evening he was hidden away in his beautifully appointed study over the garage, doing one of his favorite things, attending to his rock and mineral collection. He had been thinking about labeling a newly acquired specimen when he was so rudely interrupted by his window image. This particular specimen was a puffy-looking apophyllite from India and a gift from his wife Jo.

Phillip and Jo had a very unusual relationship; it worked. Phillip took time out from his apophyllite labeling to actively think about her for a moment or two. Actually, as so often happened, she was probably thinking about him at that exact moment and the two joined thoughts. He sensed her broad smile, blue eyes, and fiery red hair. He pictured her reaching for the top shelf of the kitchen cabinet to fetch something he himself was unable to reach without a chair. It's not that she was inordinately tall at her five eight or he short, they were just screwed together differently. Jo was blessed with long arms, fingers, and legs all set neatly around slender hips and long waist. Phillip, on the other hand, had a lower center of gravity, perhaps more grounded, but less agile and stretchable. She was turbocharged and he had four-wheel drive. Together they could go anywhere and do anything. Phillip often thought about writing a scholarly treatise on *The Influence of Physical Size on Martial Bliss*. He doubted his colleagues would ever get past the sexual connotations.

As his psyche returned to his Waterford study and the task at hand, he placed the apophyllite specimen gently on the big rolltop desk so as not to damage the desk or the rock. It would be hard to say which would be the greater travesty. The potential risk of damaging a prized possession was somehow exciting in lieu of rafting a river or bungee jumping off a bridge. It added an adrenaline rush to the objectively mundane. Or maybe it was Phillip's daydreaming into the nooks and crannies of the Earth that added the element of excitement. Where was this apophyllite found hiding? Was it in a small cavity in a mountainside? Did the discoverer have to dangle precariously from a rope on the side of some sheer cliff? What act of superhuman courage and adventure did it take to unearth this puffy looking thing so it might come under the scrutinous eye of Phillip Hansen?

Phillip began laughing aloud once again as he rolled a piece of paper into his almost antique IBM Selectric II typewriter and typed the number 462 within one-quarter of an inch from the top of the page. He then semi-yanked the paper out of the typewriter, risking tearing the paper and probably destroying some inner working of the machine. He couldn't help himself; he liked the sound of the gears trying to resist his pull, a minor pleasure impossible to achieve with a computer. Still holding the extracted paper with the number typed on it, he reached into one of the desk's many cubbyholes and foraged out a handheld, single-hole paper punch. Grasping paper and punch he leaned toward the lamp and, sticking the paper in the bright light under the shade so he could see the pica-sized 462 at the top, he carefully placed the punch over the number and squeezed. With a crisp snap the tiny disengaged disk of paper with the number 462 on it fluttered to the floor trying to hide from Phillip's determination to find it. Phillip's amusement at himself heightened as he imagined how he must look crawling about the study floor searching for a circle of paper about five-sixteenths of an inch in diameter. "Let's see, at $10,000 for four hours of my time, this little circle of paper is going to owe me quite a sum if it continues trying to escape. Good grief! If those CEOs could see me now, they'd ask just what principle of Mystic Management *this* is."

Chuckling mightily at himself, Phillip cavalierly licked the pointer finger of his left hand and adeptly placed the finally-captured disk on the wet tip, number up. Balancing the circle on his finger, he searched his giant desk for the Duco Cement. Securing the twisted, half-empty tube in his free hand, he raised it to his mouth and, between his front top and bottom teeth, grasped the head of the small finishing nail stuck in the aluminum tube neck. In one quick motion he pulled out the nail like a grenade pin, pinched the bottom of the tube, and aimed the oozing glue at the exposed underbelly of his new rock. With pinpoint accuracy he dropped a minuscule glob of glue into one of the apophyllite's topographical anomalies big enough to inconspicuously absorb the circumference of the numbered disk. And then, like a plate juggler, Phillip flipped the tiny circle off his almost dry fingertip and splashed the blank side down into the Duco pool.

It was about here that his amusement with himself peaked. And no wonder. In his other life Phillip Hansen was one of the country's leading psychologists and was respected as a pillar of sanity and stability in what he viewed as a world economic society in trouble. Before the Mystic Management hullabaloo Phillip rested somewhere between social psychologist and industrial psychologist. His teaching, research, and writing fell primarily in the social realm; his income was generated more in the industrial area. Somehow his mental meanderings about social systems had caught the fancy of the private sector. The corporate giants were sure Phillip could come up with the perfect strategy for motivating and empowering the masses (lowly employees) to increase efficiency, job satisfaction, and profit margins all at the same time. It seems his very presence had a positive impact. And Phillip knew why. It had to do with Eyespell. It still has to do with Eyespell.

To finish labeling his rock, Phillip pushed at the numbered circle with the glue-crusted eraser end of a #2 pencil, making sure to apply just the right amount of pressure with the Ticonderoga. When he was satisfied that the label and rock were one, he smiled a smile of accomplishment, and escorted his new prize toward the lighted curio cabinet in the far corner of the room. He stopped short of his destination and spent a moment taking in the splendor of the various crystals, metallics, and colorfully crusted bits of the Earth reflecting the directed rays of the high intensity lamp recessed into the inside top of the cabinet. Phillip finally moved those last steps to the cabinet, and carefully opened the glass door, trying not to shake the more delicate specimens from their Lucite perches. He reached in and gently placed specimen 462 in a location of honor at the very front of the second-from-the-top glass shelf.

There was just one more thing to do before settling into the often practiced routine of touching, sensing the vibration, and reminiscing about pieces of the collection in the curio cabinet. Phillip first needed to attend to the accountant-like task of entering the information about the apophyllite into his database. He had learned over the years that if such information was not recorded almost immediately, valuable tidbits were invariably lost, lost forever. He backed toward the computer table, still drinking in the images of his collection and, at the last possible moment, turned to begin his data entry task. The computer, humming in obedient readiness, displayed not the database he expected but an old paper he had written many years ago as a fledgling Assistant Professor at the university.

"Now what's this doing here? I remember this; oh dear, and I remember the lecture it got me from the dean when I posted it on my office door. I still think I'm right, so there. I see I still have that spark of rebellion, if more tempered; tempered is a good word for older, wiser, and more sophisticated. God I'm funny tonight! Let's see, how did this go?

The Parable of the Wheel

In a kingdom called Academia, there lived a populace ascendingly cast into Lecs (Lecturers), Assfessors (Assistant Professors), Socfessors (Associate Professors), and Old Farts (Full Professors). The Old Farts ruled and said it was good. The rest said nothing. And it was good.

A merchant brought a wheel down from the mountain one day for the Old Farts to spin upon. They liked it. For a week they spun upon it most of the day and sometimes, far into the night.

More time passed, and the Old Farts decided it was not good in Academia. They were the only ones spinning. So, to keep the kingdom good, they slowly drew the Socfessors, Assfessors, and Lecs to the spokes and rim of the wheel, keeping only the hub for themselves.

God looked down upon Academia and decreed that it was selfish of the Old Farts to hoard the activity-of-the-hub (known as the hubbub). So, God created a huge wind. In the wind's fury, the wheel began to wobble, and everyone came crashing to the ground, landing on their behinds.

God, in his mercy, allowed the Old Farts to continue to rule Academia from what they landed on. And they are continuing to do so to this day.

"Now that's hysterical," thought Phillip, "considering I now qualify as an old fart. I wonder if I'm like that? I remember how I really disliked the know-it-all attitude of some of the older faculty members. In fact I hated the university games in general. It wasn't just the old guys, some of my peers were incorrigible. I wonder if that other thing I wrote is in here? Something about "bigger is better"; no, no, that's not it; "mine's bigger," no; ah, I've got it, "mine's longer." Okay computer, do your thing and search for "mine's longer." Whoa, that was quick. Let's see here. Oh, I remember this; I was having apoplexy about the relevance of education." He started to read.

The most serious error thwarting ethical educational leadership is that educators take themselves and their credentials much too seriously. They all too often lack the ability to laugh at themselves. It seems that the all-too-serious attitude of the sometimes pipe-smoking, patched-sleeved, academician is counterproductive.

I once read a story about these two newly introduced professors at a meeting openly sparring about whose credentials were better. In fact, the introductions opened with that nauseating question, "What's your degree in? And where did you go to school? And when did you graduate? With honors?" As the sparring between the two was drawing to a close, the chap who seemed to be losing the battle, in a classic statement, stood upon the conference room table and simply peed all over the other guy. The poor guy so hideously christened literally started dissolving and cackling something about, "And what methodology did you use to statistically verify the null hypothesis?" The scenario ends with everyone leaving the room careful not to step on the pile of empty clothes, all that remained of a once smart fellow.

This leaves the sanity of educators in question. There is, also, a certain legacy with numerous idiotic concepts that education carries forth. For example, one might consider fertility in ancient Greek drama, chimneys as phallic symbols, or, perhaps, the untold problems Gulliver caused by relieving himself in Lilliput! There are LIFO and FIFO, the twin brothers, raised by wolves, who discovered Rome. There is the marginal utility of a loaf of bread, if you've already eaten one. And, there's the distinction between aggressive and assertive behaviors, both of which will get you in trouble with the arresting officer.

The fact that students actually pay tuition for their own torment is an amazement to me. They pay educators to assign some of the most boring reading in the world. Over time, students read thousands of pages of it. And then, one of those academic types might whip out an obscure quotation and demand the author, the work, the genre, and ultimately, the relationship of the quotation to the mating behavior of French bread.

What kind of legacy is this to carry forth? The bottom line is that without all that education we probably wouldn't have the critical thinking ability to know the difference. We wouldn't know as we passed through life how bad some of it really was, and how good other parts were, and how desperately education needs changing. The good and the not-so-good in education are all part of who we are and who we are not. It is simply a part of our identity.

"My, my, Dr. Hansen, aren't we a bit angsty. And today it's the brilliant Phillip and Christian Hansen espousing the Principles of Mystic Management. Sometimes I think the mating behavior of French bread would be an easier sell. Oh please, give it a rest and get back to what you were doing. I want to talk some more with that funny fellow in the windowpanes. Oh wondrous computer, find my mineral database and spare me any more of my ramblings as a younger man. Poof! There we go, let's see number 462."

After entering all the technical data such as specimen name, origin, size, color, and so on, Phillip finally came to the memo field of the database. This is where he would tell the story of the specimen. This final part of the meticulous and mundane recording task was fun and creative.

For Specimen 462, Phillip began writing, "It was no special occasion at all. I came in from the garage mumbling something about how I'm the only one who ever empties the trash around here. Jo was standing in the kitchen with that smile she gets when she's up to something."

That up-to-something smile always made Phillip uncomfortable because it invariably meant he would probably have to think about doing something fun, something not on his agenda for the day. Don't misunderstand, he always loved her ideas; that is, afterward. In fact, she is personally responsible for ninety percent of his fondest earthly memories. But, at the moment of inception he almost always found her ideas unsettling to his routine. There are two kinds of people, those whose initial reaction is "yes" and those who need to think about it. As one of the latter, Phillip automatically says "no" to most things in order to give himself some time to become grounded in whatever the new twist is going to be. Four-wheel drive.

He continued the entry writing. "I took one look at her and blurted out, 'No way, I'm not even slightly interested in whatever it is.' "

" Okay," she said, "if you don't want it."

"What do you mean, want it?"

And so it was that she pulled a little sack from behind her back and said, "You look like you need a rock."

And so it was that he came to possess the magnificent apophyllite. Number 462 will always hold a special place in his heart. He could feel Jo's vibration when he touched the stone. It was the only turbocharged apophyllite on the planet. Phillip finished the memo field of his database and leaned back in his castered chair to review his fun-with-himself evening.

Phillip had been a rock hound for years. However, he hated being designated a "rock hound" in spite of his having amassed a collection both striking and valuable. He had a basic knowledge of geology and was an expert of sorts on the history of mines and mining around the world. Phillip would be the first to admit that he could get lost in some of the most objectively boring reading about old mines and prospecting. In his reverie he could sometimes almost feel the hairs on his mule's back as he imagined climbing menacing switchbacks in the High Sierra or searching the parched desert for some sign of nature's mineral wealth. He could almost feel the freezing cold or the burning heat tearing at his aching muscles, and all endured in anticipation of that one big strike! Phillip would become almost confused if the phone rang or an airplane jetted overhead reminding him that it was not 1860, and that he was not prospecting, except perhaps in some of the finest rock shops in the country. And it was that line of thinking that got him to laughing at himself again on that May evening. He was the civilized Dr. Phillip Hansen, "the rock shop prospector."

In all honesty Phillip didn't do all of his collecting in rock shops. He was actually in the field a few times. He loved being back off the main drag where it was often silent and beautiful. These times brought memories to Phillip that fused his very soul with the earth he was standing on. These experiences were nothing short of awesome, the kind of inner dimensional experience that makes one lose one's balance, almost.

Phillip refocused on the new specimen in his curio cabinet, apophyllite from India, number 462. His hand then almost unconsciously reached into the still open door of the curio cabinet and emerged with a flat polished sheet of purple lepidolite interspersed with pink tourmalines.

He was drawn to the pastel-colored specimens, especially the pinks. They spoke to his soul of another time and another place.

Phillip ran the palm of his hand along the smooth surface of the lepidolite. He smiled as he recalled that day at The Collector in Fallbrook, California. Fallbrook was just outside of San Diego. Phillip had read about it in one or another of his books. This was California tourmaline country. There were mines everywhere, the Pala Chief, the Tourmaline Queen, and the Himalaya to name a few. Of course Phillip was looking not for a mine but for The Collector, a rock shop. The Collector turned out to be more than just a rock shop; it was owned by the Pala Mine and afforded him a special opportunity. This was Phillip's chance to collect tourmalines "in the field." The proprietress brought him huge drawers filled with rough tourmaline crystals to rummage through. With Phillip's imagination at work it was irrelevant that he was comfortably seated in a leather chair, leaning over a beautiful oak and glass table. Phillip was "in the field." His journey through the boxes of tourmaline was no less perilous than Indiana Jones' in "The Temple of Doom." The Collector proved to be the highlight of one of those marvelous vacations with Jo and their son Christian.

Christian was in his teens at the time, and his fondest memory of The Collector was seeing his father as childlike, excited as he picked through those boxes of tourmaline. It was, perhaps, the first time he saw his father for who he really was. Or it might have been one of the few times his father made it possible for Christian to "see." The memory of sharing his true self with his son was important to Phillip. Moreover, Christian's insight from that memory was somehow a catalyst that made all things possible for him later in life as he would champion a new paradigm for a new world. The exact words of their interaction rang through Phillip's consciousness.

"So, Dad, what are you doing? You've got a really silly look on your face."

"I am searching for tourmalines and it's hard to see in the dense forest."

"But, Dad, you're sitting at a table in a well-lit room looking through some drawers."

"Am I?"

"What do you mean?"

"I am doing exactly what I've created in my head. And if my mind is searching for tourmalines about a hundred and fifty years ago on this very spot, then that's my reality. You ought to see it. It feels like summer. The forest is dense and the sun is peaking through the trees. As I look down, the ground is shimmering with colorful rays as the sunlight bounces off tourmaline crystals scattered on the ground virtually everywhere. It's absolutely magnificent. Would you like to join me?"

"Why not."

"Create it in your head and it will be. Sit beside me here in the forest and let's search together."

Christian Hansen was a lot like both his father and his mother, a blend of the best of each. He stood six-feet-two-inches tall and had a self-concept to match, not unbounded ego, just a healthy self perception. And he was not average looking, but downright handsome. There was an interesting aura about him. His demeanor was unassuming and friendly. There was no need to draw attention to himself, not yet.

Phillip started to laugh again as the psychologist in him caught the errors of his free associating with his curio cabinet "friends." Everything was just as he remembered it, except that the slab of lepidolite sparking the reverie about Christian was not from The Collector at all. That particular piece of lepidolite was purchased at The Comstock Rock Shop in Virginia City, Nevada, and some three years after the wonderful experience at The Collector. It always fascinated Phillip how the "feeling mind" has no regard for linear time.

He unconsciously reached into the confines of the curio cabinet once again, this time pulling out a substantial chunk of rose quartz. He just smiled at it as if it were an old friend. "This piece of quartz was not purchased in any rock shop," thought Phillip. "No sir, this piece of rose quartz comes directly from the local pet store." The rock shop prospector had stooped to a new low. While looking for some aquarium gravel, Phillip had happened upon a large chunk of rose quartz. The shopkeeper told him just to take it, he had no idea what it was or where it came from. How unusual.

Unusual in more ways than one. Not only did Phillip have no idea where it came from, whenever he held the smooth yet indented and striated pastel pink rock in his hands, a pink world floating in a star-bespeckled galaxy far from the feeling of Earth entered his consciousness. This time was no exception. Phillip Hansen's hands clung to the rock as his mind soared beyond the confines of the study in that old Waterford house. He focused on that beautiful pink planet beneath two suns and four moons, the planet he knew was home.

CHAPTER 4

▼

WATERFORD

The phone rang, interrupting Phillip's otherworld experience. He jumped, startled that pink could be so loud. Sight and sound were fused to a point of distraction so intense he just stood there trying to make the ringing stop. The pink began to clear and he recognized the sound as the mellow ringing of his digital telephone. He approached the phone with caution, not yet totally sure of himself. Finally his brain returned to its earthly location and he answered the phone, chuckling at his confusion over such a complex task, "Hi, Phillip here."

"Hi Phillip, this is Koy Sosa; hope I'm not interrupting anything. You sound a bit distant."

"Distant would be a good word for it but I'm back and I'm all ears."

"All ears on the phone, is that a pun?"

"Probably, I'm having a very amusing evening with myself. So, are you here?"

"Yep, I made it from Dulles to Leesburg all by myself; I just need to know how to get to Waterford from here and to that mystic house of yours."

"How about if you stay right where you are and Jo and I will come get you. We'll have dinner out and after dinner Jo can ride back to the house with you in your car. It's a bit of a tricky drive the first time out, especially in the dark. And once you're settled in I promise to answer all of your questions. You are the honored guest of Phillip, Jo, and Eric Hansen. Eric's the dog. He will be waiting for us when we get home, and I promise you, barking his disapproval that we were gone too long. Friendly, but the let-me-lick-you-to-death-and-ruin-your-stockings type. By the way "Reflections on Mystic Management" was pretty impressive. I really think you got it. See you in about twenty minutes. Like Italian?"

"Italian's my favorite, and I was touched that you and Jo invited me to stay with you. I was just about to make a motel reservation when Jo called me yesterday."

"We wouldn't have it any other way. So, Bella Luna it is. It's right on King Street. You shouldn't have any trouble finding it."

"Okay Phillip, see you guys in a few; can't wait to meet Jo in person. Bye."

"Bye."

Just as Koy was putting the phone down she got a call from Sam. "Hey Sam, what's up?"

"I was wondering where you were staying tonight. Thought I'd get off early and join you for dinner."

"That would be great except I'm meeting the Hansens for dinner in just a few minutes and they invited me to stay over at their place. I was a little nervous about the prospect of staying with them but Jo, Phillip's wife, was so friendly on the phone I feel really okay with it."

"Well at least you're not heading overseas on assignment. I don't think I could stand losing track of you again."

"Does that mean we are seriously an item?"

"Yes, Ms. Sosa, that's exactly what it means."

"That's very cool. It almost makes me want to cancel with the Hansens."

"I don't think I believe that; you are a terrible liar."

"You're right. I can't wait to find out what Phillip thought of 'Reflections on Mystic Management.' I chatted briefly with him on the phone the day after it came out but we didn't really get a chance to talk a whole lot. That's when the idea of me coming to visit them in

Waterford came up. I have a very strange feeling that what happens with the Hansens this evening is going to be life changing."

"All joking aside that's really why I called you. I have had that very same feeling. Something life changing is about to happen. Something even more amazing than the seminar at the Governor's club or your article on Mystic Management. But more than that, I see us immersed in a future together."

"Is that a proposal?"

"On the phone, please. Even I have more couth than that. Call me tomorrow."

"Love ya, Sam, bye."

A bit moonstruck, Koy made her way to Bella Luna to meet Phillip and Jo. Koy and Jo turned out to be two peas in a pod: dinner was great and the conversation was non-stop, pleasant, and at times provocative. The after dinner ride to Waterford included seeing three deer and smelling the delicious scent of honeysuckle hanging in the misty early evening air. When they rounded the last turn and followed Phillip into the driveway, Koy could see that the Hansen house was a classic colonial, white with forest green shutters, a circular gravel drive, pink dogwoods and pink azaleas popping out of the landscape, and the family dog Eric, as promised, barking his welcome. The lamps at either end of the drive and the Malibu lights shining up through the trees and around the bushes gave the whole scene an otherworldly aura. Koy thought that the pink shading was familiar, kind of like the sun glinting off that vase in the restaurant and the windows in the seminar room at the Governor's Club. "How appropriate," Koy said softly to herself.

Jo hopped out of the car hoping in vain to stop Eric from licking Koy to death and said, " I should have warned you about Eric."

"That's okay, Phillip already did. I just love friendly dogs. What kind of dog is he anyway?"

"Best we can tell he is purebred mutt. He just showed up one morning and decided he lived here. Phillip over here wanted to name that cute thing Guido. But, he wants to name everything Guido: the dog, one of the cats, the bird, even the stuffed toy moose in the family room."

"You have a stuffed moose?"

"Well, yes, doesn't everybody?"

Phillip maneuvered his way between Eric and the ladies and held up one hand in a halting gesture. "Stop! I think Guido is a great name for a pet and, Jo, I find your unbending and emphatic *no way* exceedingly shortsighted, small-minded, and a disservice to the animal kingdom."

"What about the moose?" piped in Koy.

"Wow, I sense our intellectual-sounding conversation has been usurped by a stuffed moose. How sad," said Jo. "I think it's time to go inside, have coffee and cheesecake and let Phillip answer those burning questions you must have. How about it, off to see the moose. He's six-feet tall, by the way, and his name is Joseph."

The threesome settled into the family room couches. With the gas logs pretending to be real and Eric pretending to be human, and Joseph surveying the whole scene, everything seemed to be in order.

"I almost hate to spoil things by attending to business," said Koy, "but you promised me some exclusive stuff on the mystic Dr. Hansen."

"That I did and you shall have your fill. You ask, I'll answer, and then I'll tell you the real story behind Mystic Management, a story you will never print."

"Okay, I'll save that mystery for later. I have a sneaking suspicion, however, that I should have brought a lovely pink pad instead of this yellow one."

"Oh my, how perceptive," Phillip said with a smile and a twinkle.

That certainly didn't get past Koy. "Anyway," she began, "one of the things I have been asked over and over since my article on "Reflections" came out, is what do you think is the greatest stumbling block to getting people to listen to and buy into the Principles of Mystic Management? And before we're finished I'm going to get you to tell me about that pink stuff, Dr. Hansen."

"I'll ignore that, Ms. Sosa, and answer your stumbling block question. Plain and simple, fear of the unknown poses the biggest threat. The title, Mystic Management, scares people because they aren't sure what it means. One reason they're afraid of it is that they are pretty sure it means changing something and that's always perceived as trouble. Let me tell you a story about my son Christian to illustrate. In fact, I drafted an article awhile back but never did anything with it. It's in this pile of notes someplace. Ah, here it is. Sit back and relax and

I'll read it to you. It has a wonderful title: 'Never Call a Kid a Dirty Kookamonga.' Okay, here goes."

"Before you get started, does anybody need anything?" asked Jo. "Coffee, more cheesecake, maybe a Drambuie or Bailey's? No takers? Okay, but just holler if you need anything and Phillip will be happy to get it for us." Jo gave Phillip that devilish smile and sat back in her corner of the couch.

"I think I hear your mother calling," said Phillip with his own version of the devilish smile. "So, back to the Kookamonga Effect and our son Christian." He turned ever so slightly in the moose's direction and said, "Pay attention, Joseph, this is important."

I discovered the Kookamonga Effect early one spring morning. My son was sitting on the sidewalk in front of the house peacefully dismantling a bearded iris. He was about six years old at the time. Another youngster approached and, for no apparent reason, began calling my son names that reflected poorly upon his heritage and alluded to acts disgraceful and abusive committed by both him and his reputed parents.

Somewhat annoyed by the harsh and polluted consonant sounds, my son pulled slightly harder at the iris. Distraught at being ignored, the other youngster started to walk away. However, in a last-ditch, over-the-shoulder effort he yelled, "And besides that, you're a dirty kookamonga!" My son leapt from the sidewalk screaming, "I am not," and punched the other kid right on the top of the head.

I am ashamed to admit it, but evidently "dirty kookamonga" was the only unfamiliar phrase in the long list of insults thrown my son's way. Now, why do you suppose my son did not simply ask the other kid what a dirty kookamonga was? Why did he deem it necessary to react in anger and hit the other kid on top of the head with his fist?

And so my discovery of the Kookamonga Effect. The Kookamonga Effect is the inability to constructively deal with the unknown. We do not seem to have effective coping behaviors for handling anything unfamiliar.

When we are truly young enough and objectively ignorant enough, we might show curiosity rather than hostility toward foreign circumstances. However, by the time we learn even a few things, as we become more socialized, our innate coping mechanisms begin to deteriorate dramatically. We choose to distrust that which is not familiar and we develop a compulsive need to maintain the status quo.

We are plagued throughout our lives with this tendency toward non-acceptance of the unknown and aversion to change. Picture that same child twenty years later as a young executive. He is sitting behind his desk instead of on the sidewalk. He is peacefully dismantling a wooden elephant puzzle instead of a bearded iris. Someone says something annoying. He pulls harder at the elephant's leg. Someone says something not only annoying, but unfamiliar, something that he simply does not understand, something absolutely unknown to him.

The child-on-the-sidewalk awakens within the man and in a fit of anger he smashes his fist right on top of the desk.

Koy looked at Phillip and said, "Now that's a cute story, certainly none of the psychologist spilling out."

"Well, I am a psychologist by profession after all."

"So you're saying that a title like Mystic Management sparks the Kookamonga Effect in people."

"Exactly."

"Yeah, but really, the jump from bearded iris to elephant puzzle, what would Freud think?"

"Now you see, that kind of reasoning is troublesome. I'm not Freudian at all, I'm a Jungian type and my imagery of irises and elephants is correct by its very existence. I don't need to prove it or spend years in therapy trying to work out the penis part of it."

"So that's it then, the penis."

"Seems like Ms. Sosa has your number, my dear," interjected Jo. "Koy, I have been telling him the same thing for years; it's the penis thing."

"All right, you two, stop picking on me, I'm just a stupid guy who is changing the world of business with my Principles of Mystic Management. And I assure you there is nothing penile about them, overt or implied."

"Okay, okay, don't get your male ego in an uproar ala penis," said Jo. "Besides, we just don't want you to get a swelled head."

"No pun intended, I'm sure," said Phillip, giving the stuffed moose a sideways glance. "So, any more questions, Koy?"

"Actually yes, and you two had better behave; after all I'm company. I was thinking, you say you're not a Freudian type, but somewhere in my reading about you I saw an article about the ego, superego, and the id. Now, isn't that about as Freudian as it gets? I can't remember the title. Oh yes I do. It was in *Psychology Today* and it was called 'Joe Sent Me.' "

"Boy, you really have done your homework. That was a pretty interesting article if I do say so myself. But it was not Freudian and had nothing to do with Jo here. It had to do with Joe, not Jo. Not only wasn't the article Freudian, but I was actually trying to show how we can bypass all that Freudian stuff with a very simple visualization. 'Joe Sent Me' is an approach to getting rid of old psychological baggage, and its visualizations fall close to the tree of Jung not Freud. And, it's a perfect solution to the Kookamonga Effect to boot. I don't remember the exact wording of the article but I'm pretty sure that an understanding of both Joe and the Kookamonga Effect can go a long way toward helping gain acceptance for Mystic Management, an objective both you and I share. The Kookamonga Effect poses the problem and Joe demonstrates the solution, or at least one possible solution."

"So, how does the Joe thing work? I'm all ears," said Koy.

"Actually, Joe was dreamed up by of one my patients. And I mean literally dreamed up. My patient dreamed that this young man was thinking about committing suicide. In the dream the young man was leaning against an old walnut tree, feeling very sorry for himself and seriously thinking about suicide. And then this old codger came along and somehow talked him out of it. The ideas in the dream struck me as so provocative, yet simple, that my patient and I ended up coauthoring the article you read in *Psychology Today*. I know you've already read the article, but I can give you something truly unique. I can share his actual dream with you, the raw material from which the article was wrought."

"That would be really neat, what a new twist. By the way, this room is absolutely delightful and both of you are so welcoming. I feel like I've known you forever."

"Thanks, Jo is the decorator, and you probably have known us forever, you just don't remember. You're too young to remember."

"Phillip, leave the poor girl's mind alone and get on with your story. I'm curious, I don't think you've ever shared the original dream with me. I know about it of course, but we just never got to the exact details. How fun."

"Okay, it was a really cool dream. My patient said it started with this guy. His name was Antonio and he was seriously contemplating suicide. Just for the record, I am not violating any patient-doctor confidentiality. The whole story became public record after we collaborated on the article for *Psychology Today*. So, here's my patient's written account of how his dream went. This is the material from which we crafted the article."

Antonio was leaning against an old walnut tree not far from a rundown store just off the highway. He was on his lunch break. He was thirsty and hungry and had no money. "Today is Tuesday," he thought. "I get paid on Wednesday and I'll be able to eat well through Friday. Next week will be the same. What I really want is simply to die peacefully against this old tree."

Antonio's thoughts continued in the same vein for a long while. His existence had been harsh in almost every respect. He did not have a safe or pleasant childhood. While his parents loved him they felt guilty that in their poverty they could do almost nothing for him. Then all hope for his future seemed lost with the death of his mother. Antonio was sent to live with relatives. Image after image of despair and hopelessness passed through Antonio's brain.

Time shifted and he found himself left with his thoughts and still sitting under the old walnut tree, seriously contemplating taking his life. An old man, one hand on a finely turned yet simple walking stick, worked his way toward Antonio and perched over him like a curious bird, more like a vulture thinking about lunch.

"You know the problem, now, don't you son?" He cackled an old man cackle, slapped his knee and said, "Yep, that's it, son. Life's a bitch and then you die."

Antonio, unable to raise his head, whispered, "Why are you mocking me?"

"Well, son, it's simple, you need a new coping strategy. I don't suppose you ever read Dr. Freud, hey?"

Antonio laughed, almost, "It should be fairly obvious that I've never read much of anything!"

"Well, there you are then. Let me tell you a story about Dr. Freud and a guy named Joe. When I'm finished you'll be able to figure out why you feel so bad and how to get rid of all that negative mental baggage. Understand what I'm saying?"

"Not really, I just want to die, old man, go away and let me die."

"Well now, I can't do that. At least not until I tell you that story I promised. Anyway, this Dr. Freud says that the ego is the manager of the mind. And I happen to know that the ego watches the outside world from a control booth located directly behind your eyes. This ego character sees what you see and experiences what you experience. Unfortunately, he has nowhere to hide when you get feeling this bad about things. In fact, in your whole life, whenever you've been laughed at, rejected; or felt confused, ignored, not worthy, and not loved, this ego fellow has been expected to absorb all that pain and cope with it. He is expected to continue to manage your life effectively. Get my drift so far, son?"

"No, and you're holding up my death. Go away!"

"I already told you, I can't do that. Here's your problem. There's a relationship between all the hurt in your life and your inability to develop effective coping strategies. That is, strategies that will relieve the pain and allow you to go on with your life. Now, clearly, you've failed in this regard; you want to die. Anyway, not only aren't you coping, but you've also got this bag of psychological junk weighing you down. The bag is so heavy you can't even raise your head much less get up. So it looks like you'll just have to sit under this old walnut tree and die! Unless, unless you use Joe."

"Okay, old man, I can see you're not going to leave me to die until you have your say. So who's Joe? And make it the brief version so I can get on with my death."

"Well now, that's better, well sort of, part of it anyway. Okay then. It's not exactly *who* Joe is, but *what* Joe is. It's actually called 'Joe Sent Me,' and it's a strategy designed to keep the ego intact and in touch with your present moment, in touch with what's going on right now. Joe is designed to keep you from psychologically protecting yourself into continued illness by insisting on ineffective, outdated, coping strategies."

"What does that mean, old man?"

"Here's the way it works, Antonio. Each time you didn't effectively deal with your feelings about something, whether it was your mother dying or the fact that you're hungry, your ego, your mind manager, called on the Mind Team for help. Now the Mind Team is composed of two other fellows, the id and the superego. One thing is for sure, they are very reliable; they always answer the ego's call for help."

"Well that certainly cleared things up! You're quickly becoming one more reason I want to die, so could you get on with it and leave me alone."

"This is not a simple idea, Antonio. Stay with me here. So, the ego calls the Mind Team. Now, while the team is reliable and willing to help, their methods are indirect and secret. They travel deep within your psyche and make some secret deal, a secret trade-off, with somebody in there; we're not sure who, remember it's secret. But the ego doesn't care and agrees to live with the final outcome of the deal, whatever that may be. Bottom line, the ego gets instructions from the team about how to behave, how to cope, in order to survive a particularly bad moment in time. Now, mind you, the ego does not complain. Whatever coping strategy the team comes up with is okay with the ego. The alternatives to what the team comes up with, depending upon how bad the situation is, may be things like stress, a breakdown, insanity, or, like in your case, contemplation of suicide, the ultimate and final stress reducer.

"Now in the short run, the trade-off made with the team allows you to cope with the difficult situation. However, the trouble starts after years and years of secret trade-offs. The bottom line is that you end up stuck with all kinds of neurotic behaviors that were originally designed to help preserve your sanity. You can end up like you are now, against an old walnut tree, wishing death.

"The problem is that once the team makes a deal or trades something off, it never gets traded back. Even when a particular coping strategy outlives its usefulness, it doesn't automatically get traded back; you're stuck with it. Take you, for example, you've had nightmares forever and you just want them to stop, so suicide seems better than continuing the way you are. Your nightmares recount the time surrounding your mother's death and at that time in your life the nightmares actually helped preserve your sanity; they gave you something to focus on besides the reality of losing your mother. Now, today as you lean against this old tree, those same bad dreams are in the way, they are no longer useful. They essentially serve no purpose and you can't make them go away. Unfortunately, the ego cannot take the initiative to correct the situation because the ego never knew what was traded off in the first place. The ego has no idea that you traded nightmares for your inability to accept your mother's death, your inability to grieve effectively and healthily."

Antonio interrupted, "I see, I think I know what you mean. Say some kid is being laughed at all the time and it gets pretty painful. His team might make a trade-off and the kid starts wetting the bed instead of feeling the pain and going nuts. Is that it?"

"Exactly, my son, exactly! Now the problem created by the trade-off becomes serious when that same kid is still wetting the bed twenty years later and nobody knows why! There's no way the young adult will figure out the connection between bed-wetting and being laughed at as a kid. Maybe years of therapy, three times a week at $125 a pop might work. So, the kid could go through intensive psychotherapy or he could use 'Joe Sent Me.'

"For example, you don't need the nightmares anymore. I think you have appropriately grieved the death of your mother. That's not to say you don't miss her, think about her and so on, but a continuance of the nightmares about her death is useless; it's a leftover strategy; it's a trade-off that the team made that simply has not been traded back. I think Joe can help you get rid of those nightmares.

"Anyway, this is how Joe works. Although we have used your nightmares as an example, you normally would not have a conscious connection between your nightmares and trying to deal with your mother's death or anything else for that matter. Remember, you would not be aware of the connection between an inappropriate coping strategy and its root cause. For Joe to work all you have to do is understand that there are all kinds of inappropriate strategies still operating within your head, strategies that are the result of *psyche trade-off residue* or PTR as we pros call it."

"Good grief, old man, what's your thing anyway? PTR, like I care. I'm sorry I showed any interest. Let's go back to square one; you go away and I'll die."

"Okay, okay, just hear me out. What you've got to do is get your ego's attention. For example, visualize yourself experiencing a major psychological crisis."

"Oh, I get it now. Wanting to drop dead is not enough of a crisis for you?"

"No, no, that's not what I mean. You need to visualize a past crisis you have experienced, something really tough, something the ego will recognize. If you do this part right, your ego will immediately jump up from the chair in the control booth behind your eyes and start running around frantically inside your head waving its arms and yelling for the Mind Team. You have to convince your ego that you are totally unable to cope. Imagine that you are on the verge of a nervous breakdown."

"You're definitely pushing me further in that direction."

"Quiet and listen, we're almost there. In desperation, the ego runs as fast as it can toward the back of your head, looking for the Mind Team, searching for help. And then, smack! Visualize your ego slamming to an abrupt stop against a thick wooden door with a slide opening of prohibition-era ilk."

"This is great, old man. I won't have to commit suicide; you're fucking killing me! Prohibition-era ilk? Please."

"Just deal with this, Antonio; visualize your ego banging on the door with both fists as hard as it can. When they pull back the slide, and they will, say out loud 'Joe Sent Me.' You will not be allowed in the back room, but they'll ask, 'Yeah, so what, whad'ya want, buddy?' Then you say with total conviction, 'Joe said the deal's off! Trade back, now!' And, poof! No more nightmares. And that's how Joe works. You don't need to know the specifics. Just keep going back to the door; keep trading back until you start to feel better. And that's it. Now remember, the catalyst to get Joe working is to visualize a past crisis, one in which some unconscious trade had probably been made. You can't rely on present circumstances to get the ego to react and ask the Mind Team for help. For example, your death wish could not spur the ego into action because at this point you are too far gone and the ego just gives up. So, that's it, Antonio. Use Joe or have a lovely death."

"And that was the rather strangely detailed dream my patient had that we transformed into the *Psychology Today* article you read. My patient still puzzles over who the old man might have been. I see all kinds of people: executives, housewives, teachers, everybody running around with bagfuls of inappropriate strategies, especially when it comes to dealing with the unknown or anything perceived to be pushing one's personal envelope. And so it is with the Mystic Management thing. Fear of the unknown triggers ineffective coping strategies. I've heard them all with regard to what Christian and I are espousing: same old, same old; can't be done; it's impractical, costs too much; we've been in business for fifty years, why should we change; and so on and so on. It's a bunch of big people pulling on the elephant puzzle leg and wetting the bed trying desperately to make it all work out!"

"I get it," said Koy softly into Phillip's momentary frustration. "But you two, you and Christian, seem to be achieving incredible success in spite of fear of the unknown and inappropriate coping strategies to boot. Not once did you mention any of these things in that morning seminar I attended at the Governor's Club. You said nothing about fear of the unknown possibly stopping those executives from choosing the Mystic Management path. You didn't use any gestalt that I could see, Joe or any other. There were no visualizations. You and Christian talked and they listened. Not one person took you up on your offer to return the seminar fee if he or she felt the seminar was not worth it. You would think they would be eager to get their money back and run like hell. How is it that they continued to listen, almost mesmerized by what you and Christian were saying, even though all of it probably meant change to "prophets instead of profits"; a change for which they had no effective coping strategies? How did that happen?"

"Now, Koy, you have asked the right question. It's about Eyespell and the Eyespell connection and that is the story you will never print."

PART II

THE EYESPELL EXPERIMENT:
Eyespell, Earth, and the Emergence of
Mystic Management

CHAPTER 5

▼

THE RETURN TO EYESPELL

The pressure on his chest felt like an eighteen-wheeler coming to a crushing stop in the deep gravel of a runaway truck ramp. His head hurt so badly he couldn't tell if the pounding at his temples was causing double vision or if there were two suns in the desert sky. He remembered being hideously depressed, suicidal. He also remembered being in his dingy rented room in a small Northern California town. He knew it hadn't rained all month, and it was getting hotter by the day in preparation for another summer of drought.

Antonio, a young man of twenty, found his life in as much a drought as the parched lands of the Central Valley. As the lack of rainfall reduced the flowing Sacramento to a mere trickle, he hoped maybe his lifeblood too could be dried to a mere trickle and he would just die. He was an icon of hopelessness. He imagined himself withering to death in a walnut grove. He pictured being found with his back against the grafted stump of a walnut tree, his hands palms-down in the dry dirt, and his face expressionless. The cause of death would be a giving up, sort of like dying of an empty life. The headlines would read "Antonio Gomez Died Today and Nobody Cared, Especially Antonio." Antonio spent a great deal of time thinking about his death scenario. More than anything he wanted to die and be done with it.

As he stood in an unworldly desert and rubbed his grayish eyes with his cool, tanned fingers, his head began to clear and there were, indeed, two suns in the sky. One shone directly overhead in the familiar yellow noontime zenith and the other was due south, hanging low on the horizon, and an azure blue. The sand under his bare feet felt alive. The undulating dunes moved over the landscape breaking like waves in an excited sea. There were massive trees dotting what he thought of as a comfortably cool desert at what appeared to be high noon. Some trees had the appearance of old, massive oaks only brimming over with myriad colored leaves instead of the expected green foliage. Others approximated huge banyans with roots walking in all directions. They donned the same colored leafy display as the oaks only bigger. And still others appeared to be mangroves in the sand, each a different brilliant color. And they seemed "happy to see him."

His six-foot-three-inch frame tensed as he realized he stood stark naked with muscles rippling where, seemingly moments before, there were only the *meagerest* of biceps barely covering the bony frame of an undernourished field worker. Antonio was sure he wasn't dreaming; he was not afraid; and he was not depressed. He felt wonderfully at home and alive in this unfamiliar desert and unfamiliar body.

But, he clearly remembered fading out against that old walnut tree.

He pivoted in the sand to take better stock of his surroundings. The sand purposefully tickled his feet, the trees seemed to bend ever so slightly in his direction, and his shadow danced in all the wrong directions. Antonio marveled at the scene before him as the light caused shifts in shadow, shape, and color. He felt wonderful inside. He tickled the sand back with his toes. The ground laughed and Antonio dropped over backward and pressed a sand angel into the landscape. It was an impossible feeling. He wanted to talk to the ground and reminisce with the trees.

"I have died and gone to heaven." With one eye on the setting blue sun Antonio continued his angel-making. He had never really considered that heaven would be a place with sand and trees and suns. He thought it should be more ethereal with angels playing harps on puffy clouds. "Why is it like this? Why am I alone? Where did this body come from? How did I get here? What! All very interesting, indeed.

Bottom line, it feels great and I guess I'll just have to wait and see. This place must be heaven though and I'm sure God will be here soon."

As he got up from his angel-making Antonio stopped, crane-like with one foot in the air and his head slightly cocked. He was almost sure he heard one of the nearby trees "giggle."

Under the strange suns, Antonio-the-sand-angel-maker moved toward one of the oaks and sat with his back against the trunk, palms down, squeezing the living sand through his new fingers. He reflected on his past as if reading a biography. A tiny white cloud floated just above him. His thoughts displayed like a page in a book against its puffy underside. The tree branches bent a little closer as if to read over Antonio's shoulder.

> Antonio Gomez was the eldest of four children. His parents worked the tidy strawberry fields west of Santa Maria, California. Those were good times with hopes as bright as the often-visited flower fields of nearby Lompoc. Just when his father was promoted to field foreman his mother died with the birth of their fourth child. Antonio was sent to live with cousins farther north and inland. The flowered fields faded to endless days of hot summers and drafty winters. Antonio, as the child of poor relatives, while welcome in his uncle's house, got what was leftover. For some, this situation might spark courage and an undaunted need to achieve great things. For Antonio the situation was less motivating. The will to survive became cloaked in the will to do God's will, and allowed him to seek some pseudo-peacefulness in the single hope of achieving heaven as a final reward. And finally his spirit broke altogether and he moved further and further into the grips of an unbearable hopelessness. Antonio Gomez was found dead under a walnut tree.

The reminiscence was broken by the sound of a man's voice and the cloud popping out of existence. Startled, Antonio banged his head against the tree trunk; it gently gave way to cushion what would otherwise have been a painful blow.

"You would think that you could come up with something more creative than fading out against an old walnut tree." The voice came from behind Antonio and belonged to an elderly man dressed in baggy white shorts, a blue and lavender polo shirt, and sandals. He sported a shortly cropped gray-white beard and badly balding head with some longer gray-white strands along the edges. He was about six feet tall. For a moment Antonio thought he had blue skin but then realized it was the setting blue sun reflecting off the desert floor. The man seemed very happy to see him, even happier than the trees.

Antonio was caught too off guard to be embarrassed by his nakedness as he instinctively slipped into the clothes the man tossed to him. Everything fit, perfectly. His outfit seemed to mesh with his newfound body. His shorts, like the man's, were white, but sleek rather than baggy and his shirt was a pale yellow mesh that allowed his skin to reflect his aura. He did not put on the sandals, preferring to stay in touch with the friendly sand.

"You're the first one back," the man said as he pivoted on the white sand and casually motioned over his shoulder for Antonio to follow.

Antonio just stood there for several moments trying to take in this sudden development. Sprinting, almost breathless, he glided alongside the man and asked, "First one back? What's that supposed to mean? I'm just a bit confused. I feel like me, but I sure don't look like me. And this place, a cool desert with lots of trees and two suns, I don't think so?"

The man laughed. "Indeed, it must be a bit strange, but you instinctively know everything is okay. This place feels familiar and you feel like you've known me for a long time. Am I right? Oh, by the way, I'm Leo. It will all become clear with a little time in this place. For now just enjoy."

"This place is heaven, right?"

Chuckling and shaking his head back and forth Leo said, "No, son, this is not heaven. In all the universe this may be the most beautiful place, but it is not heaven and surely, I am not God. Let's go to meet the others."

"What others?"

"Like I said, you are the first one back." The twinkle in Leo's eye shone like a third sun in Antonio's consciousness as they moved in unison across the sand.

The trees rustled in the windless desert and the sands carved out a pathway as they moved ahead. The blue sun dropped below the southern horizon and left mountain spires glowing against the light of the yellow sun. It was like the scenery on a large theater stage, one thing rolling into another.

A small, vibrant blue-colored bird landed on Leo's shoulder, and then another, and another and another until there were dozens of the small birds draped over his back like a cloak. With a gentle wave of his hand Leo dispersed the birds and they fell into the sand rolling ahead of him like tiny blue snowballs. As they gathered speed and mass they rose into the air forming a beautiful blue dragon.

Leo stopped short and turned to face Antonio. "Impressive, don't you think? They're called morphbirds." Leo roared with laughter at the look on Antonio's face. "Trust me, son, you're going to like this place. Watch the puddle, by the way."

A pool of deep green water began to form just in front of Antonio. "Are you sure this isn't heaven? How can this be, birds forming dragons, and water just appearing out of nowhere? Trees that giggle? Sand that walks and forms itself into a pathway? And you, old man, are you sure you're not God?"

"Of all the choices available do you really think God would pick my looks?" Leo walked up to Antonio and gave him a bear hug that all but crushed the poor young man. "Having you back is wonderful! Now stop your gawking and let's get going. Watch the puddle."

Too late. Antonio tripped on a small boulder that seemingly jumped in his path and he fell headfirst into the water. The water, like Leo, gave him a bear hug and then heaved him back onto the sand. He went to brush the water away, but was perfectly dry.

Leo was bent over with laughter. "Take heart, the planet is playing with you." A swirling hole opened and Leo disappeared, his hearty laugh left echoing in the air.

For a moment Antonio panicked only to look up and see Leo a little farther along the sand-carved path, feigning impatience at Antonio's lagging behind. "You coming, son?"

Then the scene disappeared from Antonio's consciousness as he saw himself playing with several other children in a different desert under what appeared to be four colorful moons. A woman he knew to be his mother stood in the doorway of a beautifully sculptured house and called him in for dinner. In fact, he heard her call in his head; she did not really call out. The door to the house was an archway that, as he approached, ushered him into the spacious interior. The lighting was indirect and coming from a domed ceiling much like the sun splaying filtered light on a lush meadow in spring. Antonio's heart was full.

"Are you coming, son?"

"What?" Dazed out of his reverie Antonio stumbled toward Leo with uncertain steps.

"Looks like you've had a flashback. I'll bet that's enough to raise a few more questions. We suspect you will continue to have them, at least for a while. You will begin to remember things, like a person coming out of a prolonged amnesia. You're going to just have to ride with it. Your own memories will be your best explanation of who you are and where you are. As for me, you're going to have to trust me. Reach inside of yourself and you will find that trust. The path beckons, come. I don't want to miss the next one back." The sand curved and arched up creating a luge-like raceway purporting speed as essential.

Antonio again fell alongside Leo, reluctant to ask any questions just yet. As for trust, Antonio was acting a bit like the cat who allows you to feed it and talk nice to it but not let you pet it. Leo sensed this in Antonio and found it unsettling.

* * * * * * * * *

Melissa was wandering along a Boca Raton, Florida, beach trying to decide what to get high on. She accidentally dropped a twenty-dollar bill in the sand and could not be bothered to chase it as a mild ocean breeze gently caressed her golden hair and flew the money into the sea. As she felt her hair play around her neck and bare shoulders, she didn't need a mirror to remind her that she was the epitome of "hot." She was about five feet eight inches tall, slender, and tanned. Her skin-toned bathing suit left little to the imagination as it barely rode along the curve of her hips and the tips of her breasts. If the light hit her just right you had to look twice to be sure she wasn't naked. She was beautiful, rich, and smart to boot.

Melissa was going to be twenty in a few days and seemed strangely obsessed with how to die. She was depressed. She often thought of just walking into oblivion, walking into the Devil's Triangle ocean. "Now that would be a death scenario with a message," she mused. "Beauty, brains, and wealth were not enough to save Melissa Commings from a ravaging hopelessness. Her body was found washed up on the beach, white-crusted with salt, ghost like, and expressionless."

Melissa's death would not go unnoticed. She was the only child of Samuel Commings, world-class cardiologist, and Gloria Stein-Commings, world class bitch. Her father's position and her mother's abrasiveness always made anything Melissa did seem either much better or much worse than it really was. Melissa Commings was society page stuff. She was often subject matter for the *Boca Raton News*, or the *Palm Beach Post*, and sometimes even the *Miami Herald*. Living under the shadows of her parents turned Melissa cold and left her skating downhill through life at breakneck speed. For Melissa, an early death was just a matter of time and place. She couldn't wait.

The blue sun almost directly overhead startled Melissa even more than her nakedness. She didn't remember getting high although she was clearly hallucinating. The sand was whiter and the humidity lower, and, although it was not possible, it looked as though another more familiar yellow sun was setting in the west.

Everything around her seemed alive. She felt a bit self-conscious; she felt like the trees were staring at her. Uncharacteristically she tried to cover herself and sat cross-legged in the sand. The sand tickled almost like tiny ants. She shooed the sand away from her bare bottom and it obediently drifted into a neat pile about a foot away. Melissa chased it with her outstretched hand and the sand moved a little farther away, just out of reach. It also seemed a different color somehow. She turned away pretending to ignore the sand and then swiftly turned back trying to catch it. It again escaped and she was certain she heard giggling as it rolled itself into a small vortex spinning out of sight. "Some drug," thought Melissa.

She closed her eyes, trying to get hold of herself. She still didn't remember getting high. The last thing in her recollection was simply walking into the ocean off Boca Beach. Then it hit her. "Oh my God, I drowned, I'm dead!" She reeled at the very idea, never having thought she'd have the guts to do it alone. Her eyes sprang open and she began to pinch herself all over. It really hurt. "Dead should not hurt."

The sand opposite her curved itself into a big smiley face. Before she could react a huge blue dragon swooped from overhead and crashed in front of her. It broke into loudly chirping pieces and rolled off at high speed in all directions. The nearest tree seemed to jump out of the way tilting its branches in a mock "After you, dragon bits."

Melissa lay back in the sand, a calm peacefulness overtaking her where panic should have been. Her soul sensed playing children and loving parents. She sort of saw herself, but a plainer self who did not stand out so much from others. She liked who she was. Her clothing hung about her body like silk over a malleable chairback. The colors played in unison with her surroundings, pastels everywhere. Her reverie was broken by a loud thump on the sand.

A neatly folded stack of clothing caught her eye as she looked behind her where the ocean used to be. "Get dressed and follow the footprints in the sand," was neatly inscribed on a piece of metallic-like paper that did not move with the wind. The clothing was all pastel and draped her body like a silk cocoon. Footprints led straight over the dunes and toward the folded mountains that were not there in her recollection of just moments before.

Melissa was sure this was not a dream. She was not afraid and she was not depressed. With each step forward, the footprints behind her disappeared like invisible ink into parchment. When she looked up from her footprint-following task, she met the friendly gazes of a white-bearded elderly man and a good-looking, tall young man. Leo just smiled and motioned for her to follow.

Not being at all shy Melissa edged her way between Antonio and Leo and said, "Okay, guys, what's the deal? Is this some sort of virtual reality game or something?"

Antonio quickly replied, "Or something is more like it. I know this sounds like a terrible line but I feel as though I know you."

"Well, maybe you do. Are you from around here?"

"I don't exactly know where here is."

"You sound serious. This isn't a game? This is not Boca?"

"This isn't a game, and we're not in Florida, California, or heaven. By the way, I'm Antonio and this is Leo, and Leo isn't God. I feel better than I've felt in my whole life and I'm sure I know you. That's everything I know and Leo's not talking."

"You are serious. Well, Mr. Leo, what's the deal?"

Leo's enormous twinkle caught Melissa as he smiled and said, "No deal, young lady, you're just finally home where you belong."

Antonio and Melissa exclaimed in unison, "Home?"

"Yes, home. You were both part of a grand experiment and now you're back. Enough chat, we need to catch up with the next member of your team." Leo bent his head slightly forward and led them swiftly over the dunes. For the moment Antonio and Melissa felt content to follow, immersed in their own thoughts. The trees seemed to follow along.

* * * * * * * * * *

Nancy vaguely remembered that she was supposed to die at twenty, but she couldn't remember why. It didn't particularly bother her though. She was quite used to not remembering. Only scattered blotches of her past touched her memory. At barely eighteen she had awakened one day in a hospital bed in a small Southwest town. She had been found stumbling out of the Superstition Mountains, her family apparently victims of the Superstitions' curse. Those mountains have an uncanny propensity for just swallowing up folks. Her parents were found brutally murdered in their camping trailer. Fingerprints and the effects found around the campsite identified the surviving family member as Nancy Mellon. She took the authorities at their word, having no recollection of the incident. She only remembered bits and pieces of a life that may have been hers. As sole heiress to the Mellon estate of $42,416.84, Nancy set out on her own. She remained a recluse, lived simply and communicated primarily through her meditative world.

Hers was a spiritual path and she was very much in touch with those she perceived to be her spirit guides or angels, especially a being named Kathryn. On her twentieth birthday, encouraged by Kathryn, Nancy simply leapt off the top of a mesa somewhere in New Mexico. She had complete confidence that she would not die. When she awakened naked under the two suns, she was neither surprised nor betrayed by this confidence. She was very much alive. She did, however, feel ever so slightly depressed. She did what she always did in times of uneasiness; she stilled her mind and began to meditate.

This meditation was like no other she had ever experienced. She seemed to connect almost instantly with what seemed like an entire planet! The experience was outrageous while familiar and unfamiliar, and deafening and quiet. Most interesting, however, was the feeling of connectedness to the physical planet itself. This was a dimension Nancy had never experienced.

Nancy sensed three figures coming toward her, an elderly gentleman, a tall young man, and a very attractive young woman. Her mind went out to greet them. It was a feeling of old and deep friendship renewed.

It was curious, however, that for the first time in recent memory Nancy did not sense the presence of Kathryn during meditation.

She was startled out of her unusual and powerful meditation by the realization that Leo and the others were actually there in her reality. She absent mindedly dressed in the clothing obviously put there for her and joined them, puzzled and still ever so slightly depressed. She found it curious that such a magnificent meditation had failed to heal that nagging depression.

Leo extended his arms in a welcoming hug and said, "Welcome home."

Nancy tactfully shrunk from his grasp and addressed the three of them. "Who are you people?"

A bit flustered, Leo said, "I'm Leo, this is Melissa, and this is Antonio."

"What do you mean 'welcome home'?"

Antonio piped in and said, "It's a big mystery to all of us except Leo. Melissa and I are also recent arrivals. Although we don't know much about this place, it sure feels good. I'm sorry we sort of sneaked up on you. Anyway, won't you join us?"

"I don't seem to have much choice."

"Let's go then," said Leo. As they moved on he had an uncomfortable feeling about Nancy. He mumbled to himself, "When was the last time an Eyespellian denied someone a hug?"

* * * * * * * * *

Nancy's aloofness upon her reentry stemmed from telepathy link bleed-through between her and Kathryn, Earth Overseer of the Eyespell Experiment. Kathryn's existence had bled into Nancy's semiconscious awareness during Nancy's deep meditations. As a result of her beliefs, Nancy perceived this presence simply as a spirit guide named Kathryn.

Since this proved to be a convenient way of making sure Nancy avoided any conscious memory of Eyespell or the Eyespell Experiment, Kathryn let the deception go. It was through this deception that she was able to keep her Eyespellian identity hidden. What made it so difficult was that Eyespellians simply do not lie or deceive one another. To have to do this was the first unwelcome fallout of The Eyespell Experiment.

The underlying problem was that Nancy's premature recognition of anything Eyespellian prior to her planned reentry posed a great risk. While still in Earth-fusion a telepathy bleed might accelerate and reverse mind-set polarities, causing not only memories of Eyespell but actual premature reentry to Eyespell. It was hypothesized that such a sudden and unplanned reentry would generate severe Earth-plane vibrational leakage. The havoc such vibrational leakage could wreak on Eyespell was the single greatest perceived danger of the Eyespell Experiment and needed to be avoided at all costs.

* * * * * * * * * *

By the time he was twelve Pete was an alcoholic. By thirteen he had donned his backward Raiders' Cap, carried a baseball bat, and was loose on the streets of New York. Pete was a born leader and had he not thrown himself in front of a NYC commuter train on his twentieth birthday, he surely would have achieved a place of stature among gang lords.

Peter Capellini was first generation American. His parents, Carmen and Angelina, had moved from Sicily to the Bronx for a better life just before his birth. And a better life it apparently was. The Italian Rooster, the family owned restaurant, was one of the best hole-in-the-wall eating places for twenty blocks around. It was one of those places just waiting to be discovered by the rich and famous as one of the best off-the-beaten-path places to eat. If the neighborhood hadn't turned so bad so fast, it just might have happened. Angelina's southern fried chicken and homemade cheese ravioli were some of the best there were. On Sunday afternoons, papa Carmen kept the clientele amused with a small organ-grinder-style accordion. What papa and mama Capellini didn't know was that the only reason the Italian Rooster managed to stay open for business at all, was that son Peter and his gang patrolled the surrounding blocks with steel and gunpowder. Pete kept the illusion of business-as-usual alive for his parents. He even brought home decent report cards over the years, after making his teachers "offers they couldn't refuse."

When Pete awoke on Eyespell, his first thought was that he must have gone to heaven in spite of himself. He felt wonderful and was too elated to question either his nakedness or the four beautiful moons of Eyespell shining in the clear night sky. He was so intrigued by his newfound surroundings that it was several minutes before he saw Leo standing there, smiling broadly and gesturing for him to get dressed and follow.

"You are the fourth one back, and the fourth one of our children I have greeted this day," Leo said.

"Say what?"

"It's not important, just enjoy yourself."

Leo felt good about Pete. Within a couple of minutes they joined up with the others. Pete's presence added something dynamic and very Eyespellian to the group. Even Nancy warmed up, offering Pete both her hands in a gesture of comfortable familiarity.

Out of nowhere Pete said, "It's so great to be home! Whoops, I can tell by your expressions that you think I'm nuts. Well, maybe, but I don't think so. This just feels too right and too familiar. And all of you are old friends, very old friends. And you, Leo, you are, as always, in the middle of things."

Leo smiled broader than ever and regained whatever composure had been eroded by Nancy's earlier behavior. "Well Pete, I see you're right out front leading the group as usual. Welcome home!"

As the four followed him, Leo thought he should get in touch with Kathryn to see if there had been any linkage with the fifth and last Eyespellian scheduled to return. His concern over the whereabouts of the last to return was hidden behind his white beard and the distraction of a large dragon-shadow moving across the four moons.

"Morphbirds!" Pete hollered excitedly as he followed their leapfrogging across the four moons.

"How'd you know that? I just found out about them from Leo," said Antonio.

"And they scared the living hell out of me earlier today," volunteered Melissa. "I had just landed, or whatever, and they dropped right in front of me and went maniacally chirping off in all directions. I almost peed in my pants, had I been wearing any that is."

"Now that's a funny scene." Antonio gestured in the air with both hands as if writing a newspaper headline. "Naked girl accosted by morphbirds in the middle of the desert." Antonio lost it.

And Pete about fell down laughing, saying something like, "And she would have peed her pants had she been wearing any."

"How juvenile," snapped Nancy.

Somewhere close a tree branch also snapped.

Antonio, looking sort of sheepish, stuck his hands in his pockets and backed away. Melissa started to say something but thought better of it. Pete just sort of growled. Leo seemed to move his hands toward the earth in a calming gesture and grumbled something about, "… Earth-plane vibrational leakage."

"Okay, guys," said Leo, "we need to move it along. We have one more returnee to greet this day." The pathway again materialized to show the way. With Leo out in front the others followed silently in single file. The air was thicker than before and the desert felt somewhat hot even though it was evening. The sand stopped playing and the trees did not giggle. It was hard to tell if the planet was sleeping or just waiting to see what would happen next.

Leo placed his hand around the pouch dangling from his waist and truly hoped he would not have to open it, at least not under these circumstances. None of the returnees had even noticed the pouch much less asked what it contained. "Just as well," thought Leo.

* * * * * * * * * *

Kathryn Song, Overseer of the Eyespell Experiment and still on Earth, was trying to decide if she should leave now or take the riskier approach of waiting until the last possible reentry window. As much as she longed for Eyespell's blue sun, she knew she had to wait. The last returnee had to be given every possible chance to be found.

It had been twenty years since Kathryn had been caressed by the blue sun that daily transformed the Eyespellian landscape into a serene, pastel paradise. If one ignored the fact that there were two suns and four moons, from outer space Eyespell looked a lot like Earth, only pink instead of blue. Even though the chemical composition of Eyespell's atmosphere was almost identical to Earth's, the air was somehow different and more exhilarating to the breath. Something akin to Earth's ozone layer neutralized any harmful radiation, enhancing the atmosphere's refreshing and people-friendly essence. Moreover, the people living on Eyespell had done nothing to disrupt the pristine atmosphere. Kathryn sighed audibly and took a long and deep imagined drink of her home planet.

"I was opposed to this experiment from the onset. I had the most horrible feeling that something would go wrong, something Eyespell was not prepared for." She stretched back on the oversized floor pillows. Her flowing pitch-black hair against the white pillow offered a startling contrast to her otherwise pastel-appointed apartment. Such contrast could be seen as a microcosm of Earth and of Eyespell. Her hair, while beautiful in its sheer blackness, seemed full of danger, as if it might absorb the rest of her along with her pastel surroundings. It was a visual cue portending the subtle yet potentially disastrous leakage of one thing into another. Kathryn was too busy with her thoughts about the Eyespell Experiment to notice this cosmic clairvoyance reflected in her immediate surroundings.

From across the galaxies Eyespell had been listening and watching Earth's social progress for a very long time. The parallels between the two planets went far beyond similar atmospheres. Earthlings were very much like ancient Eyespellians in their attitudes, beliefs, and potential for fostering a world society both technologically and spiritually imposing. Earthlings even looked like Eyespellians.

The difference was that early in its development Eyespell was set on a path of enlightenment with more than a little help from the Cosmos. The Life Force had shone brightly on Eyespell and guided her peoples toward harmony in all things and all thoughts. This divine direction left Eyespell harmonious within herself with an unwavering propensity to replace discord with harmony. Throughout recent history Eyespell extended the positive healing vibration of the planet and its peoples to all she encountered. A primary dictum, however, had always been to heal from a distance, to literally shed light and love from a distance using highly developed telepathic and spiritual powers. The idea was that thought alone could produce tangible results. In fact, the whole Eyespellian existence is based on this premise.

The Eyespell Experiment was different. Due to the connectedness Eyespellians felt with the Earth, for the first time they proposed to deal with healing up-close-and-personal. The Eyespell Experiment actually proposed manifesting five participants and one observer directly on the Earthplane for twenty Earth-years.

Kathryn's opposition to the experiment was based on the nagging fear that the reentry process might be unsuccessful. There might be problems getting all the participants back or, worse yet, difficulty in neutralizing the Earth-plane vibrations picked up by the participants over the twenty years. The damage to Eyespell from such Earth-plane vibrational leakage could be irreparable and once unleashed on the planet, geometric in its progression.

In spite of such risk, the governing Elders of Eyespell had been insistent upon gaining a better understanding of the Earth and the evolution of its peoples. Much of Earth's social "progress" made little or no sense. Although Earth and Eyespell had similar potential, Earth did not seem to be getting the divine guidance Eyespell had received, or wasn't listening. Eyespellians found it most difficult to understand many of the directions the Earth took in the management of its planet and its people. The very thought, for example, of developing an economic system in total opposition to the environmental perpetuity of a planet, and ultimately its peoples, seemed insane on any collectively conscious level. How the desire for economic profit could supersede a species' instinct for survival was at best mystifying to Eyespellians. They had no parallel experience. The Eyespellian philosophy was based on long-term benefits and sustainability. The management of all things focused on a moral philosophy based in a compassion which respected the dignity of every living thing. The concept of life was inclusive of all things in the Eyespellian environment, including the physical planet itself.

Observation, research, and even telepathy across the vastness of space separating Earth and Eyespell were somewhat limited. While it was easy enough to access Earth communication modalities, this information lacked feeling. These data were from secondary sources; there was no direct Eyespell/Earth connection. Personal telepathy links with Earth were fraught with what might be best described as cosmic mental static. One could not be sure with whom one had connected or whether the connection was "clean." The possibility of picking up out-of-Earth vibrations was a constant concern. Eyespell was essentially eavesdropping on the Earth. This eavesdropping fostered a number of concerns that led to the conception and direction of what would ultimately be called The Eyespell Experiment.

It became immediately apparent that direct physical contact with the Earth, while possible, had to be balanced against the risks. It was complicated. Certainly there were reentry issues. Moreover, physical contact with Earthlings would most assuredly be perceived as an alien invasion or, perhaps, an economic opportunity. And, of course, anything economic would most likely be distorted to fit what Eyespellian researchers came to call the Species Elimination Model (SEM). There had to be direct contact but somehow cloaked, in order to mesh with Earth consciousness at a very subtle level.

A trend gleaned from various Earth media sources gave researchers an idea. One of the most severe symptoms of Earth's fragmented social evolution appeared to be the high suicide rate among teenagers and young adults, primarily in affluent countries. After careful consideration of the data, the Elders agreed upon an experiment whereby five Eyespellians would "fuse" with the Earth youth experience in the culturally diverse and affluent United States of America. They anticipated that such a fusing would offer the direct, yet subtle, link with Earth necessary for Eyespell's collection of primary and unfiltered data.

The participants would actually live Earth lives for twenty years and then commit suicide within hours of each other. The idea was that five suicides of young people within such a compressed time frame would certainly be noticed. From the Eyespellian perspective, such a series of events would be thought cataclysmic. Surely a search for reasons and solutions would ensue. This soul-search would hopefully lead to a newfound identity with community and community building. The hope was that this would ultimately culminate in a philosophy leading to sustainability instead of elimination. It was thought that success of the Eyespell Experiment might even lead to the possibility of open and non-threatening direct intervention at some later date. The exciting prospect of helping this similar planet blinded Eyespell to the magnitude of the risks. The Eyespellian perspective was ambitious and probably presumptuous.

The Eyespell Experiment was approved in spite of objections from some quarters, most notably from Kathryn. With perfect hindsight one could see that the problems with The Eyespell Experiment stemmed from its very inception. Eyespellian decision making operated in an atmosphere of consensus. How open opposition such as Kathyrn's could have been ignored remains a mystery. Actually the opposition was not ignored exactly; it simply went unnoticed in any meaningful way.

Participants in The Eyespell Experiment were meticulously screened and re-screened to determine their ability to avoid potential incidences of severe and sustained Earth-plane vibrational leakage upon their return to Eyespell. Earth-plane vibrational leakage could take the form of anything from a participant's stray negative thoughts, to his or her Earth memories of the depression that led up to suicide/reentry. A more severe problem might take the form of the angst and anger Earthlings are frequently prone to. An incomprehensible problem might be the harboring of ill will beyond mere anger or thoughts, leading to acts of violence, deceit, lust, avarice, and other deadly sins as described by some Earth dogmas. While this screening process reduced the possibility of such leakage, the overall risk could not be entirely eliminated. This is why Kathryn had questioned and was uncomfortable with the project. To assuage her perceived concern, she was officially appointed the Earth-based Project Overseer. Kathryn took on her role with a sense of foreboding and, from her Earth location, maintained close yet unobserved scrutiny of the five subjects for the twenty-Earth-years' duration of the Eyespell Experiment.

Her concern proved justified, one Eyespellian was now missing.

CHAPTER 6

▼

IN THE FAMILY ROOM ...

"Whoa, what's that?" Koy looked up, a bit surprised, and sheepishly asked, "I'm incredulous; did I fall asleep? I wasn't even tired, not one bit. I am so embarrassed."

"No reason to feel embarrassed," said Phillip. "You most certainly did not fall asleep. Seems to me you were listening rather intently and navigating a piece of cheesecake from the plate to your mouth. Check it out, you're just putting the fork down and you aren't quite finished chewing."

Koy looked at the fork gently landing on her plate and, indeed, the texture of the cheesecake was just passing her lips in an effort not to leave any crumbs in her lap. "Wait a minute! Antonio is real; he was no dream. What's going on here; I am truly at a loss."

Jo sat back smiling, as Phillip explained, "I believe your question just before taking that bite of cheesecake was, 'How is that?' You know, how is it that the executives' reaction to Mystic Management at the Governor's Club seminar was so positive and seemingly devoid of the Kookamonga Effect; no need for "Joe Sent Me" to help rid them of old and inappropriate strategies? Your exact question was 'How is that?'"

Koy's jaw dropped. "What are you saying, Phillip? Wait a minute. The pink; a pink planet, Eyespell, and you?"

"Yes, well, just relax and I'll tell you some more."

"Between bites no doubt," quipped Koy as she put her plate on the coffee table and sat back shaking her head. Not quite the evening I imagined. It must be the moose."

"Like I said earlier, it's the story you will never print."

"Don't be too sure about that, Dr. Hansen. Don't underestimate Koy Sosa, star reporter."

"Oh, I don't think we have underestimated you," said Jo. "In fact you're just what the doctor ordered, Dr. Hansen that is. He just knew the minute your friend Sam called to ask if you could attend the seminar at the Governor's Club. He came running around the corner to find me on the back deck. And he rarely runs. He was so excited, saying something about 'I think she has finally found us.' Don't let him fool you or intimidate you. We are thrilled that you are here and Phillip has never shared his story openly with anyone outside of our immediate family. His admonishment that it's the story you will never print is just a bit of his reverse psychology. It needs to be printed and you are the one to do it! That said, Phillip, would you like to share a bit more?"

"My pleasure and, Koy, your look of disbelief becomes you. So, ..."

"Wait just a sec," said Koy, looking just a bit uncomfortable. "I sort of get what's happening here; somehow you conveyed your message directly into my feeble brain, right?"

"More or less," said Phillip. "On Eyespell it's called a mind-link."

"So, I really hate to put it this way, but at the Governor's Club if you, as you call it, mind-linked with those execs, they had no choice but to go along; you were literally in their heads. I'm not sure how I feel about that. I feel really bad bringing it up this way. I've been enjoying our relationship and the intimate things you are sharing, but I'm just not comfortable with you using such a technique to make your point with the CEOs. In fact, the more I think about it the more uncomfortable I get."

"That's a good thing," said Phillip. "One of the reasons I am so excited that you are here is you are not afraid to ask the right questions. I think the word you really wanted to use but were far too polite to is 'brainwash.' You're uncomfortable to think that Christian and I would brainwash those execs into accepting Mystic Management by entering their minds and depositing all the ideas we espouse."

"Yes. I would have a real problem with that even if the ends were positive. I can't abide by an ethic where the 'end justifies the means.' You know how insidious that can be."

"I couldn't agree more. Bottom line, no such thing happened. The Governor's Club experience was a simple matter of Eyespellian charisma coupled with the participants' predisposition to the Mystic Management ideals; nothing more. Believe me, not every seminar has been so smooth. It is so important that what I share with you has no chinks in its ethical armor. I could have used mind-link at the Governor's Club or any of the other seminars for that matter. But you're exactly right, it would smack of the end justifying the means. There is no question in my mind that where we are going with Mystic Management is an exceptionally positive place to go. The problem is the phrase 'in my mind.' In someone else's mind Mystic Management may not seem like such a great idea. For example, at one of the early seminars a participant had a total fit over the concept of Karmic Kindness. He got totally hung up on the word *karmic* as against his beliefs and stormed out of the seminar aggravated and indignant. And he did pick up his check on the way out. Again, the group you were a part of was the most Mystic Management oriented in their thinking, way before they ever got to the seminar, especially folks like Jack and Sam."

"Indeed, using mind-link would be extremely convenient. The mind-link is essentially telepathic communication. It can be face-to-face or over great distances, even between planets if you will. The mind-link allows almost instant communication of ideas, stories, history, and so on. It can function like a zip file, a compressed file on your computer. That's what I did with you earlier tonight; it allowed me to convey a lot of information in a compressed format. In a matter of seconds, I shared a story that would have taken a long time to *say*. The communication took place between bites of cheesecake as you put it. Now, that's the process but it does not address the ethics of the situation, the act of entering another's mind and planting ideas. The mind-link cannot influence free choice and therein lies a critical safeguard. While I can communicate to you via mind-link, what you do with that information is totally up to you. For example, nowhere in tonight's story are you forced to believe that any of it is true. Again, while I was able to communicate the information, what you do with it is up to you. Mind-link is incapable of directing choice or action; that is always left up to the individual."

"But, Phillip, you entered my mind without permission and that can't be right."

"A bit of a possible rub there I admit. On Eyespell the mind-link, telepathy, is the norm. There would be nothing unusual or sneaky about it and every person has the option of an open or closed mind-link at any time. In fact, on Eyespell an open mind-link among great numbers of individuals can literally generate a global type of communication. The entire populace of the planet can connect simultaneously, but that's another story. Telepathy as a form of communication on Earth, however, is the type of thing science fiction novels are made of and 'unannounced' use of a mind-link would be sneaky and unethical. But even in such a case there is another safeguard. We already mentioned that if a person consciously has a closed mind-link, telepathy cannot occur. The same is true if there is an unconscious block to any telepathic intrusion. Tonight you were open to new ideas. Your unconscious, or subconscious if you prefer, offered no objection to the mind-link. I could have spent time this evening explaining all of this to you beforehand. I am sure you would have consciously agreed to the mind-link.

"Gosh, Phillip, that just does not wash with me. This may sound convoluted but I would never consciously let my unconscious make decisions for me."

"Good for Koy Sosa," said Jo and Phillip simultaneously.

"I can't imagine having to write a retraction of my article. Can you picture it: 'Top Executives Duped through Mind Game' instead of 'Reflections on Mystic Management'? That would be ugly."

"And you'd do it too," commented Jo. "And good for you again!"

"So what about tonight, what really happened to me?"

"That, Ms. Sosa, was pure unadulterated Eyespell mind-link in zipped format."

"Oh. And ..."

"And, if you want to *hear* more I'm ripe for the *telling*. And if you want to hit the sack, head home in the morning and forget the whole thing, that's okay too. Or, if you're completely freaked out I'll let the moose drive you back to Leesburg right now." I admit that I violated your mind space this evening. However, I needed to be certain that you fully appreciated the power of the mind-link. All kidding aside, I am prepared to apologize for my intrusion and end our interview at this point."

"I suppose I'm feeling that Eyespellian charisma. Besides, I really want to hear more. Spill it, Dr. Hansen, and directly into my head to save time. And we can talk about the ethics of it again later. I am still a bit confused but my gut tells me I'm okay with this."

"Of course, I would never consider telling you any of this if I wasn't prepared to answer any questions you have. So take another bite of cheesecake and I'll tell you about the missing Eyespellian."

CHAPTER 7

▼

THE MISSING EYESPELLIAN

Leo spent the day and the better part of the evening intercepting Antonio, Melissa, Nancy, and Pete at their assigned reentry points. While there was much to-do about the possibility of Earth-plane vibrational leakage upon reentry, no one had seriously considered what the consequences might be if one of the experiment participants failed to return at all. The exact time and place of each reentry was established at the inception of the Eyespell Experiment. It was assumed all five would return in twenty years as planned. By now it was obvious that Phillip had missed reentry and there was no word from Kathryn Song indicating his whereabouts.

There had never been a missing Eyespellian; they are inextricably connected to each other and to their planet. Every cell or molecule on Eyespell reflects in every other cell or molecule; nothing on Eyespell exists in isolation. All things Eyespellian are interconnected and what happens in one cell affects all other cells. This is the simplest explanation of what is called Eyespell's planetary cell-matrix; the thing that makes sand tickle and trees giggle.

This cell-matrix so connects everything Eyespellian that the consciousness of the planet would, indeed, be dramatically impacted by the unexpected and premature loss of even one Eyespellian or, for that matter, even one grain of sand on the planet's surface. The question in Leo's mind was just how extreme the disruption would be to Eyespell. Even the seemingly mild Earth-plane vibrational leakage already experienced with Nancy and Antonio to a lesser degree was disconcerting. The sound of that snapping tree branch when Nancy chastised the others for fooling around, resounded in Leo's consciousness like a serpent ready to strike. He closed his eyes and unconsciously reached for the pouch dangling from his waist in an attempt to steady his nerves. It was a new and unfamiliar experience to have to steady his nerves.

Anticipated, predictable changes in the density of the cell-matrix caused by geological shifts or energy shifts as individuals move through death and rebirth transitions are routinely handled. The total consciousness of the planet embraces and absorbs the vibrations of such occurrences and restructures them into the total fabric of the Eyespellian landscape and community. In this sense the energy of every Eyespellian lives on.

The cell-matrix is in constant flux and the impact of even the slightest vibrational shift needs to be minimized so as not to disrupt the overall balance of the planet. What might be construed as an accident, or perhaps illness, is simply reabsorbed into the matrix and re-manifested in some positive way. Even something as seemingly insignificant as a stray thought is captured in the Eyespellian consciousness and translated into a fragment of the planet's overall reality. If Earth were observing Eyespell, Eyespell would appear extremely enlightened and advanced.

With one Eyespellian missing and concern about Earth-plane vibrational leakage affecting those who had returned, Leo and Eyespell had much cause to be worried. Could Eyespell's cell-matrix absorb and redistribute Earth-plane vibrational leakage and handle a missing Eyespellian on top of it all? There was great potential for skewing the planet's reality in some heretofore unknown direction, a direction that would almost certainly be undesirable and negative.

Leo evaluated the four returnees in an attempt to gauge the severity of the Earth-plane vibrational leakage. There was Nancy; she had refused to hug him and then snapped at the others for their digressions into child play. That tree branch had snapped at the vibration. Antonio was not telling all. There were hidden feelings there. Melissa and Pete seemed okay. Except Melissa was about to get into it with Nancy, and Pete actually growled his disapproval of being put down by Nancy. "Not Eyespellian, these interactions, not Eyespellian at all," thought Leo.

* * * * * * * *

In the hope of connecting with Phillip Hansen, Kathryn remained on Earth until the last possible moment, catching the final panes of the reentry window. When she finally arrived on Eyespell she was alone and somber, in disbelief that she had returned without Phillip. All attempts to reestablish the telepathy link with him had failed. Even the more earthbound approaches of checking missing persons and hospitals and scanning newspapers for accident victims produced nothing. It was as if Phillip had simply vanished into thin air. During the entire twenty years of the Eyespell Experiment he had been the easiest to track and seemed the least likely to experience any serious reentry trauma. It was ironic that he was the focus of this last minute crisis.

Kathryn reviewed the telepathy procedures a thousand times and could come up with only one explanation of how the telepathy link with Phillip could have been broken, a near-death experience. If Phillip had entered the white space Earth people call the tunnel, at the exact moment reentry was to occur, a total telepathic amnesia was possible. In that one extraordinary case, one in tens of millions, Phillip could be cut off from Kathryn and could be earthbound forever. This was a frightening prospect. Eventually Phillip would intuit his Eyespellian heritage, finding himself trapped on what would suddenly become an alien world, alien even though part of his memory would recall the event of his Earth-birth on that alien world.

Kathryn wept for Phillip Hansen and for Eyespell.

Thus manifested another complex tangle resulting from the Eyespell Experiment. There would be more and each tangle would be unpredictable and each shrouded in its unique ambiguity.

It was uncertain whether the sadness Kathryn experienced was an indicator of Earth-plane vibrational leakage or merely a residual energy flow confined to her own psyche, possibly even relief at her own successful reentry. Although she had been on the Earth for twenty years, she had never technically Earth-fused. Therefore, Kathryn dismissed the possibility of leakage, but who could be sure? In any case, unless she were to close her telepathy link and keep it closed, her thoughts and feelings would ultimately become part of the cell-matrix and would become assimilated into the Eyespellian consciousness and dispersed in some positive redirection. That was the way of Eyespell.

Her thoughts ran swiftly. "The upcoming debriefings of the four who have returned will answer the critical questions. Perhaps all my worry has been for naught. Maybe there is no significant vibrational leakage. Just maybe, my crying jag was not such an extraordinary event after twenty Earth-years away from home. Just maybe, Phillip is not separated from Eyespell. He's probably already home. Such optimism," she thought, allowing a brief smile.

By the time Leo met Kathryn at her reentry point, she had manifested her clothing. Her jet black hair clung to her tangerine top which overflowed onto her lime green pants and matching sandals. It was hard to keep Kathryn confined to the typical pastels of Eyespell. She was a truly vibrant energy. Although she was no longer crying, Leo had not arrived too late to catch the telltale redness in her eyes. For now he chose to keep the observation to himself, giving Kathryn a twenty-year-overdue hug as he mind-linked twenty years of Eyespell's "news" to Kathryn, filling in any details she may have missed through their long-range and often static-filled communications between Eyespell and Earth.

"It's wonderful to have you home, Kathryn Song. Did you really mean to manifest tangerine and lime green or were you thinking of the miniature citrus in the pots I promised to take care of for you for twenty years?"

Kathryn looked at her outfit and began to laugh hysterically. "Oh, my. It looks like I am a bit out of practice. Even I would consider toning this down a bit. Yes, I was thinking tangerines, lemons, limes, and grapefruits. I'm surprised I didn't come out all polka-dotted. Oh look, my sandals do have orange dots. So, how are my beloved plants, smarty?"

"Actually, they look a lot like you. Alive and garish as hell."

Kathryn looked up at Leo, thrilled to see her close friend again. "And the four that made it, how are they doing?"

"They are doing fine. The reentry trauma is no worse than we expected. They don't really remember much about Eyespell, just a flashback here and there. Except for Pete, he's quite sure he's home although he can't explain it, not yet anyway. It's too soon to tell if there has been significant Earth-plane vibrational leakage. I am somewhat concerned about Nancy. She is definitely out of sorts. She seems a little depressed, and certainly acted oddly when she first returned. She shrunk from my hug, can you imagine that? With Antonio it's nothing specific, just a strange feeling I can't quite put my finger on. All four are more or less still playing out their Earth-roles. Melissa is such a tart; it's actually funny to watch her. And what about Phillip? Any thoughts?"

"Nothing we haven't already discussed in our recent communications. Leo, did you know that I actually cried after reentry? When I was hit with the full realization that Phillip was left behind I simply lost it. I feel it's my fault. I can't believe the telepathy link was broken. My sole purpose for the past twenty years has been to keep track of the five of them. How could this have happened?" Tears again began to well up in Kathryn's eyes.

"Let's take things one step at a time." Leo grasped Kathryn's hands in a gesture of reassurance and continued. "Our four returned explorers are just chomping at the bit to meet with the Elders' Council. I told them we would do so as soon as you returned. Let's focus on the joy of the five of you having returned. Together we will figure out what has happened to Phillip. Although he is not here I do not sense that he is gone from us forever. By the way, your tears have not gone unnoticed in this connected place. Together we will make them tears of joy."

Kathryn smiled and felt comforted by Leo's words. She turned her attention back to the issues at hand. "Have you told them anything of their mission or their identities as Eyespellians?"

"Very little, except that Eyespell is home and that they were part of an experiment. As I mentioned, they have been having momentary periods of recall, but nothing that makes complete sense to them, nothing specific enough. They have lots of questions. Pete almost has it figured out. Like I said, he knew immediately that this is his home. Oh, and he recognized Antonio and the others as old friends. He even remembered me. Even though he couldn't fill in the details he very much trusted his feelings. Pete's state of mind made me feel very encouraged. On the other hand there is Nancy; there is definitely something amiss there. I still can't get over that she actually shrunk from my hug. Maybe

I'm just being too sensitive, you know, hurt feelings. Of course, that in and of itself is symptomatic that something is wrong. But, things seemed better after Pete's arrival. Nancy seemed more settled and the peculiar vibrations dissipated, that is until Nancy chastised the others for acting like children. I'll fill you in on the details later, but let it be said that there was enough discordance to cause one of the sandgrove trees to snap a branch. Now that was unsettling and gave me pause. I reached for my crystal charge and it was very hot to the touch, even through the pouch." Leo unconsciously folded his hand around the pouch dangling from his belt.

Looking somewhat pensive, Kathryn finally said, "After twenty years of clandestine observation, it will be nice to deal with them face-to-face. Especially Nancy. Having to lie to her because of that thing with the telepathic bleed-through really bothered me. Such deception is so counter to what we believe. Imagine Eyespellians lying to one another, for any reason. Without a doubt that was the most uncomfortable task in my twenty years as Experiment Overseer. At least until today when I was forced to return without Phillip. Oh, Leo, I missed you. It is so good to be with you again."

"Having you and the others back makes our planet almost whole again. It has been more difficult than any of us imagined letting six souls leave the planet at once. The whole planet can feel your presence, Kathryn Song."

Leo and Kathryn moved purposefully over the sand to gather up the other four returned adventurers and take them to the Elders' Council as promised. Leo felt a mounting yet unidentifiable apprehension as they continued their journey. His apprehension would find its target when Nancy and Kathryn met soon after.

* * * * * * * *

Kathryn was very introspective as they continued walking their silent path. She thought to herself, "Why do Eyespellians have to be so curious? We have manifested an almost perfect world and yet we risk it all out of curiosity or the quest for a little more knowledge. There was no reason to get mixed up in this Earth business in the first place. And then to lose a loved one, to actually have Phillip not return. Unforgivable!"

Leo looked at her quizzically, "Surely, Kathryn, if you wanted to keep your thoughts private, you would not leave your telepathy link wide open. Have you forgotten such basics after a mere twenty Earth-years? And surely, you do not mistake our motives for mere curiosity. Curiosity is not our motive. Interest, love, empathy, compassion, caring, and the potential to help a struggling world, now these come closer to our motives. On Earth it is said of curiosity that it killed the cat and, certainly, we are beyond the cat in our thinking."

"Leo, I am not myself. Of course I know what you say is true. I feel like a, like a, a confused Earthling." For the third time since her return tears shone at the corners of Kathryn's eyes.

Leo let love flow from himself to Kathryn in an expression of unconditional acceptance. "Don't worry. There is nothing Eyespell can't handle." He did not believe that for a minute as he closed his own telepathy link lest his own doubts spill into the cell-matrix.

"Antonio, Melissa, Nancy, and Pete have been awaiting your arrival for almost three Earth weeks now. The foursome has expended most of their energy getting reacquainted and learning more about Eyespell and Eyespellians. I've been in my teaching mode, just like when they were kids. The reentry trauma is moderate to severe and none of the four has regained their Eyespellian faculties. While each returnee has had many and varied flashbacks of Eyespell, they were still mostly limited to the Earth concepts of linear time, three-dimensional space, and oral communication."

From the conception of the Eyespell Experiment, reentry trauma was expected as a result of being immersed in Earth vibrations over a long period of time. The best *guesstimates* of the time necessary to dissipate reentry trauma ranged from three days to six months. It was thought that most symptoms of reentry, such as not remembering or general disorientation, would go away of their own accord through flashbacks and simple re-exposure to the Eyespellian environment. However, reducing and ultimately eliminating more serious symptoms such as lost faculties or vibrational leakage would probably take active therapeutic intervention and connection with the cell-matrix under close supervision. It was anticipated that most of the surface confusion would dissipate almost immediately while direct interventions in the first few days or weeks would help the returnees regain their Eyespellian faculties, such as telepathic and manifesting abilities.

While flashbacks might make telepathy an obvious possibility, it was doubtful that such information in and of itself could actually restore telepathic ability. There would have to be much practice where each of the returnees would attempt to communicate without words to each other and to Leo. While it was easy to "hear" communication from another, it was far more difficult to initiate telepathic communication. Even on the listening side of telepathy, one had to develop the ability to discriminate between one's own thoughts and those coming from outside oneself. And there was the trick of opening and closing the telepathy link so that one could enjoy personal privacy in either direction. And then there was the sheer number of communications that might come through at one time; telepathy was not strictly a one-to-one affair on Eyespell. It was possible for the entire planet to be tuned in at once. It was important that the returnees did not experience this level of telepathic communication without being fully prepared and reoriented. This was one of the reasons each of the participants reentered Eyespell in a somewhat desolate location; someplace where they would be alone. Every Eyespellian was informed of the reentry times and places and asked to take particular caution to avoid sending any thoughts in those directions.

Manifesting presented a far more intriguing problem than telepathy. Even Kathryn, who was not expected to suffer from reentry trauma, didn't get it quite right upon her return as evidenced by the garish outfit she manifested simply by thinking about her potted plants. Eyespell is a place where thought can consciously and immediately produce reality, physical as well as psychological reality. This, of course, is at the core of the worry about Earth-plane vibrational leakage. If extremely negative Earth-thought consciously or unconsciously emanated from the returnees, how would these undirected, random, and uncontrolled thought patterns be absorbed into the cell-matrix? How would these thoughts, or could these thoughts, be dissipated and redirected into positive patterns? The snapped tree branch was a clear sign of uncontrolled manifesting and disruption of the cell-matrix, however slight it might first have appeared.

While awaiting Kathryn's arrival, Leo had led the participants in many activities designed to reignite telepathic ability and to consciously push thought patterns in constructive and positive directions. The returnees spent most evenings sharing flashbacks and checking with Leo for confirmation of their accuracy. There was constant telepathy practice. There was practice receiving, practice sending, practice sending and receiving multiple messages, and practice looking for that internal switch that turned the whole process on or off. After three weeks there was much progress from a cognitive perspective; the returnees seemed to understand the concepts of telepathy and manifesting. However, there were only minimal results from an actual behavior, or doing, perspective. There seemed only slight progress with regard to telepathy and no progress in the ability to manifest.

Each day Leo led the four through the desert and each day exposed some new facet of Eyespell. One particular day Leo demonstrated how light could be manipulated into patterns and how those patterns could be collected into physical constructs. Mostly he "created" everyday things like dishes, clothing, knickknacks of various design, and even a New York Mets bobble head at Pete's request.

Most evenings the sand itself formed a comfortable bed out in the open for the returnees. One evening, to further demonstrate the possibilities of manifesting, Leo used light to build a complex and beautiful shelter. He held out his hands, commanding a blue laser-like beam, and the sand gathered in an upward stream dropping back in the shape of five small huts placed around a circle. Each hut came fully equipped with a comfortable bed, change of clothes, bath, and any amenity one might find in an expensive island resort. At the center of the circle, trees had gathered around a beautiful pool fed by a waterfall bounding across translucent blue rock slabs lit from underneath. The morphbirds settled in the nearest trees singing peacefully as the moons began to rise in the Eyespellian sky. The sandgroves circled the outer perimeter of the "resort," lighting the area in a panorama of color.

As the five gathered near the pool, the evening meal of flatbread, cheeses, fruits, and nectars of varying colors and tastes manifested on a blanket like the perfect summer's evening picnic. The four returnees surveyed their surroundings in disbelief. They were awed. Melissa pinched herself a few times; Nancy unconsciously began to repeat her mantra under her breath; Antonio mumbled something about heaven and God; and Pete repeatedly flicked the Mets bobble head. No one spoke. Leo hoped he hadn't shown them too much too quickly.

Finally Pete broke the silence. "How far can you hit a baseball, Leo?"

"As far as I want," answered Leo with that twinkle in his eye.

From there the questions came fast and furious. Leo spent the rest of the evening trying to explain the principles behind light manipulation, manifesting, and how thought and the cell-matrix combined to produce the intended result. All five sat by a warming fire until three of the four moons had set. The Eyespellians retired to their respective huts that would be gone in the morning along with the breakfast dishes.

"That particular evening sent me to bed feeling a lot better," said Leo. "For a while, excitement and Eyespellian magic seemed to replace any signs of Earth-plane vibrational leakage. In my gut I knew the tranquility was temporary but at least it gave me a bit of breathing room to think while I was waiting for your arrival, Kathryn. And now you're here."

* * * * * * * *

Leo and Kathryn rounded a smooth bend in the path and then walked down a moderately steep dune. The other four excited returnees stood waiting about one hundred yards ahead. After what seemed forever-in-an-instant, Antonio, Melissa, Nancy, and Pete were finally going to meet with the Elders' Council, still not remembering that Leo was, in fact, a member of that Council. Kathryn and Leo neared the waiting group. Nancy's eyes met Kathryn's and Nancy instantly knew of the deception, knew that Kathryn had feigned to be her spirit guide. Nancy faced Kathryn and screamed, "You lying bitch! How dare you deceive me! How dare you!" The unmitigated hatred in Nancy's eyes and the contempt in her voice stunned the group into an awkward silence where a merry greeting should have been. The smooth bend in the path behind them began to tear and crack at the curved stress points. Thunderheads began to gather directly above them and the pastel serenity of the blue sun became engulfed in the thick pitch-blackness of swirling clouds.

There was a sharp snap in the air, a psychic cracking of a whip. The planetary cell-matrix shifted and both the social and climatic environments began to refocus in a more positive, typically Eyespellian fashion. Nancy's anger dissipated and the path mended itself as the blue sun peeked through the rapidly-scattering thunderclouds.

"Earth-plane vibrational leakage," Leo muttered to himself as he motioned to gather the small group into a prayer circle. "Gather in a tight circle, and quickly," shouted Leo. "Nancy, I want you by my side."

"Why?"

"This is no time to argue, please do as Leo asks," said Kathryn.

Nancy continued in an argumentative tone. "What's the big deal? Why are you so upset over a little thunder and lightning? What's the disaster, what's the big deal?"

Melissa chimed in, "Yeah, what's the urgency here? I don't understand."

As the group irritably questioned Leo's instructions, thunderclouds began to reform in an even more menacing fashion than before. Leo ignored their questions and removed the crystal pyramid from the pouch at his waist. It was attached to a rope of light. Placing the rope around his neck, he held the crystal between his skyward-lifted palms. Within moments, all instinctively gathered into a prayer circle and were bathed in an umbrella of blue light as the blue rays of the planet's sun were focused through the crystal. Each also instinctively knew to remain in the light until Leo lowered his crystal. They prayed as one until the yellow sun set in the western horizon and the blue sun barely hung in the north. They waited in stunned silence for nightfall and moved toward Elaysia under the light of the first three rising moons of Eyespell.

Antonio was the first to speak. "What just happened? Where did the daylight go? And where are we going? Sorry, I feel like I just dropped into a time warp or something."

Kathryn answered, "The planetary cell-matrix was disrupted. We have been in a meditative prayer circle for the last several hours reversing the negative vibrations initiated by Nancy's outburst and the group's irritated questioning of Leo's instructions. And we are going to Elaysia to meet with the Elders' Council."

"Oh yeah, now it's coming back," said Antonio. "Nancy, are you okay?"

"Yes, thanks to Leo. I feel totally embarrassed to have caused all this commotion."

Leo's concern continued to increase. Nancy's embarrassment, while not negative per se, was a further sign that the Earth-plane vibrational leakage was still manifesting itself. Embarrassment was truly an Earth-plane emotion. The path was mended and the clouds dissipated, but to what end, what result? Leo couldn't help but wonder if there was any permanent shift in the cell-matrix that perhaps was running deeper than the sand or higher than the clouds.

The feelings generated by the prayer circle sparked several questions. Nancy began, "I know my outburst caused a potentially serious situation; I can intuit that much. But why? Like I said before, what's the big deal? I don't mean that nastily, I really don't understand."

Leo decided there was no point in hiding anything. He tried to explain the situation. "This is the planet Eyespell, as you already know. This is your home. The physical planet and its people are one, each mindful and respectful of the others' aliveness. Those thunderclouds are as alive as we are. And that, young lady, is what the big deal is."

The concept of "aliveness" got Pete's attention. "Leo, I almost understand, or I should say, I feel what this aliveness is. I feel totally connected to each of you and to this place. Tell me more about Elaysia."

The group had been back long enough so that much of what Leo had to say made sense, at least at some intuitive level. "Elaysia is a beautiful and magnificent gathering place. It is this planet's only city and I use the term loosely. Elaysia is one with its natural environment like two snuggling kittens one upon the other in an afternoon nap. The glassy spires of the city are hardly discernible from the intertwining mountain peaks. Bathed by the two suns by day, and the four moons by night, the pastel hues of the city blend with the landscape. Ordinary city noises enhance the music of its birds and waterfalls rather than create the harsh cacophony one might expect in a typical city.

"Elaysia is central to the created reality of Eyespellians. There is a synergy about Elaysia. Eyespell's collective consciousness is manifested in every molecule, animal, plant and mineral and that manifestion is gloriously apparent in and around Elaysia. As I have explained before, everything on Eyespell is alive and part of what we call the planetary cell-matrix, only somehow even more connected around Elaysia.

"The cracking of the pathway on the dune and the ominous forming of thunderheads at the same instant as Nancy's negative outburst were examples of the force of this cell-matrix. The comings and goings in this place demand a wholesomeness of purpose and uncontaminated thought patterns in order to maintain its skewed lightness.

"Eyespell, your home, is a planet of the light-skew. Earth-plane vibrational leakage is the negative vibrations potentially integrated into your beings as a result of your direct contact with the Earth's environment and people for the twenty years of the Eyespell Experiment. Any display of this negativity, whether outward or internal, threatens Eyespell's existence as a planet of the light-skew. A stray negative vibration, thought, or feeling, if not immediately compensated for, could potentially come alive on Eyespell, creating itself over and over and over, and with ever-increasing intensity. Eyespell is not a place of opposites. It is a place of light, a place of positive in the absence of negative. The enlightened consciousness of this planet Eyespell is a fragile thing."

Antonio, not understanding the inescapable magnitude of what Leo was saying, changed the subject and asked, "How many people are there on Eyespell and how could the vibration of a single person possibly disrupt things?"

Sensing Leo's disappointment at seeming to fail to communicate the seriousness of the situation, Kathryn took up the charge and said with a broad smile, "That's a practical question, Antonio. The entire consciousness of Eyespell and its light-skew centers around community and unconditional love. Eyespellians number only about 250,000 in physical body at any one time. The total energy of the planet incorporates another million or so souls out-of-body within the planet's aura, in transition between physical and non-physical reality, birth and death as Earthlings call it. We have no machines on Eyespell and use no technology in the hardware sense. Eyespell is a manifestation of the thoughts and spirit of the total populace within its aura. We Eyespellians literally create our reality from thought translated into the cell-matrix. This beautiful desert, waterfalls, shelter, food, even existence itself are without exception, thoughts manifested. The formula is simple. We have manifested unconditional love and compassion as the basis for our planet's reality. As Leo said, this is a fragile thing and its takes very little to create an immediate, serious, and potentially harmful response within the cell-matrix. Remember, even a single stray thought can impact reality on Eyespell. So in that context, the entirety of a person's thoughts, if I can put it that way, could be potentially cataclysmic if those thoughts were negative."

Leo interjected, "A negative vibration such as that produced by Earth-plane vibrational leakage could contaminate Eyespell with the dark-skew, manifesting a different and undesirable reality."

Taken by Leo's words, Nancy embraced Kathryn as her anger was temporarily assuaged. Leo returned the crystal to its silk pouch and pulled the cords together, closing it with a sigh of relief. The tension had dissipated and Eyespell once again moved in love and light. With the gesture of a herdsman, Leo swung his hands in the air and exclaimed, "Off to see the Council we go!" There was a true sense of excitement and Leo could feel a sizzle in the air. He said nothing further, feeling that he and Kathryn had finally made their point about Earth-plane vibrational leakage and its potential consequences.

The dome of the Council Chamber stood above the city and was the first thing visible from any direction. On second or third glance, the dome might seem to disappear into the round crest of a multi-colored dune, then seem to reappear. The whole of Elaysia took on this melting-into-the-landscape vision as one approached the city. The desert sands melted into multi-colored hues and the space between the grains filled with thought. Feet crossed those chasms of thought like giant mental bridges. As the returnees moved through Elaysia they began to sense their Eyespellian heritage.

As Leo, Kathryn, and their following reached the Council Chamber, it took several minutes for them to become grounded enough to focus on the finite dimensions of their surroundings. The feeling was out-of-body and utterly expansive. Elaysia was alive around them. The sands were transformed into smooth granite blocks with an undulating serpentine stairway leading to the Chamber entrance. Fountains splashed in every direction and colorful trees lined shaded walkways. There was the sound of birds and the sound of children. It was as if the populace of Eyespell had materialized before them.

There were people everywhere. While they had the appearance of Earthlings, at the same time, they didn't. They had an ever so elusive glow about them. There was a sense of belonging that encompassed the entire plaza. No one spoke but everyone was heard. There was an aura of excitement surrounding the group's return.

The buildings off the spokes of Council Plaza, as it was called, shone with that same granite. While there were no streets, the walkways were as wide as boulevards, boulevards broken by planters with every imaginable type of flower. There were dazzling purples, pinks, blues, and they seemed to change hue as one focused on them. The building entrances were inset; there was a slab of granite that hung at about a sixty degree angle and several feet out from each doorway. Then the building went straight up like a sheer cliff. Each entrance had multi-colored banners displaying pictures and words. Some were shops, some were dwellings, some were eating places, and all blended like soft cotton candy clouds.

People sat on the benches between the huge flower pots. Some appeared to be chatting while others were meditating. The movement of the people around the city was more of a gliding or ice skating than a walking. The whole feeling was one of a Sunday outing with close friends and family.

The birds in the trees ranged in size from hummingbird to eagle. All were colorful and songful, mostly soft and never intrusive. Other colorful insect-like bugs darted among the flowers. There were butterfly-like creatures hovering here, there, and about, and colorful rabbits and squirrels dancing in and out of the maze of walkways and massive flower bowls.

Most of the people were dressed in light clothing and either sandals or bare feet. And some appeared naked, their skin shimmering a color of the rainbow. There was a softness, a smoothing of the body. It looked like one big yoga class with the beautiful and coordinated stretching motions as people moved about.

Leo, Kathryn, and the four made their way up the serpentine stairway and entered the Council Chamber. It was like entering a huge crystal. There was an instantaneous and conscious fusing with the atomic structure of the planetary cell-matrix. The returnees fully and instantly regained their Eyespellian identities and looked around the now familiar surroundings.

The Chamber was an enclosed amphitheater. There were twenty-seven descending and curved rings of stone-like seats. Like all of Eyespell, the amphitheater was alive. As Eyespellians met stone, perfectly contoured cell-chairs enveloped their physical bodies. A raised stage formed the twenty-seventh and center ring. With Eyespell's six Elders at the center and all perimeter rings occupied, the Council Chamber could hold three hundred thirty-seven Eyespellians in manifested physical presence. Such a configuration of Eyespellians was called a Full-Round Session. During a Full-Round, the three hundred thirty-seven maintained total telepathy link with all other Eyespellians as their collective consciousness sought enlightenment born of the very life force of the universe. The Eyespellians, in a very real sense, would "talk to God." All things imagined and all things real would fuse into the same cosmic stuff. The Full-Round had always been the ultimate reality-creating experience on Eyespell, channeling the energy of the planet toward specific outcomes.

On Earth, a personal definition of "God" depends on where and how and to whom a being is born. On Eyespell, God is God. There is no fragmentation. There is so much more to the definition - God is bigger and all-encompassing. God is energy and compassion.

The Full-Round was reserved for special occasions. The vibrational weather needed to be particularly clear and positive to guard against unwanted outside influences. During a Full-Round the slightest stray negative thought anywhere on Eyespell or within the planetary aura extending far into Eyespellian space could easily and instantly translate into an unwanted reality. With the positive light-skewed nature of the planet it would take little for the Universe to impose, matter-of-factly, its typical balance of light and dark upon Eyespell.

Eyespell's defiance of the continuum of opposites suggests that if balance were to happen on this planet it would mean destroying its skewed lightness. Eyespell's light-skew leaves it open to a chaos unmatched. In the normal scope of a more balanced, if less enlightened planetary evolution, diverse factors of light and dark would have less of an impact. Eyespell's absolutely positive bent is its most dangerous enemy. This seemingly perfect planet suffers from an innate, fragile, and potentially self-destructive intolerance for anything unlike itself. Earth-plane vibrational leakage is a force unlike Eyespell and represents that cataclysmic diversity in the face of Eyespell's absolute intolerance for any blend of light and dark.

The small group began to descend toward the center of the chamber, chatting excitedly among themselves. Leo moved ahead of his companions to take his place as an Elder on the raised center stage at the twenty-seventh and lowest ring of the domed amphitheater. The other five members of the Elders' Council were coming into body at center stage. Each had a pouch containing a crystal at his or her side on a rope of light like Leo's, only of different colors. Each crystal's color vibration corresponded to the bearer's custodial charge for a portion of Eyespell's light-skew.

Using their crystals, the Elders could bend light into the colors of the Eyespellian rainbow, a rainbow with an infinite range of hues, all in harmony with the primary colors of the planet's two suns and four moons. It was this type of light bending through his crystal that had enabled Leo to bathe the prayer circle in blue light. Leo's crystal corresponded to the blue sun and the Blue-Light-Corridor, the Corridor of Peace. Color fusion, the making of rainbows, and light bending are more than esoteric or aesthetic pastimes on Eyespell. Light is always the first manifestation of Eyespellian reality. Therefore, anything of the light-skew on Eyespell is serious business.

The group members continued making their way into the Council Chamber. The Full-Round had been called in honor of their return. Each of the twenty-seven circle-rows in the Council Chamber had a specific vibrational level and each Eyespellian resonated to a specific row. The closer to the center, the more powerful the vibration, and the higher the row number. This did not, however, represent a hierarchy of power; each of the vibrational levels was regarded with equal dignity and as essential to the total community of Eyespellians. Different intensities of vibration were needed for different things. Kathryn, like Leo, moved ahead of the group and she proceeded to the twenty-first ring of the amphitheater to take her designated place. The four Eyespell Experiment participants moved to the third ring and stood waiting, intuitively knowing not to move closer to the center at this time. The rare meeting of the Full-Round was about to begin. The amphitheater was rapidly filling to its capacity of three-hundred-thirty-seven, and Antonio, Melissa, Nancy, and Pete found themselves surrounded by a multitude of various, flowing pastel-hued robes. All were finally gathered in physical presence. The Full-Round of Eyespell commenced.

CHAPTER 8

▼

IN THE FAMILY ROOM …

Koy just sat there for several minutes looking at Phillip, then Jo, then Erio, then the moose, then Phillip, the moose, then Phillip. Finally she tried to speak but her voice simply failed her. Aside from a funny little squeak nothing emerged.

"I take it you're gathering your wits," said Phillip with a soft smile. "I assume the reality of what I am sharing with you is beginning to really settle in."

Koy gave the stuffed moose one long last look and managed to blurt out, "Well, for Christ's sake, Phillip, you're a goddamn alien! And I don't mean from some other country either. I get it, I really do; you're from another planet. I mean I thought I got it before, you know on the last bite of cheesecake. But I don't think it actually sunk in; it was a novel idea, but I don't think I actually processed it. I mean you are going on about the Eyespell Experiment, these returnees, Leo, Kathryn, Elaysia, the Council of the Elders. Holy Christ, Leo; I mean Phillip. Maybe the moose should drive me back to Leesburg."

"Like I said, it's the story you will never print."

"Or what, you'll send little telepathy bugs into my brain and make me forget I was ever here? Okay, I think my panic attack is over. I could really use a stiff drink though."

99

Jo walked into the room, her absence having gone unnoticed by Koy, balancing three short glasses of ice with an amber liquid coming up to the second cube. "I figured it would be about time for a drink. This is a great single malt scotch, hope it does the trick." She handed Koy a glass, gave one to Phillip, and settled back with the third one comfortably resting in the palm of her hand. She got that smile of hers again and raising her glass, toasted, "To the rest of the story."

"I don't even drink," said Koy as she downed her scotch in one easy motion. "Boy I needed that," she said, tipping her glass to the moose. "I can see why you guys have such a big moose in your family room; you need it as a distraction as you share the impossible with your unsuspecting guests."

"Not fair," said Phillip. "You are hardly 'unsuspecting.' You wanted to solve the mystery of the pink, now you have it. Actually I think you are recovering rather well. Wanna hear more?"

"How about I have a refill on my coffee and then you tell me more after you answer a couple of questions; would that work? Jo, where's the pot? I'll get it, if I can still walk."

"Just around the corner to the left." When Koy left the room, Jo gave Phillip a big wink and said, "She's the one, Phillip, you are absolutely right about that.

"Okay, I'm back. Can I pour for anyone else?"

"That sounds good, more coffee is always good," said Phillip.

"How about you, Jo?"

"I'm going to pass for now. I'm dying to hear what questions you have for the alien doctor."

"Well, you can imagine how taken aback I was when the fact that you are really an alien from another planet finally sunk in."

"Careful there. I am only sort of an alien if you really think about it. I was actually born right here on Earth, in the good old US of A, right here in Virginia in fact."

"Keep this up and I'll need another drink, several perhaps. You had me convinced you were an alien from Eyespell and now you're not?"

"Well, I am but I'm not. It's a technicality surrounding the Eyespell Experiment and how I actually got here. But that part of the story is for later. Just be careful who you're calling an alien, that's all. I'm sensitive."

Jo about choked. "Yeah, Mr. Sensitive, excuse me, Dr. Sensitive. You bring Koy out into the wilds of rural Virginia, ply her with dinner, introduce her to your loving and normal wife, sit her down next to the dog and the moose, and then fill her head with impossible stories between bites of cheesecake. Yeah, that's definitely sensitive. Thank God she's a woman. Can you picture some guy sitting here trying to deal with this with the male, linear, non-multitasking brain? Non-linear, straight; you know, the penis thing."

Phillip threw his hands up in supplication but before he could say anything Koy volunteered, "Yeah, ply me with dinner and fill my head with crazy stuff. Okay, alien or not, here I come. You claim to be an Eyespellian; in fact you told me or mind-linked me that you are in fact, the missing Eyespellian. You were supposed to go back to Eyespell at the end of the Eyespell Experiment, the details yet to come, but got stuck here somehow. Is that accurate?"

"Yeah, close enough."

"So, somewhere in this yet unfinished tale you must have discovered you were not from here, not from Earth that is."

"Exactly right, Ms. Sosa."

"Well now, that had to be a pretty weird discovery."

"Do you think? Weird is an understatement. Instead of ending up back on Eyespell, I woke up in a hospital with absolutely no memory and no identification. So for a while I was from nowhere. I affectionately call this period in my life 'the time of madness.' It's fitting that I ended up a psychologist."

"That sounds terrifying."

"Trust me, it was pretty scary. That's when I met Jo, at the height of my insanity. She truly saved me didn't you, hon?"

"Oh yeah, he was definitely certifiable when I met him." With that devil smile she added, "I had to save him, they told me to. You know Phillip here is not the only one in the room with super powers."

"Good grief, don't tell me you're from elsewhere also."

"No, not to worry, I'm full-fledged Earthling, just special, sort of like you actually."

Koy blushed under Jo's gaze. "Maybe you had better tell me the rest of the story."

"Oh, one more little tidbit that's kind of interesting," said Phillip. "When I finally recovered my memory and even later when I became aware of Eyespell I realized that I knew Melissa."

"Really."

"Turns out we were in school together in Florida and had actually made plans to commit suicide together. In fact, I was on my way to meet her for our final event when the unthinkable happened, and so to the rest of the story."

"My mind is all yours," said Koy, giving Phillip one wide eye, a scrunched up nose, and slightly twisted mouth."

"It's hard to mind-link with a face that looks like that, but I'll do my best. I bet I can finish zip-driving you the information before you can get that silly look off your face. One, two, three, go!"

CHAPTER 9

▼

MANAGING THE LIGHT-CORRIDORS OF EYESPELL

Still standing at the third row of the Council Chamber, Antonio, Melissa, and Nancy were engaged in highly animated conversation while Pete, a few feet away, stood silent, completely mesmerized by the flurry of activity around him as the Full-Round was about to begin. Falling deeper into his apparent daydreaming, Pete slowly became aware that the goings-on he perceived were not coming from his surroundings at all, but from inside his own head. It was as if he were greeting and being greeted simultaneously by everyone present in the Chamber, maybe even everyone on the planet. Pete was experiencing complete telepathy link for the first time since his return to Eyespell. Having difficulty managing this newly rediscovered faculty, he simply sat down where he was and allowed his mind to receive and reach out best he could.

In addition to all of the telepathic commotion, Pete began to flash back to a time when he was one of Leo's students. He envisioned Leo sitting cross-legged with a small group of youngsters also sitting cross-legged in a semicircle facing him. They were hanging on their teacher's every word.

"Now pay close attention," said Leo. "This part is very important. As we have already discussed, the maintenance of the light-skew on Eyespell is a complex matter. Our legends tell of the very creation of the light-corridors of Eyespell and the simultaneous creation of a very special system to manage those light-corridors. That system containing the principles upon which Eyespell is managed to this day was simply called Mystic Management. The history of the creation of the light-corridors and Mystic Management are recorded in the *Book of Dreams*. Who can tell me about the *Book of Dreams*? How about you, Pete?"

Still watching his daydream, Pete chuckled as his younger self all but fell face-first in the sand in his enthusiasm to answer his teacher's question. The young Pete blurted out, "The *Book of Dreams* is a book of, a book of, ah, a book of dreams."

Leo laughed and said, "And a green and purple songbird is a green and purple songbird. Actually, Peter, you're not that far off, and your enthusiasm more than makes up for your imprecision. The *Book of Dreams* is composed of complex symbolic images rather than simple text pages, and a single image has been known to keep our historians and scholars in lively discussion and debate for hours, even days, at a time. It is, indeed, a book of dreams, complex ones laying out fundamental Eyespellian truths. Our task today is to review and synthesize a number of the basic images relating to the light-corridors and Mystic Management. The *Book* provides much practical information about these matters. Look at the chart I have given you. In unison, tell me what the six essential elements of each light-corridor are. Come on now, don't be shy."

Leo cupped his hands behind his ears and leaned toward his students. They sat at attention and pretended to be the instruments of a symphony responding to the conductor's undulations. Not exactly in unison they sang out in sing-song fashion, "The first essential element of each light-corridor is its crystal."

"Good," said Leo. "And what do you know about these crystals?"

This time Pete jumped in without hesitation. "Each Elder is in charge of a crystal that reflects the same color as one of the light-corridors. There are six crystals and they've existed nearly forever. They have been passed down from Elder to Elder, and each is a polished double pyramid, pointed at both ends. They are identical in size, exactly

1.33 inches square at the center and exactly 3.33 inches tall, tip to tip. Each crystal is formed from a different gemstone, each displaying perfect clarity. And each crystal weighs exactly 9.99 grams despite its density. An Elder is never without the crystal of his or her light-charge, carrying it either in a silk pouch at the waist or around the neck on a rope of light. The crystals focus energy on the spirits and emotions of our people."

Leo responded like a proud parent, "That's quite a dissertation, young Pete. You are quite sure of yourself after all. Does anybody here know the color of my crystal?"

The reverie continuing, Pete smiled again at the image of his much younger self. For the first time he realized that Antonio, Melissa, Nancy, and even Phillip were among the group attending Leo's history lesson of long ago. Pete felt so connected. He found it hard to imagine that Phillip was not with the group in the Council Chamber on this day. He could feel him so clearly in his daydream.

As if on cue, Phillip popped up and tugged gently at Leo's robe and said, "Leo, show us your crystal. Yours is the blue one."

In unison the children said, "Please, Leo, oh please, can we see it, please?"

Leo undid the drawstring of the pouch at his waist and produced a perfect double pyramid of clear sapphire. It dangled from a rope of blue light as he held it in front of him, almost touching the now misshapen semicircle of students below him. The crystal flashed blue light that could be felt as it caressed the small group. An overwhelming peace came over them.

"My crystal's not blue," said Leo.

Nancy looked at him and said, "You're just trying to trick us. Your crystal doesn't have to be blue, only its light has to be blue."

"Exactly right. You are all just too smart for this old man. So then, what's the next essential element of a light-corridor?" Leo straightened his back and the semicircle of pupils regained its shape.

This time Antonio spoke up. "The second essential element of a light-corridor is its affiliation with one of the suns or moons. And I know the answer to your next question. Your crystal is of the blue sun."

"Wonderful, Antonio. And does anyone know what trait the blue sun represents?" asked Leo.

"You're getting at the third element," chimed in Nancy. Peace is the trait for the Blue-Light-Corridor. We could tell that just by the way we felt when you held out your crystal."

Pete, both in the present and in his flashback, thought, "How odd sitting no more than three feet away from Melissa, Antonio, and Nancy right here in the Council Chamber while at the same time being with them in a childhood daydream that is so real." His thought shifted and he again heard Leo talking softly to his pupils.

"Okay, you've got the idea. You have the essential elements a little out of order but no matter. An image from the *Book of Dreams* will clear it right up. I would hate to squelch your enthusiasm in my desire for perfection. I have given each of you a copy of an image that lists the six essential elements of each light-corridor in the proper order, beginning with the color of the light-corridor and ending with the Elder responsible for that corridor. The order is corridor color, crystal color, celestial body, trait, mystic principle, and Elder in charge."

Pete looked down and could see the image Leo was talking about. It was as if he were seeing it both now and back in time, and Pete easily recalled the chart in its entirety.

CORRIDOR COLOR	CRYSTAL COLOR	CELESTIAL BODY	TRAIT	MYSTIC PRINCIPLE	ELDER
RED	RUBY	FIRST MOON	ENERGY	COLLABORATIVE CREATIVITY	MATTHEW
BLUE	CLEAR SAPPHIRE	BLUE SUN	PEACE	EGO EMPOWERMENT	LEO
PINK	PINK TOURMALINE	FOURTH MOON	LOVE	GENTLE GENEROSITY	MYANA
WHITE	CLEAR QUARTZ	THIRD MOON	ONENESS	INCLUSIVE INTEGRITY	GRACINA
GREEN	EMERALD	SECOND MOON	NATURE	KARMIC KINDNESS	NATHAN
YELLOW	CLEAR DIAMOND	YELLOW SUN	KNOW-LEDGE	SYSTEMS SENSITIVITY	DANIEL (Head Elder)

Leo gave his students several minutes to ponder the image. He continued, "The combined infinite hues of the six light-corridors make up Eyespell's light-skew. Even though each Elder is appointed to manage a single light-corridor, responsibility for the maintenance of the light-skew is shared by every citizen. Each of you is part of this sharing. Our being here together is an example of this. Our planet is a totally empowered society, to a person, even you kids."

A young boy sitting beside Antonio spoke up, "I don't understand the word 'empowered'."

"Excellent point. To empower is to share, to allow everybody to participate, to contribute; to make everybody feel good about what they are doing. It's that kind of thing. This kind of empowerment, although based in high ideals, does demand a kind of social structure. This is where the Elders and Mystic Management come into play. The day-to-day management of the planet's affairs rests primarily with the six Elders who make up the Elders' Council. The Eldersix, as we are often called, are looked to for leadership in both spiritual and corporal matters. Our leadership style is that of consensus and respect among all Eyespellians, not of power held exclusively by the Council. Does that help explain empowerment or have I raised more questions than I have answered?"

Everyone looked at Leo and sang out, "We think it's time for a break!" With that they jumped up and surrounded Leo, threatening mischief.

Pete watched the scenario continue to unfold. He thought, "I'm literally a part of my daydream." By the time he had finished his present moment thought the daydream had jumped ahead of him. His mind fast-forwarded through the break and picked up where the teachings resumed.

After a short time, Leo said, "Okay, settle down. The break is over. Now, back to the day-to-day management of the planet. Due to our telepathy links there is never a question of miscommunication or hidden agendas among Eyespellians. The net effect of this level of openness is that there are no politics necessary in our Mystic Management."

Pete was particularly interested in this part as he saw his younger self yell out, "Are we going to learn about Mystic Management, Leo?"

"Relax, Peter, I'm getting there," Leo said with approval in his eyes. "Mystic Management is our planet's culture, our style. It is the antithesis of the typical power structures developed on some of the other planets we have already studied, Earth for example. Our structure revolves around six tenets that are geared toward sustainability. Notice how everything seems to come in sixes on Eyespell. Six is the number that represents personality, magnetism, and the community that is Eyespell. Anyway, the Elders have managed Eyespell in the Mystic Management tradition since the creation of the light-corridors. This tradition, as explained in the *Book of Dreams*, dictates how we manage our lives and our planet. So now it's time to study the six principles themselves. Okay, can anyone name one of the principles?"

Pete saw himself enthusiastic and again yelling out, "My chart lists Collaborative Creativity as part of the Red-Light-Corridor."

"Yes, and Collaborative Creativity, is, in fact, the first principle. It promotes a style that examines all ideas. Creativity for its own sake holds a position of respect and is an integral part of decision making in virtually every aspect of our lives. The decision making process itself is managed by one or more Elders depending upon the light-corridor or corridors needed to accomplish the task at hand. This is no simple process. Even with the aid of direct telepathy links, examining all available information and allowing for maximum creative input literally from everyone on the planet can be a lengthy process. Everybody's ideas are welcomed all the time. So, here on Eyespell *creative* is rarely synonymous with *rapid* and, of course, as you know, time is essentially irrelevant anyway.

"Because we have no medium of exchange as such, the inherent conflict that is caused by the correlation between time and money is eliminated. Since time is not money on Eyespell, and there is no economic gain or loss in terms of how long creative decisions may take, all things can be explored until consensus is achieved. Our lack of a typical economic system, like the ones we have seen on other worlds, allows Collaborative Creativity to exist in the purest sense. Moreover, our ability to manifest necessary resources through manipulation of the light-corridors eliminates the concept of scarcity. In the absence of concern over scarce resources and with no time constraint, Collaborative

Creativity easily maintains a paramount and unopposed position in our society."

The reverie split apart for a moment and Pete found himself connected to another set of thoughts. "The lack of scarcity discussed as part of Collaborative Creativity is one positive result of the light-skew and good reason for Eyespellians to eschew balance. Balance would imply alternating cycles of plenty versus scarcity and a lesser ability to maintain a Collaborative Creativity. Earth-plane vibrational leakage has the potential to create a balance, not a good thing for Eyespell." Pete recognized these thoughts as Leo's, but not from the daydream. He looked up, caught Leo's glance from across the Council Chamber, and began to understand how telepathy link can take several directions at once. He again heard Leo's voice in his head, "It's time to get back to your reverie."

The daydream picked up without losing so much as a sentence. Leo was again talking to the semicircle of students before him, "The second principle, Ego Empowerment, also speaks of our rule by consensus. The focus is on shared ideas and a group centered leadership. The orientation is other-directed rather than I-directed. There is a mutual respect for the unique talents and abilities of every member of the Eyespellian community. We do not operate in a hierarchical fashion. While the six light-corridors are different each from the other, no corridor is considered better or more powerful than another. For example, Daniel, head of the Eldersix and Keeper of the Yellow-Light-Corridor, is no greater or lesser than any other Eyespellian. His focus is on knowledge and he brings his personal qualities to bear on his light-charge. He is a focal point, a beginning point for sharing. He provides a starting place, a point of departure in what would otherwise appear totally chaotic."

Nancy waved her hands in the air with a question that just couldn't wait, "We shine with color. Does this have anything to do with what you're saying?"

"Now there's an interesting question, young lady, and pretty perceptive. I'm sure your parents have discussed this with you in a general way, but not in relation to the light-corridors or to the principle of Ego Empowerment specifically. Each of us has a primary affiliation with one of the six light-corridors. You might say we resonate with that light-corridor. The color of our affinity corridor is reflected in the shading of our skin; the stronger the resonance with a particular corridor, the more obvious the skin tone. You used the words 'shine with color.' You're exactly right. These skin tones are not flat and consistent hues, but a shimmering fire of colors like those of an opal being slowly turned in the sunlight. If one were to look closely, for example, Daniel flashes distinct yellow tones aligned primarily with Systems Sensitivity and the Yellow-Light-Corridor while I give off an obvious blue more aligned with Peace and the Blue-Light-Corridor. These various flashes of color among the populace are a perfect blend with the hues of the planet and its two suns and four moons. Eyespell is literally a place of color diversity that culminates in a feeling of oneness through acceptance and all-inclusive community. You have already been taught total acceptance. What might be new to you are the broader concepts of oneness and inclusive community as extensions of that acceptance."

Again Pete picked up Leo's present moment thoughts, "And the impact of Earth-plane vibrational leakage would be to fragment community. Even the physical color of Eyespell could potentially change. Balance could cause a blending of colors across the planet resulting in colors different, and probably darker, than we currently experience. The balancing vibrations from the Earth's dark-skew of negativity would produce a planet definitely darker in color. It would be like metaphorically mixing black pigment into a can of pastel blue paint in the hope of lightening it. The concept is disconcerting." Leo waved from across the Council Chamber and said into Pete's consciousness, "Sorry, I've interrupted again. Continue with your daydream; it is important that you fill in the details about Eyespell. You have an important role to play in our future."

Pete did not have time to be puzzled by Leo's comment as his mind again reached out and captured the continuing daydream. The dream-Leo was back at his teaching. "Gentle Generosity is the third aspect of the Mystic Management. This refers to our always going the extra step to encourage others. It is the giving to someone else while simultaneously freeing one's own insecurities. Eyespell is a planet of positive self-concept and continuous positive identity formation. Our studies show that many peoples from faraway planets are plagued with identity crisis. Unlike us, they do not know who they are or where they are going either individually or collectively. We experience identity-building through a collective conscious that each of us can relate to. Other places experience identity fragmentation through inconsistent interpretation of a collective unconscious fraught with confusing and stereotypical imagery. There is little ambiguity in Eyespellian identity. The *Book of Dreams* is filled with identity-building images that can be manifested through light combined with thought. A magnificent example is an image called 'The Identity Garden,' which is found in Dream V, Image 1. Mind-link with me and let's image together."

Leo closed his eyes and brought the image of "The Identity Garden" into his head for his pupils to share.

The Identity Garden

The young monk had a dream about the most beautiful place he had *never* been. He was hiking up a subalpine meadow. The snow, freshly melted, revealed carpets of wildflowers in honor of summer. And there, high above his path, hiding in the mountain's mist, he could make out a curlicue wrought iron gate hanging between the parting ends of a massive wall that hugged the steep slopes. As he approached the gate, the dream stuff stretched and he found himself amidst a pleasant crowd of people making their way through. The cornerstone in the wall named the place "The Identity Garden." Immediately inside and stuck in the middle of the pathway, a little keep-off-the-grass-type sign instructed: "PICK WHAT YOU WANT."

The monk awoke with a host of new metaphors from the dream garden. There was the wall, constructed of the building blocks of short-term goals and sustained positive motivation. There were the tall and skirted firs of aspiration and inspiration in the alpine meadow. There was the fountain of unconditional love at the garden's hub. From the myriad flowers abounding one could fashion a bouquet of identity. There were curiosity, compassion, truthfulness, trust, self-assuredness, and a non-judging attitude, all in full bloom. There was limitless possibility for choosing psychological healthiness among the objects and flowers in the garden of identity. In a word, there was hope.

Leo opened his eyes to find his pupils still immersed in the garden, each selecting a bouquet of identity. Finally Leo spoke, "The sharing of these images is a celebration and brings us to our greatest vibrational level. Constant sharing and giving produce a state of planetary self-actualization. Gentle Generosity is truly the heart of Eyespell."

Pete's consciousness returned momentarily to the Council Chamber. He was profoundly affected by the imaging in his daydream. He now knew exactly who he was. He recalled the details of the Eyespell Experiment, his role in it, and the concern about Earth-plane vibrational leakage. He also knew that he resonated with the Yellow-Light-Corridor and that his natural place was in the twenty-sixth ring of the Council Chamber. For now, however, he chose to stay where he was and to finish his daydream. Leo looked up and smiled in confirmation.

The students were reluctant to leave imaging, and Leo had to coax them back to their lesson: "Bring your image with you into the next principle, Inclusive Integrity. Inclusive Integrity celebrates the light-skew as the coming together of six diverse light-corridors. It allows for the complementarity of different qualities merging into a synergistic whole. While the guiding principles of Mystic Management must remain intact, the specific style within each light-corridor is directly tied to its Elder and the Eyespellians affiliated most closely with that corridor. The manner in which I empower within the Blue-Light-Corridor need not be identical to how Daniel empowers within the Yellow-Light-Corridor. Equifinality, the ability to do things in more than one way, is the concept in play here. We maintain the light-skew through an empowered society. Exactly how that is done may vary from light-corridor to light-corridor and from individual to individual. Any questions?"

Leo paused for a few moments and then continued, "Of course I know there are never any questions in response to the question, 'any questions?' It's just a technique I use when I really want to move along. And so on to Karmic Kindness, the simplest principle of all: what goes around comes around and kindness is the only way. Kindness is the nature of all things on Eyespell, whether one is speaking of the nature of relationships or literally the natural environment as reflected in the cell-matrix. Eyespell is compassion personified."

From across the Council Chamber Leo again added a footnote to Pete's dreaming. "Imagine the negative possibilities of Earth-plane vibrational leakage with regard to this principle. It would be difficult enough to lose creativity, to lose empowerment, to lose diversity of color, or to not be self-actualized; but imagine the dark-skew balancing Eyespell's kindness with different types of unkindness, like violence for example. This is a most frightening prospect. Nancy's recent outburst toward Kathryn is a prime example. This minor confrontation was almost instantly translated into the cell-matrix and began to wreak havoc. You saw the thunderclouds and the path beginning to crack. While temporarily averted, the overall effects of this leakage have yet to be felt, I'm afraid. I've done it again. Get on with your daydream lessons."

Leo's teaching voice again drifted to the front of Pete's mind, "And finally there is Systems Sensitivity. This is the understanding that all things, whether of mind, physical reality, or spirit, are interconnected. What happens in one part affects all other parts. This is an essential element in manifesting everything on Eyespell. It is the linking-pin between the light-skew and the planetary cell-matrix. Since a single thought can be captured and manifested within the cell-matrix, positive thinking in the absence of anything negative is vital. The impact of negative vibrations could prove to be impossible for us to handle.

"The Elders always maintain their light-charges in the Mystic Management tradition, holding the six principles paramount in the management of the light-corridors of Eyespell. In a nutshell, that's Mystic Management. Let's sit in silence for a few moments to capture the spirit of what I have said and what you have learned."

Pete watched as the children reflected upon their lesson. Phillip was the first to speak, "Leo, if the light-skew is the manifestation of all six light-corridors into the planetary cell-matrix, is it the cell-matrix that gives Eyespell its physical reality of total connectedness?"

"Yes, yes, now you're getting it. The body of Eyespell, its physical being, is manifested through the reality-creating process itself, and this process is a most fascinating aspect of our planet's culture. Observing an Elder manage a light-corridor for the purpose of creating, within the light-skew, a new vibration that is ultimately manifested within the physical cell-matrix, is truly a magic show. It is Mystic Management in action."

"Can you give us an example, Leo?" asked Melissa.

"Ah, let me think of a good one. Yes, yes, a wonderful example of this reality-creating activity was solving the problem of transportation. We had a need to get from one place to another on the planet's surface as well as travel among the four moons. The Elders' Council met, and using the principle of Collaborative Creativity, opened the transportation issue to all ideas. There was much discussion. The gathering of information and consensus-reaching among all Eyespellians took a very long time. Nonetheless, this was a joyous process and is an integral part of our culture. There was no hurry to complete the task. That's not to say we worked only on the transportation problem. It is not uncommon for us to have hundreds, even thousands, of reality-creating tasks occurring simultaneously, some very complex and some very simple.

"Ultimately, a fascinating decision was reached; it was decided to keep the planet machine-free. Any transportation system would, therefore, have to be energy based and capable of instantly transporting Eyespellians from place to place. Since energy was the focus of this task, it was placed squarely in the Red-Light-Corridor, and under the auspices of the Elder Matthew.

"Matthew gathered all Eyespellians within his light-charge and together they walked in prayer to the Red Sand Desert in time for the rising of the first moon. By the way, the Red-Light-Corridor has the greatest number of people affiliated with it; a full 30 percent of the population is needed to manage its skew. What a sight! A team of approximately seventy-five thousand gathered into a great spiral moving slowly in a clockwise direction. Already in deep meditation they began to focus on Matthew's ruby crystal now extended by his fingertips toward the heavens. Suddenly the Red-Light-Corridor opened. Its energy exploded like a volcano through the crown chakras of seventy-five thousand Eyespellians set on the identical conscious image of the agreed-upon transporter system."

Leo had become effusive in his description and his pupils sat transfixed and wide-eyed, fully imagining that they were there, themselves creating the transporter system. Pete stood up waving his arms and making explosion noises, "Was it like this, Leo?"

"Even greater. After the defining thought, an explosion of light is always the first kernel of reality-creating. As the light passed through the consciousness of those seventy-five thousand set in prayer, the image was projected like a laser onto the red sands. This was the connection with the cell-matrix and, poof, the thought was converted to physical reality. Deeply resonating, single-syllable chanting and tremendous fireworks of red light accompanied the whole process. Then it ended as abruptly as it began. The Red-Light-Corridor closed. What was left behind was the comprehensive system of energy vortices that allow us to freely and almost instantly travel in physical body around the planet's surface and to its four moons. And we're all familiar with that."

"Wow, what a story," said Melissa. "Is any of this dangerous?"

Leo thought for a moment, then said, "I'm not sure dangerous is the right word. The most important conditions for accomplishing this are the purity of the color in the light-corridor and the sameness of the image in each person's consciousness at the time of the corridor opening. Any stray color or thought would produce a result different from that intended. The only thing that might be construed as dangerous is the possibility of negativity entering the system during reality-creating. This has never happened."

Leo practically yelled into Pete's head, "Until now, anyway! I never really thought about it much back then because the possibility seemed so remote. Sorry, finish up your daydream, Pete."

"Just one more thing, then we'll quit for today. The most dramatic, exciting, and beautiful outcomes of our ability to reality-create through manipulation of the light-corridors are exhibited in our natural surroundings. Just look around you. In the scope of things, Eyespell is a comparatively small planet, about the size of Mercury in Earth's solar system, for example. We are located at the fringe of the Pinar Galaxy in a small solar system with only two sister planets, both uninhabited. But you already know this. Our planet's most unusual characteristic is its configuration of two suns and four moons. In the entire universe known to us there is nothing quite like it. We have spent much time and energy designing the natural environment of both the planet's surface and the four moons. Although Eyespell appears pink from outer space, it's actually made up of an infinite-color array. Each of our six deserts, for example, displays the full color range of a particular light-corridor in its shifting sands. The Green Desert shows off streaks of every imaginable shade of green in constant and shifting blend. How many of you have been to the Green Desert?"

Everyone in the group raised a hand and the girl next to Nancy said, "I've been to all six deserts and I think the green one is the most beautiful." As she turned her head in the soft light, barely perceptible flashes of green reflected back from her cheeks. She continued, "From my other studies it seems that the term desert is a misnomer. Other than the sand itself, our deserts display none of the parched characteristics commonly associated with them. For example, they are neither overly hot nor dry like the deserts on the planet closest to our yellow sun. Our deserts are wonderful places to walk."

"And to meditate," added Leo. "Meditation is something you will spend a great deal of time doing. Walking meditation is indeed the great Eyespellian pastime. Our deserts are also places of beautiful mountains, streams, waterfalls, meadows, small forests and all manner of other undesert-like topography. I am pretty sure we just love the word *desert* and we are truly fond of creating colored sands."

"Except on the moons," blurted out Antonio. "I've been to the first moon with Matthew, keeper of the Red-Light-Corridor and I didn't see one grain of sand."

"And what are the moons like?" quizzed Leo.

Melissa volunteered, "They are like magnificent gardens. Each moon favors a light-corridor in its color array, but there's no sand. I have only been to the fourth moon. It's a wonderful, predominately pink garden; there is every imaginable flower in every shade of pink the mind can comprehend. The birds and cats are shades of pink, and even the water has a pinkish glow. However, I've seen pictures of all four moons. Well, we all have, and I think the most spectacular picture in the art gallery in Elaysia is of the third moon. It is a garden of white light taking in and reflecting back the entire light-skew in an explosion of color that is beyond all imagination."

"Indeed," added Leo, "the third moon is within Gracina's light-charge and is truly a place of unparalleled beauty and oneness. On that wonderful image let's stop for today."

Pete awoke from his daydream and again caught Leo's glance from across the Council Chamber. Leo sent yet another message to Pete, "A looming concern with Earth-plane vibrational leakage is the manner in which the dark-skew might change the colors of Eyespell. As I said, the current threat is like putting black pigment in a pastel-colored paint. I think I need to close my telepathy link before I contaminate the Council Chamber with my worrisome thoughts if I haven't done so already. I am glad you have finished your daydream lesson." Leo smiled and prepared for the Council opening.

Pete got up from where he was sitting and made his way down the Council Chamber aisle, greeting Antonio, Melissa, and Nancy with a broad smile as he moved past them on his way to take up his place in the twenty-sixth ring.

CHAPTER 10

▼

IN THE FAMILY ROOM …

"Well, I'll be," said Koy. "I really like this mind-link in zip format. What you just told me would have taken half the night. Can't say I'm used to it, but I like it. It's really hard to catch up in real time. In fact, it's amazing that the information sticks as well as it does. But it's not just planted there; it still comes through as though we had been talking for hours and my normal processing is intact. What I mean is that even though things appear to be happening almost instantly I still recall my mulling over a lot of what you have presented. I don't exactly get that."

Phillip interjected, "You are thinking linearly, or I should say in terms of linear time. Eyespell does not always work that way. Time is, well, it's time but not an a-to-z thing. Did that make any sense?"

"No, sort of, not really, kind of."

"That clears things up."

"You know what, Phillip, I am not going to try to figure the time thing out just yet; I'm going to let that one simmer some more. What I am intrigued by, however, is that while I finally get that you're Eyespellian, the missing Eyespellian to be precise, I never thought to connect Eyespell with Mystic Management. So all that stuff I wrote about in *Reflections on Mystic Management*, is, in a sense, Eyespellian dogma. How did you come to be privy to all of that?"

"I'm not sure I like the word dogma, it makes Mystic Management sound like a religion. Then we'd have to start a crusade and go out and kill people in the name of it."

"You could always start your own church; maybe something like the Church of the Intertwining Minds and Foot?"

"Boy, you just don't let anything go, do you, Ms. Sosa?"

"Hey, you don't get to be a star reporter by letting things go, right Joseph? she said, giving the moose a sideways glance. So, how did the tenets of Mystic Management make it to Earth anyway?"

"Now there's a story and I'll get to it, I promise. Christian and I had quite an experience in Sedona awhile back."

"Wait a minute. Speaking of experiences, you were going to tell me about the time of madness as you phrased it. You never so much as mentioned it in that last download, if I may call it that."

"Oh gosh, I'll get there, I promise. I just can't say when. The parts of the 'story you will never print' all happen together, not sequentially. It's an Eyespell story and not tied up with that time thing we don't want to discuss."

Jo leaned forward and said, "Don't even try to keep up with the Eyespellian over there. We've been together for years and I still get mixed up. Sometimes I feel as though today is the first time we met; other times I feel we've known each other for eternity, and other times I just want to strangle the goddamn *alien* as you so aptly put it."

"That's really low, Koy did not mean it that way when she called me a goddamn alien; she was only venting her surprise, no nastiness intended."

"Yes, but wait until you've finished your story and scrambled most of what she thought was true before she showed up in Waterford this evening. Isn't that right, Eric? Come here and let me scratch your ears. Oh God, not you, Phillip! Go sit down and behave."

"That's it," said Koy. "Time for a potty break. I need to clear my head."

"Okay, but before you are allowed to leave the room I think a three-way hug is in order. All kidding aside, Koy, you are handling this better than I could ever have hoped for. I think Jo is right, I think you are special like she is."

"I suspect that's the nicest compliment I have ever been paid. Thank you, thank you both and now I'm going potty."

Eric barked that "I think that's a wonderful idea" bark and everybody got up; Koy headed for the bathroom, Jo for the back door with Eric in tow, and Phillip just wandered about stretching, and thinking what an amazing night this was turning out to be. "I think she will tell the story," he mused.

A few minutes later everyone returned to the family room. Koy got things started, "What an amazing evening. I thought I was going to get a few interesting insights about you, Phillip, that I could use as follow-up to the *Reflections* article. Instead, I'm getting the story of a real ET trapped on the earth, the history of a planet of the light-skew that's God knows where in the universe, and I think I'm getting why it's called Mystic Management."

"Just for the record, Eyespell is in the Pinar Galaxy."

"Well, that ties it up neatly. I'm afraid to ask where that might be and how one might get there. From the little you've said so far it sounds like a wonderful place; better to move there than to Europe or Costa Rica even. Okay, I'm still a mere Earthling and I still operate in linear time and I would love it if you would fill in a few gaps. Please, before total insanity sets in; I feel my own time of madness coming on."

"Okay, I'll try to package it up for you, honest. What would help you process at this point?"

"A couple of things would go a long way for me about now. I would like to get back to Earth for a moment and find out more about that time of madness. I would like to know what actually happened to you and how you and Jo got together. And I would also like to know how Christian got involved in all of this. Did you have a heart-to-heart talk with him at some point? 'Now son, your father and I have something to tell you. No, you're not adopted, but your daddy is from another planet so that makes you half alien.' I can't imagine."

Jo and Phillip were laughing hysterically at Koy's impromptu heart-to-heart. Jo popped up with, "You know, that might have been a better approach, we just never thought of it."

"Interestingly enough," said Phillip, "my time of madness and how Christian came to know of Eyespell are actually related. We had no way of explaining things to Christian when he was younger so we decided to put some clues around and let him come to his own conclusions; at least give him enough evidence so that the concept of me being from elsewhere did not totally freak him out. As you kiddingly said that would make him half alien. Try dropping that one on your kid. I think Christian always knew something was up; I mean, after all, look at his parents. And then there is the Eyespellian mind-link; it would open within Christian now and again in some rather interesting ways. He used to tell me that he just sensed things; that he knew stuff and that he had thoughts of another place. He would periodically do a sanity check with his brilliant psychologist father. Over time the unusual did not surprise Christian much. After punching that kid on the head, Christian began to quickly separate from the Kookamonga Effect. He never did grow up to be that guy pulling at elephant puzzles and pounding his fist on the desk when something new came along. Christian embraced change with a passion. When he began work with the environment in Death Valley and started Used Water Works, he was definitely hanging out there by himself at the forefront of a new paradigm. And one of the things about new paradigms is that there's no history to them, no proof that they work, and yet they demand an unwavering faith from their proponents. That's Christian. As my cohort in the Mystic Management arena, well, he's the one who will ultimately make the difference."

"Just from the little time I spent with him at the Governor's Club I was truly impressed. I have a confession to make. I called Christian first about a follow-up interview. He said 'talk to dad if you want the rest of the story.' Does that make me a bad, deceitful person?"

"No, that just makes you intelligent and perceptive. I think Christian is far more approachable than I am. You know that Eyespellian charisma I said made the difference at the seminar? Well, about twenty-five percent was mine and the other three-quarters belongs to Christian. And besides he called me right after you talked to him. If you hadn't called me I was going to call you, so there."

"I love it. So what about the time of madness, you meeting Jo, and Christian figuring things out?"

"Let's begin with the time of madness. But let's not forget about Eyespell. If you think I was having problems, mine were nothing compared to what the poor Eyespellians were going through. Remember, there was a goodly amount of that Earth-plane vibrational leakage running rampant on Eyespell and, to boot, I was missing. At this point they had no idea what had become of me. If it wasn't for Leo, I don't think Eyespell would have survived the ordeal, but that's another story."

"See, there you go again. Stop it and just tell me about the time of madness, meeting Jo, and ultimately Christian discovering who you are. I think I can follow that much."

"Okay, ready for a download?"

"Fill my mind with thoughts, Dr. Hansen. Wait a minute, stop! I do have one burning question. You know when Pete was going through the lesson as a kid with Leo, but he really wasn't a kid but just got his telepathic powers back? Oh my God, I sound totally whacko and I think it's your fault, Dr. H. What I'm trying to say is when Leo was teaching the kids about Mystic Management and such, his vocabulary sounded more appropriate for a graduate seminar rather than talking to a bunch of kids. And only once did a question come up. The one kid asked about what empowerment meant. Are you Eyespellian types awfully bright or did I miss something?"

"I never even noticed that, but you're right. Language and communication are simply not issues. With telepathy and mind-links, everyone is so connected. Everybody just knows, most of the time, what the words mean. There aren't reading grade levels. The lessons like the one Leo was teaching are conceptual; they don't have anything to do with words. Language is different in a telepathic society. And remember, time is not linear. This sounds ridiculous but, in a sense the kids could go forward in time to glean the meaning of the words per se. Does what I'm saying make any sense?"

"To an Eyespellian, I'm sure. To me, Koy Sosa, well, you are stretching my limits. I don't think I get the *how* exactly, but I do get the idea that language, words, and the meanings of words, don't cause a problem. I think I'll just have to leave it there for now."

"I don't think I explained it all that well. I appreciate your being able to take some things on faith. Thank you. So, ready for the next installment?"

"Ready."

CHAPTER 11

▼

FILLING IN THE GAPS

It was no accident that Jo had come to be Phillip's wife and Christian's mother. She was a special individual. Although of Earth, Jo shared many Eyespellian-like characteristics; her vibration could easily resonate with those of Eyespell. She would feel perfectly at home in Elaysia's Council Chamber. Aliveness, connectedness, and compassion were integral parts of her personality. She was said to have a healing solvent; just being around her was enough to put one at ease. Testament to that healing presence is that, without Jo, Phillip would never have survived his time of madness and the aftermath of having missed the reentry window.

Shortly after missing the reentry window, a confused Phillip Hansen, still in the grips of partial amnesia, arrived in Washington, DC, where he would soon meet Jo. He was barely recovered from a near fatal accident in Boca Raton, Florida. The impossible had, in fact, happened. At exactly the moment of his planned reentry from Boca Raton to Eyespell, he was instead sent spinning toward the light of a near-death experience just as Kathryn Song had deduced. The statistically outrageous coincidence did indeed occur and sever his telepathy link with her and with Eyespell. Phillip's missed reentry and near-death experience left him in a coma for several days. He awoke remembering only select bits of his past. He read about Melissa Commings' suicide and felt a horrible pang in his gut, even though he did not know the girl; she was washed from his memory. Melissa and Phillip were the only two Eyespell Experiment participants who had had direct contact with each other while on Earth. Of course they felt a natural attraction and remained very connected from the moment they met on a public Boca beach. As reentry approached they had even planned a double suicide. None of this was yet a part of Phillip's consciousness.

The combination of a missed reentry, telepathic separation from Kathryn, slipping into a coma, and the gripping awfulness of the death of a girl he hadn't even known pushed Phillip into what he later dubbed the "time of madness." He felt compelled to leave Florida for Washington, DC, where he would, to all outward appearance, serendipitously connect with Jo. It was imperative that he meet Jo before the onslaught of panic attacks and free-floating anxiety that would plague him on and off for the better part of the next fifteen years. For both Earth and Eyespell it was critical that during the ensuing "time of madness," he not reach total despair and actually commit the suicide originally planned for his twentieth birthday. If he killed himself now, it would mean the end of his physical incarnations both on Earth and Eyespell. There would be no Eyespell connection; there would be no Mystic Management for the Earth.

While the Eyespellians had no contingency plan to account for defects in the Eyespell Experiment, the Universe, seeing the total cosmic picture, did have an alternate plan. Through a series of prophetic dreams, Jo learned of Phillip and was made privy to Phillip's Eyespellian identity, his missed reentry, and his anticipated move to Washington. The dreams clearly foretold the tremendous loss to the two worlds should he commit suicide. Jo sensed it was her duty to meet Phillip and to become his protector. It was her cosmic responsibility to intervene. The gift of her solvent was needed to protect Phillip during his "time of madness." This period would eventually pass, Phillip would rediscover his Eyespellian reality, and Jo would go about her own worldly business.

The prophetic dreams, Phillip's identity as an Eyespellian, and her role in protecting him did not fall outside of Jo's experience. She was particularly sensitive to issues surrounding death and dying, and to put bread on the table worked as a counselor with a local hospice. However, her sensitivities went far beyond the worldly. She often connected with the energy of a dying person and literally helped the soul's transition to another plane. In this work she was constantly in touch with spirit and frequently took direction from her higher self and from all manner of Beings of the Light beyond her own consciousness. The dreams about Phillip were particularly lucid and specific about how, later in life, he would bring Earth toward something positive. However, at the time of their meeting he was a very fragile Earth-bound soul teetering between survival and suicide. Meeting Jo and being immersed in her special and unique personal qualities would be the essential ingredient to survival winning over suicide. The Universe elected and hailed Jo as Phillip's protector.

Early one evening, Jo slipped into her jeans and a peach-tone sweatshirt and headed for Georgetown. She decided to walk. Her mood was light and reflected in the rosy glow of her cheeks. Excited and filled with an inner joy, she intuitively sensed an imminent encounter that would begin her mission to save an Eyespellian. Absorbed in these thoughts, she finally looked up to get her bearings. She was surprised to find herself wandering the narrow path next to Georgetown's canal. She spotted a young man coming from the opposite direction. Everything inside of her told her this was the man she was to meet. As they neared one another, he moved aside to let her pass, a little late. Their eyes met, and Phillip's Earth-life was changed forever.

Transfixed, he was barely able to speak. Finally he said, "Excuse me. I didn't mean to crowd you, I guess I was daydreaming."

Looking into the murky canal Jo said, "It is a bit chilly for a swim. What were you daydreaming about?"

"Meeting a beautiful and intelligent woman along this canal and having a cup of coffee, buying a beautiful house in the country, and having one perfect child."

"Done! Where shall we go, for the coffee that is?"

"How about the first place we come to?"

"I always like a well-thought-out plan. In fact, I think you should feed me as well. Or, you could watch me eat and you don't even have to pay for it. I just think eating is great fun, as long as it's a vegetable that is."

"You're a vegetarian?"

"And an Aquarius."

"How impressive. Me too."

"Vegetarian or Aquarius?"

"Both and proud of it. You know we've only just met and I feel better than I've felt in some time. That must sound like a terrible line."

"Indeed, but I like it coming from you."

"That's it then, a veggie burger and coffee."

From the moment they met, in what appeared to be a chance encounter, Phillip perceived Jo as a filter of light, a healing solvent. She soothed those innermost thoughts still so terribly pained by the recent events in Florida. Her very presence was enough to heal his mind. The relationship between Phillip and Jo never stopped evolving. They balanced each other. While her solvent protected Phillip from the subtleties of the dark-skew from within his own mind, he protected Jo from direct attacks of the dark-skew coming from others. Jo did not initially realize that their relationship would become part of an intricate cosmic dance. Her *choice* and Phillip's *choice* to become permanently involved proved good for them and good for the cosmos.

Phillip's point of greatest weakness in protecting himself against dark vibrations rested within the workings of his own mind. He was his own worst enemy. He had frequent bouts of negative thinking, depression, worry, guilt, and discouragement. The possibility of suicide as an answer for Phillip was not an imagined concern. His vulnerability was life threatening and, indeed, very real. While in one of his funks there was the danger of his committing suicide out of sheer confusion between his Earth-born thoughts and his then unconscious Eyespellian-born thoughts. Somewhere in his brain was still implanted the Eyespell Experiment's directive to commit suicide even though his twentieth birthday had passed. Connection with this thought process, however veiled, was uncomfortable in even the best of moods. In times of despair and confusion, Phillip relied on Jo for comfort and the assurance that he was not totally mad.

Jo, on the other hand, relied on Phillip to protect her from negativity embodied at times in the physical life force of other beings. Sinister others, given the chance, would take pleasure in destroying Jo's purity of soul, destroying her solvent. Phillip had an intuitive gift for recognizing and protecting Jo from those who would either maliciously with intention, or accidentally in their own selfish need, deplete her of her solvent. It was one thing to simply be around Jo and let her healing aura soothe you; it was totally another to try to psychically steal her gift, destroying the healing solvent in the process. For Phillip, being bathed in her aura was enough to comfort him.

Each truly benefited from the relationship created through Jo's dreams and her belief in a higher purpose. For her, what may have begun as duty ended in love. She joyfully and freely married Phillip and it was etched in the cosmic plan that she give birth to their child, Christian Hansen. His heritage, Eyespellian from his father and of "special personal qualities" from his Earth-born mother, would come to serve him and the planets of the light-skew during the approaching time of Mystic Management.

* * * * * * * *

Christian Hansen was rummaging through a big trunk in the attic. He came across several notebooks of his father's writings that he had never seen before. His parents had lived in that house in Waterford, Virginia, for a long time now. He was born and raised there. Christian had great fun exploring the attic during visits home. He felt like such a kid whenever he was home. It was hard for him to believe that he was approaching mid-life and that his father was gaining on *old-codgerdom*. It was even harder to imagine that the new millennium was well under way. He remembered all the talk of its approach and all of the horrible things that were going to happen at exactly midnight ushering in the year 2000.

On this particular day, the rest of the family was on a trek to Harpers Ferry, West Virginia. Mom and dad, his wife, and the kids never seemed to tire of wandering through the old Civil War graveyards or standing on the famous rock outcropping that overlooks Virginia, West Virginia, and Pennsylvania. Sometimes they were sure they could hear the shouts of distant foot soldiers and see the lights of their campfires across the river. It was as if John Brown himself walked out of the past and gave personal tours inside people's heads. It was like that a lot when his father Phillip was around; he had a unique way of bringing things to life. There was a unique aliveness about him that seemed to connect everyone and everything around him.

Earlier that day in his attic exploring, Christian had come across a bunch of old photographs. His mind wandered to his favorite one, a picture of his father in an idyllic setting. He was standing in a field of gorgeous wildflowers with a waterfall in the background and an absolutely magnificent double rainbow framing the whole scene. His dad must have been in his early twenties when the picture was taken. What intrigued Christian the most was the faraway look on his father's face. The look hinted at a sadness or disappointment with the beauty surrounding him. It was as if it paled in comparison to some incredible vision in his head.

The only time he had seen his father cry was years ago when the two of them were looking through these same old albums and they happened across this very photograph. His father had taken one look at himself as a young man in the picture, held the photo against his chest, and sobbed for several minutes. Christian vividly recalled that when his father had stopped crying, he had looked him deep in the eyes and said, "Thank you, Christian, for sharing this moment with me and allowing me to be human."

Christian was about twenty at the time, around the same age as his dad had been in the photograph. He had hugged his father and said, "You are the most human man I know. Somehow, your tears give me hope for my own future and my own humanness. They give me permission to just be." Christian never really understood that moment, nor did he question why the photograph brought his father to tears. But Christian had felt the penetrating and almost mystical impact of that interaction ever since.

His mind moved from reflecting on the old photograph to the pile of manuscript pages in his lap. Just as his awareness peaked, the pages seemed to intentionally slip onto the rough-planked attic floor. As he leaned over to collect the loose papers, a breeze sneaked through the attic and several sheets tried to escape behind an old bureau. He deftly stopped the getaway by maneuvering the entire stack of papers speedily upward and under his waiting chin.

He chuckled to himself as his eyes caught the words trying to fall off the page before he could read them. With his head still cocked from the capture, one eye shut, and the other eye almost parallel to the page, he managed to negotiate a few sentences.

... and still another book was started but never finished. There is no way to rationally describe what I think I have experienced. Every time I try, the spaces between the words are more provocative than the words themselves. Anti-synergy! The whole is smaller than the sum of its parts.

"Anti-synergy?" Now that got Christian's full attention; he loved it. He grabbed the pages firmly in both hands, settled back in the broken-down redwood lawn chair and, by the dusty light of the sun's rays spilling through the cobwebbed window, he began to read. Christian now focused his attic exploration on the neatly typed, age-yellowed pages.

Somewhere in the flatness of the land, the relative sameness of the weather, and the contrast of excessive wealth along the ocean and excessive poverty less than fifteen miles inland, there was a terrible disconnectedness. Out of this sense of despair arose the theme of community and community building as a starting place. There needed to be a new paradigm if the Earth were to be saved.

Less than half a page into his reading the neat typing gave way to scrawled notes which unevenly marched down the page and onto the back of the first sheet. With some effort Christian was able to decipher his father's handwriting.

Community building is essential. A bridge somehow needs to be built between the microcosm of one person's experiences in the world, and the macrocosm or commonality among the experiences of all of us. Maintaining the dignity of every human being must be paramount while focusing on team building as a core strategy, eventually working toward a global team to solve global problems of economic and environmental incompatibility. In order to get enough attention I need to focus on something that is part of everyone's tangible experience. I need to highlight and restructure community from the fundamental building blocks of a collective unconscious and bring it slowly to a conscious and purposeful level. Through this process, Earth's healing journey might be initiated. But how can I presume to take on such a task? And where might I begin?

The handwritten text ended with these questions and picked up again in typed format in the middle of the next sheet. The pages weren't numbered and Christian couldn't be sure of the order of things, especially after chasing the pages around the attic. The perplexities of the puzzle, however, only increased his interest. He read on.

The Eyespell Experiment focused on the desperation of America's youth. The five planned suicides, with four that actually happened within hours of each other, were designed to get Earth's attention. However, they had little impact on anyone's consciousness. There was such a lack of community that the suicides went virtually unnoticed. They appeared as disconnected and isolated incidents fed into the national statistical mean for suicides, raising it ever so slightly. I am glad I was not the fifth. I am glad I did not die with the others as planned.

Christian thought the manuscript was becoming "curiouser and curiouser." The Eyespell Experiment? Although quite a scholar, Christian could not recall anything called the Eyespell Experiment. He could not even begin to process the reference to his father's suicide nor did he try. He continued reading with renewed fascination.

Americans are searching to make sense of their pasts. The altruism of the 1960s brought soul-searching and revolution with no resolution. The narcissism of the 1970s made everyone 'do their own thing,' but too often at their own expense and the expense of others. The individualism of the 1980s made Americans self-centered, but certainly not self-actualized.

How can we fit into our chosen life without becoming a mere reflection of someone else's values and beliefs? We learn conflicting truths that play havoc with our identities. We are taught that it is important to be an individual and to stand up for what we believe in. Yet we quickly learn that to get ahead, it is seldom who we are that matters, but who we are perceived to be and who we know, that counts.

Armed with this kind of inconsistency, we tell our children that "He who has the most wins." Wins at what, life? What cognitive dissonance this creates as we tell our toddlers things like, "Now share your things with Jimmy at day care." Would we as adults share with anyone, any of our toys, our grander and equally important toys? Think about this type of clash between ideal and real culture. We also tell our children that "Honesty is the best policy." Yet, they routinely see us lying. For example, when we don't want to talk on the phone: "Tell them I'm not home or I'm in the shower and I'll call back." They know we cheat on income taxes and exceed the speed limit when we're pretty sure there's no cop around. And we do these things because that's how the game is played.

It's not really about honesty. We tell the children that "It's what's inside that really counts," and yet it's obvious that the ugly, perhaps overweight, kid with braces, orthopedic shoes, thick glasses, and acne doesn't really have much of a chance even in the kids' world. Indeed, children can be cruel as part of the socialization process.

But think about where the most noxious racism, classism, and sexism thrive. Think about where the most cruelty is. It exists in all institutions where adults live, work and play, setting the examples for the next generation. Observe the worlds of business, government, entertainment, education and sports. Where exactly are the desirable role models? What part of human unkindness is just part of growing up and what part is set up as the model to emulate when achieving adulthood? No wonder we become emotionally insulated as adults and can barely identify what we really think and feel. We don't know what we think and feel because we've grown up with so many cultural contradictions. We have all we can do to make any sense out of it and stay sane. Perhaps the insane are the only ones who have insight into the craziness of this place and time? The rifts are continuous. We are told one thing while constantly experiencing another. Identity crisis is squared and then squared again with each cognitively dissonant experience. Some of those experiences are stored into memory and, with later conscious recall become the stimuli for negative acting-out behaviors such as aggression, scapegoating, and gossip. Other experiences are placed into the unconscious for later expression through defense mechanisms such as substance and alcohol abuse, and even suicide if the stress level becomes too great.

To achieve self-preservation and to enhance the illusion of growing up, we bury the inner child. We bury the child under our perceptions, reactions, and pseudo-solutions to the anxieties of growing up. We keep this child hidden under the surface. The result is that as adults we feel impotent, hostile and anxious. There is often a free-floating anxiety whose source and solution are also buried within the psyche of that inner child. Maybe this is just another type of child abuse our culture fosters, cultural catatonia and societal schizophrenia.

Christian twisted in his chair in an unconscious physical reflection of his psychological discomfort. He continued reading.

Americans have gone from left to right and back, liberal to conservative and the opposite, liberated to traditional and still haven't found what they've needed. They've become specialists, then generalists, then specialists again. In all of this maneuvering, while they have learned to access massive amounts of information, they have not gained much wisdom. A generation once full of hope has hit old age. Their legacy is abject confusion feeding into a society fraught with hopelessness and bent on violence, sex, drugs, crime, and suicide as means of escape.

Christian read on in spite of his escalating discomfort.

All of this, and Americans have gained so little insight. For many, the inability to distinguish between what is physical and what is psychological is fashionably called a spiritual dilemma. And then there is more vacillation, a seemingly endless cycle. This is the American dilemma: Americans encircled, in the way of their own growth, and tripping over their own feet. The result is isolation, fragmentation, and an almost total lack of community.

The typeface again gave way to margin and back page notes done in Phillip's obviously excited handwriting. Christian struggled to piece the bouncing letters together.

As an off-world-observer, I feel that what is most profoundly wrong within the whole American culture is that Americans have lost a sense of community. They idealize the community that existed prior to and during World War II, know something made it sick during Vietnam, and feel alienated and truncated with the ever-increasingly mobile society and dominance of the distended family.

Christian's brain came to a screeching halt. "Off-world-observer?" He had never seen that idiom before. Twice now, in less than three pages, his father had stumped him. He made a couple of mental notes and continued to the next typed page.

America is a wealthy society. Her wealth is especially evident in her corporate structure. The output of General Motors alone is greater than the gross national product of some third-world countries. How can this imbalance be in the interest of a world community? It isn't, and in the past twenty to thirty years the term "business community" has become as much an oxymoron as "business ethics." America's wealth is achieved at great cost, lack of community. America is a high anxiety society suffering from soaring blood pressure and at high risk of heart disease. Do people realize how broad this handicap is? This is symptomatic of lack of centeredness, lack of focus, lack of community, disconnection. Without a clear center, a healthy heart, where is the point of reference in America? What is the system and what is the sub-system? How are things connected? What makes up the whole and how can one tell if something critical is missing?"

In the margins Christian could barely make out the words.

Maybe that's what this new paradigm should be about, connection. It could pull together, for example, business, art, psychology, and spirituality. It could combine right and left brain and create a synthesis that generates synergy, a whole that is, indeed, greater than the sum of its parts - a synergy that shifts America's brokenness into integration focused on community building. This could be called *systems sensitivity*.

There was an arrow from the margin pointing to systems sensitivity with a note.

"Systems sensitivity is the key, it's the exact concept and the correct terminology." And printed in big block letters on the back of the page: "FROM WHERE IS THIS INFORMATION COMING?"

Christian looked up from the manuscript, now totally bewildered. The writings revealed a side of his father's psyche that he was unaware of, to say nothing of the nagging implications of references to "Eyespell Experiment" and "off-world-observer." He had not known his father to criticize anyone or anything, much less lambaste the entire nation without offering any tangible solutions. It wasn't the absolute truth or falseness of what his father had written that seemed so uncharacteristic; it was the pounding harshness of some of the statements. There was an ill-defined urgency behind the whole theme.

Christian was not sure what had given his father such a perspective. Was he not an American himself and just as much a part of the society as those he seemed to be criticizing so severely? Looking down again, Christian discovered a poem couched within the fiery prose.

Perhaps the greatest American travesty and the direst symptom of lack of community is the prejudice which is openly displayed, one soul against another. Even to the point of murdering one another over the color of one's skin!

DAY OF RECKONING
To Martin Luther King, Jr.
By Bettie Rose

Just as "they crucified the Lord" and others...
Hatred engendered in the hearts of man,
Hammers its nails of violence,
And fresh-flowing tears add weight to the human "cross."
Angry voices shriek "black" and "white" words,
And cancerous evil festering in the souls of brothers
Distorts all truth in spiritual mutilation.
"Assassination!" the headlines scream,
And rampant destruction is born of the senseless death.
What idiocy the premise! A cause cannot be slain!

Disquieting thoughts needle the national conscience,
And racism, by its negative quality,
Shackles the oppressed and his oppressor.

What right any man to blacken his brother by deed,
To raise the weapons of inequality against him!
No deity separates the children of the "family,"
Nor rains eternal love in unjust favoritism.
Were the roles to be reversed, what reactions?
Suppose the condemning became the condemned?

The "righteous" in their supplications
Denounce the violent element among them;
They, too, repudiate what is savage uprising.
All thinking men ask: "Is ruthless murder to be discounted?
Or injustice, a permanently prevailing condition?
Our land, a jungle of fear, triggering uncivil deeds?"
It is a day of reckoning … time to listen.
Unchaste hearts are but a cacophony
In life's great symphony of brother loving brother."

Unable to process what he had read thus far, Christian stretched his
back and rubbed his eyes, and somewhere between the prose and the
poetry, he dozed off. His unconscious ear heard the family car creating
the unmistakable sound of fine gravel being pressed between rubber
tires and Mother Earth. He bounded out of the old chair and took the
steep stairs down three at a time to ask about the Eyespell Experiment
and off-world observing. He felt like a little kid on Christmas Eve.
And he was pretty sure that "Eyespell" and "off-world" were just well-
wrapped packages preventing him from seeing what was inside. Surely
his dad, Phillip Hansen, would gladly help him open them up.

He rushed out of the house to greet them as the car slowed to a
stop. Phillip instantly spotted the yellowed manuscript pages in his son's
grasp. He stuck his head out of the car window and said, "I see you've
been in the attic again, Christian."

Phillip was caught somewhere between severe anxiety and intense
relief at seeing Christian in the driveway with what he recognized
as those old manuscript pages he had stored in the attic. The rest of
the family, oblivious to the yellowed papers clutched to Christian's
breast, couldn't wait to share their Harpers Ferry adventure with
him. Christian, however, was so intent upon finding out about The

Eyespell Experiment and what his father meant by "off-world-observer," that he barely acknowledged the arrival of the rest of the family. He absentmindedly patted the kids on the head and gave his wife and mother token pecks on the cheek. He held up the manuscript and said, "Dad, I have a couple of questions about some of your writings."

Phillip strode purposefully toward his son and, putting out his hand, said, "Let me see exactly what you have there." Of course, he knew without looking; he could feel his son's questions and could sense his overwhelming curiosity.

"Oh, yes, some of my more flamboyant stuff. I sure do remember the feelings behind those words. I was a much younger man then and had some rash opinions to say nothing of the fact that I was crazy at the time."

Christian thought but didn't say aloud, "Crazy would be a monumental relief."

"I thought I had thrown all of this in the trash years ago." Phillip was well aware he had not thrown those pages away. In fact, the rest of that fiery old manuscript was tucked neatly away in a leather case in his study.

"Now, Dad, do you expect me to believe that? You've never lost track of anything you've ever written, or said for that matter. And especially something as peculiar as this. No way!" Christian stood very still and looked his father straight in the eyes.

Phillip smiled and said, "Just checking. So, what has you so overwhelmingly curious?"

"Two things, 'Eyespell Experiment' and 'off-world-observer.' I've racked my brains and can't come up with anything even approximating 'Eyespell Experiment.' The name is unusual enough that I would remember it; after all, I don't have such a bad memory myself. And the use of the phrase 'off-world-observer' is most curious, indeed. It sounds like you're from another planet or something!" Christian cleared his throat and laughed a very uncomfortable laugh.

Phillip slapped his son on the shoulder and while gently pushing him by the elbow said, "I think it's time you come with me and have a look at another part of that manuscript." Phillip led his son to the study and produced the leather case. "Sit down here and read. When you have a few more pages under your belt, call me and I'll share the rest of the story with you. And, just for the record, I mixed those pages in with the other stuff in that old attic trunk knowing that when the time was right, you would find them. One other thing, I love you." Phillip hugged his son and, for the second time in Christian's awareness, cried.

Christian sat in his father's sand-colored, corduroy-upholstered recliner. He was barely able to gather his wits about him. The rolltop desk stretched directly in front of him and across the room. His father's curio cabinet, glistening with its wondrous rock and mineral treasures stood to his immediate right. While Christian was not scientifically interested in or particularly knowledgeable about his father's collection, the cabinet always caught his attention. He was especially attracted to the pastel-colored specimens. His favorite was the large chunk of rose quartz on the next-to-bottom shelf. When he was alone in his father's study, he would often open the cabinet and just stand there holding the chunk of rock close to him, like an old friend. The vibrations were incredible.

What started out to be a typical day of attic exploring was turning into something quite extraordinary. He opened the leather case his father had given him and removed the manuscript. He picked a place at random to begin reading.

> You are all frantically fragmented, running around making money, exercising, eating right, dying anyway, breaking up relationships, and ultimately feeling isolated. There is always the nagging realization that even though things aren't terribly wrong, something is just not right. Everything looks so pretty and in place, but it often feels artificial, automatic, contrived.
>
> The environment is dead; there is no heartbeat, no heart, no center, no downtown, no community. There are just shopping malls decorated with artificial plants and chlorinated fountains.
>
> Under this pressure of having no sense of community you tend to cocoon. You go home after work and hole up alone with your families. You may be in physical proximity to your families, but there is no mutually satisfying interaction. There is just a sharing of some defined space.

Someone is watching TV while someone else is Nintendo-ing, while someone is reading, and someone else is meditating. You are all back home exhausted from being out there. You are home but not at peace. You're desperately trying to heal yourselves of all sorts of physical, emotional and mental pain.

You are missing community. You don't know how it looks, or what it feels like, or where to find it. You know that a key determinant to longevity is the degree to which you become involved in meaningful, ongoing support systems, and other-directed activity. And still you are alone.

Inner work, outer work; action-reflection-action, in an ongoing cycle. You collect lots of information about what your reality ought to be. You obsess about the right personality type, friends, job, family, children (how many and when), where to live, what to drive, and how to help yourselves if you fall short in any of the categories.

One thing is certain. As you are now, greed will bring you to a point of social disaster. Even cocooning will become impossible. If Americans do not begin to voluntarily change toward a community-based way of life, necessary change will be initiated and managed by outside forces. America needs a new paradigm of sustainability. If you don't do it yourselves it will be done by other peoples and other nations. This has always been the way of history.

It seemed like more of the same, and Christian did not feel any closer to solving the mystery. He was becoming restless in his need to confront his father directly. However, he was well disciplined and learned long ago that his father's way, while sometimes mysterious, almost always proved to be the better alternative. In fact, he honestly couldn't think of a time when his father had misjudged a situation. And perhaps for the first time on any conscious level, Christian was beginning to realize that his father was not who he appeared to be.

His father was, indeed, an unusual man. He continued to read from a different part of the manuscript.

> At the turn of the century the new management practitioners began to stir the Industrial Revolution into something more concrete. By the 1920s, schools of business actually became legitimate places for study and even a kind of worship.
>
> Many people in previous generations died unhappy because they did not make a million. Should you, too, die unhappy for lack of ten million? And will your children die unhappy? And for lack of how much?
>
> The old paradigm with its bent for success is destructive; it kills people. World resources are being depleted, the world population is soaring, there are food riots in South America, and revolutions of rising expectations in the Eastern bloc are happening. And all of that is going to affect you. Newspapers juxtapose 1000 percent inflation and food riots opposite advertisements for the must-have Rolex watch and Mercedes.
>
> Look past the front pages of most newspapers and the predominant use of space is advertising - advertising of sales, specials, and superlative labels with which you can adorn yourselves. Each week boasts its unique combination of sales. Holidays have become secularized as you see Halloween set up the week after Labor Day, to be followed by Thanksgiving, and then Xmas, taking the *Christ* out. The pre-Christmas sales cover November and most of December. January hosts the post-Christmas rush. Thank goodness for Valentine's Day and St. Patrick's Day to close the gap before Easter! In all of this hubbub malls have become an important socializing venue. For many families the primary outing they take together, once a week, is to the mall to take advantage of the week's specials and to shop for the upcoming holiday. How much can we learn about culture and community at the mall?

One can certainly assimilate all the latest trends: which tennis shoes are for executives versus those for nerds; how many earrings need to be hung in one or both ears; how tight and how short the skirts will be for half a season. And then there are the latest gadgets, gizmos, and toys offered at the high-tech stores.

In all of this there is no humanity. There is no heart. What will the turn of this century produce to offset the knowledge produced at the turn of the last? Or, will this be your society's last? How can you continue to be so blind to corporate global reality - international suffocation, asphyxiation by undigested knowledge?

It was still that same condemning tone, that same pounding. Christian thought: "A couple more pages and then I want some answers from Dad." He picked out another section of the manuscript at random.

How can it be that in some places the man-made landscape rivals God's? The only hills here are the Interstate bridges over the secondary roads. In Southeast Florida, rivers and lakes are diesel-dug deep ditches; and the closest thing to seasons is outside versus inside. The leaves fall off the trees at random, flowers blossom in what's called hard winter, and even the tiny ants bite and sting!

The neighborhoods are clothed in oscillating sprinklers and Malibu lights at dark. Palm trees and man-made lakes encircle the perfectly kept stuccoed houses. The illusion of serenity is frequently shattered, however, by screaming alarm systems in those same neighborhoods, neighborhoods that have become unsafe.

In the 18th and 19th centuries a town typically had a town square, with the city hall on one corner and the church predominantly positioned on the other major corner. In the 20th century, you switched to a different model. The bank, your new worship center, sat in the middle of town. Over the years, it became increasingly ornate and expensive as it replaced the church as the new symbol of blood, sweat, and tears. The bank became the town's primary expression of community.

By the 1950s, the concept of town began to fade into the suburbs. The bank's branch office went up first, either within or adjacent to the malls that came out of California, to usurp the town and become decentralized hubs of most activity. The new youth spend all of their weekend time hanging out at these malls. They used to go to church picnics.

Like the church picnic, the mall has an intergenerational quality. This is evidenced by the elderly who sit on the benches and people-watch in order to pass time and relieve their loneliness and boredom. As long as their roles remain passive, they are not considered bothersome. Of course, it's okay if the elderly interact with each other during the mall walks early in the morning before the stores open. So, where is America heading, where is community?

"That's it," thought Christian. "I can't stand the suspense another minute. While all of this prose is certainly attempting to corral the themes of community building, identity crisis, the decaying of America, and a mishmash of a hundred other ideas, none of it explains the 'Eyespell Experiment' or 'off-world-observer.' "

His father's manuscript smacked of its own identity crisis. While interesting in spots, the text seemed more an expression of anger than an offering of suggestions for improvement. He thought again how terribly unlike his father it was to criticize without giving accompanying recommendations toward progress.

Just as Christian was about to get up from his chair to seek out his father, demanding answers, the study door swung open. Not surprisingly, it was Phillip. "So, you think you have read enough. I suppose you have, and I suppose it's time that I answer your questions.

"What you have read was written by me during a period of tremendous inner turmoil in my life. In fact, it was written around the time depicted in that old photograph that made me cry. That far away look on my face that I know you've often wondered about, was a look of longing, a look of longing for the unequaled pastel beauty of my home, my home planet, the planet Eyespell."

Christian was frozen to his chair by his father's words. And, yet, there was a piece of him that was not surprised. He recovered quickly and darted back with, "Well, I guess that explains off-world-observer." With perfect hindsight, Christian had been sure of the meaning and implications of the phrase the moment he had first read it in his father's manuscript. His logic had simply gotten the best of him as he searched for a less dramatic but more easily acceptable explanation.

Phillip sat in the castered oak chair, rolled up to the large desk, and removed a notebook from one of its hidden panels. He handed the notebook to Christian explaining, "This contains the technical details of the Eyespell Experiment as best I can recall them. Read the notebook carefully. We can discuss it in detail tomorrow. It's quite late." Without saying anything further, Phillip reached inside Christian's mind and soothed the apprehension that was festering. Christian could feel his father's familiar presence within his thoughts and he left the room content to wait until the next day for further discussion.

Phillip tipped back in his desk chair and stared out the clerestory window of the study. He looked past the twisted branches of the huge oak tree into the night sky where, at this hour, the fourth moon of Eyespell would be rising. His thoughts flashed back.

* * * * * * * * *

He began to think about the days right around his twentieth Earth-birthday when he was making plans to kill himself or, as he now knows, when he was making plans for reentry. Thinking about that time always produced a strange sensation. Back then Phillip was never sure whether Eyespell was just an imagined memory or a different reality. Over time Eyespell had become an integral part of who he was. He remembered Eyespell as a place before birth. The memories of Eyespell were vivid, but somehow out of sequence; they did not follow a linear time frame and they were incomplete. They did not seem real but rather the outcome of an overactive imagination. He would sometimes joke with himself and call these feelings "Eyespell-plane vibrational leakage."

Phillip was going to college at a state university in Boca Raton, Florida. In Phillip's opinion, Boca, near the tip of the Devil's Triangle, was a place susceptible to negative "vibes." The university, for example, was an administrative and political mess. There had been a shooting, a suicide, and lots of psycho-junk in the air. Phillip was very vibe sensitive; he was very much in touch with how things felt on an abstractly intuitive level. Bottom line, it didn't much matter to Phillip that he was in a place that felt negative; he was intent on killing himself anyway. In fact, he had plans for a double suicide; he and Melissa Commings were going to do it together.

The two of them had finally decided on the method, and both knew it had to be soon. Their same-day birthday was only a few days away and each had a driving need to be done with life at twenty. They had planned to simply walk into the ocean off the Boca beach and never return.

Just before the agreed upon suicide time, for all intents and purposes, Phillip simply disappeared. The evening before suicide-day, unable to sleep, Phillip decided to go for a long walk. He did not bother to take any money or identification with him. He walked for hours and finally headed for the Boca beach to meet Melissa at the appointed hour. It is unclear exactly what happened at this point. He was deep into a walking meditation and evidently wandered into a crosswalk against the signal. He was hit by a car at an intersection near the Interstate, and was pronounced DOA at the hospital.

Phillip remembered hovering several feet above his physical body, looking down at himself. He was fascinated, but not concerned. The brown eyes of his body were rolled up and glazed over and he had a horrible bump on his forehead. Otherwise, he looked just fine. His blonde hair was reasonably neat and he had trimmed his beard just that morning. He was wearing pastel plaid shorts, a seafoam green Polo shirt and tan Birkenstocks. Best of all, he had on clean underwear! He could almost hear his mother's voice admonishing him, "Phillip, make sure you have on clean underwear. What if you're in an accident and they have to take you to the hospital? Wouldn't you be embarrassed if your underwear was dirty?"

Phillip started to laugh but, at just that instant, he felt himself being pulled upward. He was somewhat startled as he began moving swiftly away from his lifeless body lying on the gurney in the hospital emergency room. He thought he heard someone named Kathryn call to him and he thought he saw a soft pink planet with a beautiful blue sun. He saw Melissa with three strangers about their own age, a girl and two guys. It was as if he knew them.

Then there was a blinding flash with an accompanying sensation of falling up a tunnel. He found himself moving rapidly toward a white light at the end of the tunnel. Although this experience should have been frightening, it was not. In fact, the feeling was quite the opposite, extremely mellow and peaceful. All motion stopped as suddenly as it had begun a few moments before. Phillip lay suspended in an aura of white light and felt totally one with the universe.

Still immersed in the light, he saw a small dark figure jump from a thorn tree and race across the browned grass, arms flailing wildly, apparently trying to get the attention of the rest of the tribe. Hands cupped around his mouth for amplification, he was screaming, "The coming of the spirit! The coming of the spirit! The coming of the spirit!"

Following the shouts of this diminutive figure heralding a special event, Phillip received the message: "Mystic Management." His attention was piqued as he crossed the unseen barrier. Then it was all gone.

The floating sensation and the light were interrupted as if by a loudly ringing telephone. His conscious thoughts flashed back to the body, lying, he supposed, dead in the emergency room. He felt instantly yanked back through the tunnel and came crashing inside his head. He barely caught a glimpse of himself as he reentered his body.

Every part of him hurt. While nothing was broken, his body had done quite a dance with the asphalt and concrete at the intersection. He had absolutely no idea who he was, where he had been, or what had happened to him. He had two distinct thoughts: there was a God and he had no intention of killing himself. He was at peace like never before.

A doctor came rushing over to what she assumed to be the dead body of a young man who had been hit by a car near the Interstate. He was muttering, "Mystic management, mystic management is the way." It immediately became clear that even though he had been declared DOA, he was not dead now. His heart was beating out of his chest and he was gasping for breath. Phillip was most definitely alive but not yet aware of his surroundings. He slipped almost immediately into a coma and remained unreachable for almost three weeks. Even when he regained consciousness, he had no recollection of who he was. By the time he rediscovered only bits and pieces of his identity, the semester at college was over and Melissa had killed herself right on schedule.

There was a single nagging recollection running though his consciousness like a melody one can't help but repeat over and over and over: "Mystic management, mystic management, mystic management."

Phillip, while his brain seemed to be intact, was still uncertain of his identity. Encouraged by the people he met at the hospital he opted for a short course to prepare him for the Series Seven Examination for stock brokering. He passed the exam and took a job in the Washington, DC, area.

When he arrived in DC, his memory was still sketchy in spots and he was suffering from panic attacks. The peacefulness after the tunnel and the recollection of mystic management had all but disappeared from his consciousness. In fact, Phillip was reasonably sure that he was losing his mind. He kept a diary, intent on cataloging his madness for posterity. While working in the world of business, he rediscovered his fondness for psychology and eventually received his PhD. Over the years, Phillip Hansen had moved from successful stockbroker to renowned psychologist.

* * * * * * * * *

Phillip had not thought about his "diary of madness" for years. The new development of Christian finding the old manuscripts rekindled a rash of memories. Phillip reached behind one of the secret desk panels, and produced a badly creased clasped envelope containing three or four steno pads filled with scribblings from what seemed like a different lifetime.

Since Christian and his mounting questions had been put off until morning, it seemed like a good time to skim through the old diary. It would be interesting to review it now that he was a seasoned clinical psychologist. Moreover, Phillip thought it important to recapture some of the intense feelings he had had while struggling to come to grips with his Eyespellian identity. He felt he would be able to better answer his son's questions if he became immersed again in the events of that earlier time, his time of madness.

He pulled the spiral pads out of the envelope and, with a certain apprehension, searched for the early entries. With little difficulty he found what he was looking for, descriptions of the first hints of his horrible anxiety. He had suffered panic attacks coupled with exceedingly strange dreams and what seemed like memories that initially led him to believe he was going mad.

The first entry Phillip came across was dated February 28, or 23. The writing was pretty shaky, so he couldn't be sure whether it was an "8" or a "3." He knew the diary would be difficult to decipher in spots. He wanted to throw his psyche back in time and put as much present-moment energy as possible into his task. He decided it was 28 after all.

February 28

In the *Book of Matthew*, it is written: "... do not be anxious about tomorrow, for tomorrow will be anxious for itself. Let the day's own trouble be sufficient for the day."

While I see the wisdom in that, I am constantly plagued by the nagging events surrounding my accident. I am especially concerned about the dreams and partial memories I have been having ever since I first glimpsed that incredible pink planet as I moved through the tunnel. I still mourn Melissa's death and I still see people and places that are both perfectly familiar and strange, all at the same time. The odd phrase 'mystic management' still flows in my semiconsciousness. I fear that I am going crazy. I worry very much about tomorrow.

Phillip absentmindedly swiveled his chair around; the bottom of the seat bumped solidly against the side of the desk cavity, almost causing him to panic. It seems that it didn't take much effort to put his thoughts back to those hideously troubled times. He realized, literally with a jolt, that he still missed Melissa. Yet, back then because of his scattered memories he wasn't even sure who she was most of the time. He read the next entry in the diary.

March 3

If only I could have reached Melissa before she killed herself. While I would not have been able to explain it logically, I could have shared some undefined hope with her. I could have given her reason to go on living; I could have convinced her of a future, maybe even our future together. In the months right after the accident, I was in close touch with something, something that gave me the courage to go on. I felt close to God. And now, I'm not so sure.

Phillip got up from the chair and began to pace back and forth parallel to the bookshelves lining the study wall. He was thrown back in time to the doubt-filled Phillip Hansen who had written the diary entry of March 3rd. He remembered, as if it were yesterday, the circumstances of that first really horrible panic attack. While he had been anxious on and off since the accident, he had not experienced anything as debilitating as this. He read the next diary entry, holding the notebook at a distance lest he again feel the anxiety captured in those pages.

March 4

Although my anxieties began before I moved to the DC area and before I met Jo, I had my first serious panic attack last November. November 18, to be precise. It is the most horrible memory of my life. That lunch at that little Persian diner at Bailey's Crossroads, Virginia, will be lodged in my brain forever. I'll never forget how I came flying out of the diner, light-headed, clutching at my Adam's apple, unable to swallow. I was sure that I was dying. I honestly thought that I had contracted some rare Middle Eastern disease, a disease that attacks the throat with absolutely no warning.

I was such a fool. Now I know better. I am simply going crazy; I am losing my mind. It's been months and little has improved. I am beginning to feel more and more like I did in Florida; I think I want to die.

Phillip could hardly stand it. His memories became so vivid he thought he was going to have a panic attack right then and there. He could feel both the panic and the despair of the young man he had been. What upset him the most, however, was reliving the feelings of utter and desperate confusion. At the time, Phillip had had no idea what was happening to him. There was no logical explanation, and this was disturbing to a very intelligent person.

As Phillip continued to pace, other memories of that frightful day at Bailey's Crossroads moved into his conscious realm. He could see himself outside the diner, alternately spread over the hood of his car, face to the metal, and then madly walking around, still clutching at his throat. He remembered that he had felt totally insane.

In spite of his embarrassment at stumbling and crashing out of the diner that day, Phillip had been glad that he was not alone. He smiled and shook his head as he thought about how horrible his ordeal must have been for Jo. She was there with him that infamous day at the diner. While Jo had come into Phillip's life by this time, it was only much later that she had explained her role as his protector chosen by the Universe. If she had not consoled him, assuring him he was not crazy, it is hard to say what would have become of him. They married the following April.

Phillip finished out his thoughts of that first attack. The ordeal did not end with lunch. About twenty minutes after the first onslaught of panic, everything started over, only it was worse. He recalled how he could actually feel the blood rushing through the veins in his arms. It was absolutely terrifying. He thought death was imminent.

Engrossed in these thoughts, Phillip again bumped the chair hard against his desk as he relived the ride to Alexandria hospital, and the events in the emergency room. He was in a hospital for the first time since Florida. This time he was not labeled DOA and there was no peacefulness, no tunnel, no white light. Phillip was indisputably alive, and suffering.

After checking him over, the doctor told Phillip that he was fine physically. He explained that he had had an attack of what's called "globus hystericus." He then proceeded to tell him about a little old lady who had been in just the other day with the same thing. "The poor woman was so frightened," he could now hear the doctor saying as clearly as if he were still there, "that I just sat here and held her hand for about twenty minutes and talked to her, tears streaming down her cheeks the whole time."

Phillip threw the steno pad across the room with renewed anger as he thought about that stupid doctor and the story about the little old lady. How insensitive and fear producing. Phillip remembered that what came next was absolutely incredible, totally unbelievable. The doctor had told Phillip that he needed to talk to somebody, a therapist. Now that had really made him mad. There he was dying and the doctor had told him to see a shrink. He did not understand; he was not prepared for what the medical man was saying. He interpreted the doctor's message to be that he, Phillip Hansen, was crazy. Phillip remembered now being so overwhelmed then that he had gone home and pretty much stayed there for the next four years. He became a classic agoraphobic, terrified to leave the house. He was capable of going only a few places. He could not walk around the block, go to the store, to a movie, and certainly not out to lunch. Most days he could go to work and come right home again, but only with the aid of valium. His fears continued to multiply and the greatest fear of all, going insane, seemed to become more of a reality.

Phillip's chair, bumping against the desk yet again, banged him back to the present. He was startled by his ability to recreate the past scenario with such detailed and strong feeling. He recalled his absolute stubbornness, his refusal to see a therapist in spite of suffering anxiety and his suspicions of insanity. His reluctance to deal with his own issues in spite of his education and training as a psychologist, was perhaps the most peculiar aspect of his time of madness. The battle went on for years. Phillip read another of his diary entries.

September 25

I had to make an emergency visit to the mental health clinic early this morning; it was about 2:30 a.m. if I had to guess. Things are becoming unbearable. It hits out of nowhere and for no apparent reason. I had to work pretty late tonight. I was sitting there alone eating a stale chocolate chip cookie. I remember mindlessly staring at the remnants of a cup of coffee, a half-empty glass of water, three open and scattered packs of gum, and a messy pouch of pipe tobacco, all of which I utilized to soothe me in my times of stress and potential panic.

And then there was that dull plastic, safety-topped container of small yellow pills, valium, 5mg. I was fondling the container and reading the label: "TAKE AS NEEDED." And at the bottom, in that bright day-glow color, it said: "THIS PRESCRIPTION CAN BE REFILLED ONLY BY AUTHORITY OF YOUR PHYSICIAN." With horror, I noticed that the container was empty.

I was instantly, without warning, surrounded by that feeling that I might stop breathing, hyperventilate, pass out, lose control, begin yelling and running around aimlessly and afraid like a crazy person, like a crazy person, like a crazy person. I am absolutely terrified that I am losing my mind. I really feel as if I am going to go off the edge at any moment. Dying along the Interstate in Florida would have been much easier and, certainly, a whole lot faster.

The fear had always been so real, thought Phillip. It had been much more terrifying than he had imagined anything could be. To make matters worse, during this same period the intermittent memories of Eyespell had begun to increase. Phillip had simply added his delusions of being an alien to the mounting proof of his escalating madness. One thing fed upon another and the anxiety worsened. Phillip scanned another diary entry.

October 1

My anxiety isn't getting any better. Why do I feel like this? My stomach is twitching; my throat is tightening.

My throat, what about my throat? I can't swallow! It's happening again. It's been five seconds, ten, fifteen! Oh my God! My head is coming off, bursting. I am losing perspective, reeling. I am in a panic! I am afraid! No. There is nothing logically wrong. If only I had five magic beans, I would be Jack.

Sometime in the third year of his ordeal, and with the constant urging of Jo, Phillip had agreed to see a therapist on a regular basis. He was just too exhausted to continue on his own and, surely, the magic beans he craved could be purchased at seventy-five dollars a session.

Phillip tipped further back in his chair and propped his socked feet on the desk. He remembered his therapy well. "For my first seventy-five dollars," he thought, "I learned that anxiety could not be ignored and that I would have to assume total responsibility for getting in touch with my feelings." He was not impressed, then or now. Ultimately, there had been some talk about self-concept and the notion that the brain could not solve problems of the heart or the soul. It was hypothesized that there was an imaginary steel plate in Phillip's throat separating his brain from the rest of him. At that time Phillip was not an integrated person and he was incapable of truly feeling what was going on in his life.

Phillip remembered that no matter how hard he had pressed the issue the therapist would not concede that he was crazy. Evidently, the therapist knew something Phillip didn't know.

After about six months and one-thousand-eight-hundred dollars of what Phillip considered psychological drivel, the magic cure had finally entered the scenario of his therapy. He had been introduced to his inner child and through that child, Phillip got in touch with both his fears and his Eyespellian heritage. The imaginary steel plate had been removed from Phillip's throat and he had begun to accept the possibility of the pink planet as part of his reality. However, he never did mention the pink planet to his therapist.

Throughout this entire ordeal, Jo was his rock. Her presence soothed him on a moment-to-moment basis. Phillip Hansen did not commit suicide.

Phillip stayed with his diary and with his thoughts throughout the night. It was mid-morning next day before Christian had the courage to knock on the study door. He poked his head in and sheepishly asked, "Does this mean that I am half Eyespellian?"

Phillip smiled. He felt like the Phillip who was bathed in the white light at the end of that tunnel where there were no restrictions of either time or space. Probably for the first time, Phillip had a clear vision of Mystic Management and he knew it would ultimately come to be, through the efforts of his son, Christian.

CHAPTER 12

▼

IN THE FAMILY ROOM ...

Koy looked at Phillip with a whole new respect. She then turned to Jo and said, "I could never be special, not like you."

Jo reached out and gently placed her hand over Koy's and said, "You already are and when we're finished with you, young lady, there will be no doubt in your mind."

"So," said Phillip, "How's that for filling in the gaps? Pretty good, don't you think? In one download you have the time of madness, how Jo and I got together, and how Christian came to know of his Eyespellian identity, and mine, of course."

"Yeah, pretty good. What an amazingly difficult time in your life and to come through it to this. Now that is a story I can print, if it's not too personal that is."

"We'll see."

"Why didn't you ever seek help from your parents?"

"Good thought, but by the time I pieced together my two worlds, Earth and Eyespell, my parents were already gone. They died rather young actually."

"Did they ever find out what happened to you?"

"No, they never did; I worry that might be one of the reasons they gave it up early in life. It truly saddens me to think about it. It was definitely one of those places the Eyespell Experiment really goofed. While back in Eyespell they were all worried about reentry trauma and Earth-plane vibrational leakage; they never considered the Eyespell-plane leakage left behind. Imagine the pain of the parents and families who lost their children to suicide. Those parents and families were not privy to Eyespell's grand plan. Dealing with the death of a child probably tops the list of difficult things to deal with. Imagine my parents; I was just gone and they never found out what became of me. I just slipped through the cracks in spite of their efforts to find me."

"You consider them your parents, then?"

"Yes, that's part of what's so complicated. You have to understand that for the first twenty years of my life on Earth, I was just like everybody else when it came to parents and family. I knew nothing of Eyespell."

"Ouch."

"Here's a kicker. You remember that poem in my rantings during the time of madness? The one about Martin Luther King?"

"How could I not remember it."

"Bettie Rose was my Earth mother, and I found that poem tucked in one of my books during the time I had amnesia. What is sad is that at the time I copied it into my journal, I had no idea who she was.

"That's really touching. Are there other members of the family alive today?"

"There're a couple of aunts and uncles and a fistful of cousins. We try to get together when we can. Like most families we're all over the place and that makes it hard. Christian and I are the family celebrities and that's always fun; they seem to love hearing about our adventures around the country."

"Do they know anything about this adventure?"

"No, not yet anyway. How would your mind like to go back to Eyespell and see how things are coming along with all that Earth-plane vibrational leakage and poor missing Phillip?"

"Sounds like a plan. What about how you and Christian came to the Mystic Management stuff?"

"That will have to wait a minute. I think you will like that part of the story better when you have a more complete sense of Eyespell."

"Download, doctor."

CHAPTER 13

▼

THE VALLEY OF THE BLUE NOON

Daniel, keeper of the Yellow-Light-Corridor, custodian of knowledge, and head of the Elders' Council, stood at the center of the Council Chamber. His crystal, on its rope of light, lay beautifully displayed against his flowing yellow robes. When Daniel moved, the crystal appeared to throw sparks of light as it swayed almost imperceptibly across his chest. With eyes lifted, palms open, and arms stretched toward the heavens, Daniel "spoke" the opening meditation into the minds of all Eyespellians. "In the light-skew of two suns and four moons manifesting six primary planetary light-corridors, may the crystal charge of each Elder be preserved. The Full-Round is open."

With the final word of the meditation, a magnificent color ray emanating from each of the six Elders' crystals burst into "flame," merged in the high reaches of the amphitheater, and created a light show inside the dome. The fabric of the dome and the surrounding structures amplified the intensity of the colors until the surface of the planet surrounding Elaysia was ablaze with Eyespellian rainbows. The sight as seen from the dunes outside the Council Chamber was cosmically impressive. The view of Elaysia from outer space during a Council opening would be considered a spectacle in the category of miracles. And, in fact, the best spectator "seats" for this show were at the fringe of Eyespell's furthermost aura. Thousands of Eyespellians manifested these incredible seats through purposeful meditation that put them out-of-body above the planet hours before a scheduled Council opening. The whole ceremony was nothing less than expansive, grand, and literally out of the world.

As Daniel spoke, the planetary cell-matrix resonated with his light-charge. Daniel could not only be seen and heard, but felt. All beings on the planet were connected with every fiber of Daniel's being. He was one with the planetary cell-matrix and the experience was total oneness with Daniel and with the planet. Words do not adequately describe the depth of this experience and no image captures the spectrum of color flowing from the Council Chamber. This is truly of another dimension.

As Daniel's presence combined with the power of the laser-like lights opening all of Eyespell's light-corridors simultaneously, Antonio, Melissa, and Nancy instantly and fully regained their Eyespellian identities and faculties. This allowed them to move from the third row where they had been standing to rings fifteen, sixteen, and twenty-two respectively. Their sensor-chairs enveloped them and they finally became one again with each other and their home after twenty long and difficult Earth-years. Pete was already comfortably seated in the twenty-sixth ring and at some level still in touch with his reverie about Mystic Management.

Leo watched pensively as Nancy settled into her place in the twenty-second ring. He was uneasy as he thought about how she was the one who, just weeks before, through avoiding Leo's hug upon reentry had triggered the first, albeit minor, episode of Earth-plane vibrational leakage. And only days before she had caused the first serious episode upon her initial encounter with Kathryn. Now this same individual was in the Council Chamber during an opening of the Full-Round! Leo's telepathy link was closed so as not to contaminate the Council Chamber with these worrisome thoughts.

Pete was the only one who knew specifically what was going on with Leo; it was unprecedented for one of the Elders to go into open Council with a closed telepathy link. Leo felt he had no choice. He could handle his charge of preserving peace only if he could preserve the purity of his Blue-Light-Corridor. He was worried that his crystal might still contain even the slightest manifestation of Nancy's anger and hostility. To expose open council to such a potential risk would be unconscionable.

Leo's closed telepathy link did not go unnoticed for long. Daniel said, "This is the first time that one of our Eldersix has come to Open Council mind-shrouded. This is a dangerous sign. Leo, peace-keeper, what so threatens your spirit?"

"With all respect to you and the Council, I am gravely concerned about Earth-plane vibrational leakage. I have experienced it firsthand, and if it seeps into our planetary cell-matrix the light-skew will be disrupted. A strong enough negative vibration could cause a permanent rupture in the cell-matrix. No matter how infinitesimal, such a rupture would begin to move the planet toward homeostasis, a mixing of light and dark. And what impacts the planet impacts the people. That which is Eyespell, is simultaneously Eyespellian. The Mystic Management principle of systems sensitivity, above all others, cannot be compromised. All things are interconnected, are one. If Earth-plane vibrational leakage contaminates one part, it contaminates all parts of the cell-matrix."

Gracina, keeper of the White-Light-Corridor, custodian of Oneness, supported Leo's position. She was the essence of white light; she literally captured those around her in an aura as bright as the third moon of Eyespell. "What Leo says is true. If Oneness is broken there is no assurance that we will be able to heal ourselves. Perhaps it is time to hear from our returned children about all that has transpired in the last twenty years on the Earth-plane. Only then might we be able to determine the real dangers to our planet. With the non-return of Phillip, my ability to maintain Oneness has already been compromised. The loss of one of our children leaves a great void within the crystal energy of the third moon. I think our collective and unconditional love for Phillip is temporarily compensating for the shift in the White-Light-Corridor his absence has created. And this is to say nothing of the added energy Myana has had to expend to maintain the Pink-Light-Corridor from which unconditional love resonates. The skew within the White-Light-Corridor is still shifting even as we speak."

The pressing reality of Phillip's non-return, Leo's closed telepathy link, and the potential ominous consequences of substantial Earth-plane vibrational leakage, forced the Elders' Council into an unprecedented action: the Eldersix prematurely ended the Full-Round and moved into closed session. There could be no further contact with the returning Eyespellians or with their overseer, Kathryn, until things were sorted out. The Elders shielded the center ring from all outside vibrations and went into a state of Oneness in mind-link-orbit around the third moon of Eyespell.

This action by the Elders immediately kindled feelings of rejection within the small group returning from Earth. Dismayed, they left the Council Chamber. With Leo unavailable, Pete and Melissa looked to Kathryn for leadership and perhaps consolation. But there was immediate friction in the group.

Nancy was quick to point out, "I sit at ring twenty-two. Kathryn sits at the vibrational level of only the twenty-first ring. Why would you follow her advice? Besides, I don't trust her."

She had no sooner spoken the words when Antonio pressed between them and stated matter-of-factly, "Pete is of the twenty-sixth ring and almost an Elder. He's the one we should be following."

Pete seemed embarrassed, and Kathryn, for the fourth time since her return, became teary-eyed. It began to rain. It was uncertain whether the clouds were natural phenomena or clouds of dissent, perhaps intent upon whetting some new and unfamiliar appetite for conflict on Eyespell. For the second time since their return they were reduced to an awkwardly silenced and fragmented group of individuals, quite un-Eyespellian-like.

While the Council remained in Oneness around the third moon, events on the planet's surface were worsening. The light-skew was definitely being pulled toward homeostasis. Eyespell was suffering from Earth-plane vibrational leakage of a serious and global nature. Signs were everywhere.

One catastrophe was that the Eyespellians who had been out-of-body above the planet watching the spectacle of the Full-Round, were harshly and instantaneously jerked back into their bodies. As a result they suffered something akin to reentry trauma. There was widespread loss of Eyespellian perception, telepathy, and connectedness. Even though the negative impact on these powers was temporary, the cell-matrix had been damaged. Leo's greatest fear had manifested. The cell-matrix ruptured slightly and was wreaking untold havoc with the light-skew. The fabric of Eyespell was being compromised.

The Elders, even in their state of Oneness, were unable to immediately mitigate the situation on the planet surface. Eyespell was beginning to experience opposites. An example painfully obvious to the Elders was the contrast between their state of Oneness and the temporary fragmentation and total loss of connectedness among the general population. It was as if the planet had been thrown back several hundred thousand evolutionary years in an instant, in the reflex of an eye.

There were fractures in the cell-matrix itself. There were thunderstorms, mild earthquakes, and millions of tiny stress cracks beginning to form on the planet's surface. The healing blue sun remained hidden behind a darkened atmosphere for long periods of time. Growing things began to die. The various species of cats, birds and other members of Eyespell's animal population began to revert to an untamed and ferocious state. There was disharmony, danger, and fear among the living things of Eyespell.

Suddenly everything went still; there was an incredible electrical snap in the air and the climate of Eyespell once again quieted itself. The cell-matrix, responding to the powerful positive vibration of the Eldersix in Oneness, was able to compensate for the devastating vibrational leakage, *this* time. But what of the future? The Elders broke the mind-link-orbit around the third moon, each of them moving swiftly to manage their respective light-corridors in an attempt to protect the light-skew from further disruption.

* * * * * * * * *

The blue sun of Eyespell reached its zenith each day above a very holy place. Leo, guardian and manager of the Blue-Light-Corridor, quickly made plans to go there. The Valley of the Blue Noon, as it is called, is the most sacred place on all of Eyespell. Blue Noon is twenty-seven miles due south of Elaysia and, for Leo, a two-day prayer-walk with a company of fifty-four pilgrims. When Eyespellians devote linear time to walking meditation, the intensity of their purpose is dramatically enhanced.

In good times, the pilgrimage was a festive occasion for young Eyespellians. They typically donned their colorful rainbow-hued robes and set forth from Elaysia in good cheer. They would savor the opportunity to go off into the desert with an Elder to learn more of the light-skew and the cell-matrix. This day, however, the company was a select group of Eyespellians with special affinity to the vibrations of Leo's crystal and the Blue-Light-Corridor. The pilgrimage was not one of excitement and learning, but rather one prompted by the critical and urgent business of survival.

Leo emerged from the Council Chamber and found that the fifty-four pilgrims were already preparing for the journey. The robes chosen for this day were not of the hues of festivity, but of the solemn and serious monk's brown. The left sleeve of Leo's robe carried the symbol of the Blue-Light-Corridor. The rays of an embroidered blue sun stretched from near the top of the shoulder to the bottom of the loose sleeve. He wore nothing on his head or feet, his crystal resting over his heart on its rope of light. The fifty-four pilgrims in their plain brown monk's robes also wore nothing on their heads or feet. Around the waist of each was a silver fabric rope laced at the front in a complex series of ties forming a knotted frame around a polished talisman of blue lapis lazuli with shimmering, golden pyrite inclusions.

Leo led the group away from Elaysia's center toward the dunes to Blue Noon. It was evening as they walked under the light of the first three rising moons. The fifty-four Eyespellian pilgrims walked behind Leo, two-by-two, in a perfect line of twenty-seven rows. As Leo raised a chant each row would follow in succession in the same tone. It was an eerie-looking brown line of chanting monks with moon-glistening talismans that moved mindfully over the dunes on that uncertain evening. Arrival at the Valley of Blue Noon would be precisely at the light of the three full moons the following night. It was not unusual for an Eyespellian pilgrimage to walk and chant for many days without stopping to rest, eat or drink.

Leo's and the pilgrims' states of consciousness moved gradually to higher and higher vibrational levels. The slowly marching column became one with each grain of sand turning and rolling under the forward motion of each monk's soles. The lapis talismans swayed gently back and forth in sync with the crystal of the blue sun pressing against Leo's heart chakra. The chanting tones gathered and rose like an invisible force field against the waves of Earth-plane vibrations still threatening to fragment the planetary cell-matrix. The ground upon which the pilgrims passed was instantly healed. With each footfall the cell-matrix responded as if it were alive and itself the fifty-fifth pilgrim. At two full moons on the second evening, the planet healers reached the fringe of mountains overlooking the Valley of the Blue Noon. The third moon, the White Moon of Oneness, was rising in the already two-moon-lit night sky. Later in the evening, when the monks reached the worn path overlooking and encircling the valley, the fourth moon would also rise, the Moon of Unconditional Love and Compassion. Four full moons would light the Valley of the Blue Noon as the monks continued to chant their unbroken vigil.

The valley itself was a crater totally surrounded by jagged peaks rising sharply out of the beautiful Eyespellian desert. It was exactly one and one-half miles across with a tower-like formation jutting out of its center and standing one-hundred-fifty feet above the highest of the encircling peaks. The valley had sheer sides dropping like vertical glass sheets to the valley floor several hundred feet lower than the crater's top. Adjacent to the worn path around the top perimeter there were four sets of steps carved out of the stone leading downward in steep descent, one stairway at each point of the compass.

The pilgrims began to slowly walk the perimeter path above the valley. They ever so gradually spaced themselves at long and equal distances until the entire circumference of the Valley of the Blue Noon was encircled by chanting monks revolving counterclockwise at an almost imperceptible pace around the valley. This living circle continued its ceremony under the light of the four full moons of Eyespell.

Just as the blue sun lifted from the northern horizon and the four moons set, Leo began to descend the staircase at the north point of the compass. The encircling monks immediately realigned the space between them, and stopped their movement at fifty-four equal intervals atop the crater. Arms at their sides with palms open, and facing the valley center, they chanted in a tone that focused the very molecules of air toward the tower at the valley's center. As the sound sent its energy toward the tower, the talismans at their belts began to send points of light following upon the sound waves.

Leo continued to move down the stairs, eyes focused on his destination at the center of the valley. As the blue sun moved higher in the sky he made his way to the base of the tower. The monks above continued their energy focus and chanting. Leo removed the double pyramid crystal from around his neck and held it, points vertical. With this gesture, he appeared to float to the uppermost plateau of the tower. Waiting for the Blue Noon, when the blue sun would reach its zenith directly above the point of the rock tower, Leo sat cross-legged facing north with upward pointed crystal at his chest. The fifty-four pilgrims ringed the tower in prayer.

At exactly Blue Noon, Leo lifted the crystal directly above his head with the fingertips of both hands. The clear crystal caught the full intensity of the blue sun. The rays of lapis blue and pyrite gold from the talismans inched up the tower with the monks' concentrated meditation. The sound of their chant reverberated against the glassy walls, and the entire Valley of the Blue Noon turned an all encompassing iridescent blue as the rays of the sun flowed into and back out of the crystal. There was Peace in the Valley of the Blue Noon as heretofore only described in accounts of the dawn of Eyespell's light-skew. It was as if the planet were reborn.

Leo and the fifty-four stood their vigil for three consecutive Blue Noons. Leo then replaced the rope of light and crystal around his neck, floated down from the tower, and purposefully ascended from the valley floor by the stairway to the south. The pilgrims journeyed the two days back to Elaysia, still in prayer and chant.

Seven evenings after the beginning of the pilgrimage and with only the fourth moon lighting the landscape, Leo reentered the twenty-seventh row of the Council Chamber. The peace had been preserved; Eyespell again moved in the uncontaminated light-skew. The Council of the Elders was to meet the following day.

By the rising of the yellow sun, the Elders, the four returned Earth travelers, and Kathryn were at their places in the Council Chamber. Matters of the Eyespellians' adventures on Earth were to be taken up directly. Leo and the other Elders were still in monk's garb, each having barely finished specific tasks to try to repair the cell-matrix and to help reverse the effects of Earth-plane vibrational leakage. While there would be no meeting of the Full-Round, the four returnees and their overseer were happy to finally be meeting with the Elders' Council. They were anxious to share their Earth experiences.

Daniel stood and faced the five Eyespellians in the Council Chamber. "Please forgive our delay in hearing your stories. Our sincere interest in each of you who spent twenty years on Earth for the Eyespell Experiment is shared by all of the light-skew. Antonio, you were the first to reenter, and you shall be the first to share your Earth experience with the Council. Give us just a few minutes to complete our check of each light-corridor. We need to be absolutely sure we are clear of Earth-plane vibrational leakage."

CHAPTER 14

▼

IN THE FAMILY ROOM ...

"Now that's incredible," said Koy, gently shaking off the mind-link. "You know, the mind-link gets easier each time. I don't feel disoriented at all."

"Like we've been telling you, you're special," said Phillip. "What did you think of the Valley of the Blue Noon? Quite the place, don't you think?"

"I'll say. I think Leo is nothing less than amazing. I'd like to meet him."

"Me too, I'd like to meet him in the flesh."

"What do you mean, in the flesh?" asked Koy.

"Well, that's another story," said Phillip with that maddening twinkle in his eye.

"Do the surprises ever cease? I'm still waiting on how you came by the Mystic Management Principles."

"Ah yes, that story. Soon enough. It's still early. How about we take a break from Eyespell and you tell us a little more about yourself. A little distraction will do us good and then I can answer more of your questions."

"Well, I'm an Earthling, I'm thirty-four years old, and unmarried by design."

"You're a smart aleck, don't look a day over twelve; and unmarried by design, no, that's got to be an accident. How is it possible that an intelligent and beautiful young lady such as yourself has not been captured? If it wasn't for Jo over there I'd put a bid in myself. For the next life of course; I'm way too old in this one."

"You got out of that one just in time, Dr. Hansen," said Jo, laughing.

"Actually, I thought I'd go after Christian in the next life. Do you mind waiting?" bantered Koy.

"I suppose. So, seriously, how is it you don't have a special beau?"

"I didn't say I didn't have a special beau, I just said I wasn't married. I've had my designs on Sam Simpson since college. You know, Sam who called you to get me invited to the Governor's Club seminar."

"Ah, that Sam Simpson. Good choice I think. As soon as he grows up he'll make one hell of a husband and father."

"God Phillip, is there anything you don't know? Sam behaved very adult-like at the seminar; in fact I think he was the most intelligent one there."

"I didn't say he wasn't intelligent, I just said he needs a little growing up."

"So again, how could you possibly know that?"

"Because he hasn't married you yet. I saw the look in his eye and the look in both of your eyes."

"Jo, is he always like this?"

"Pretty much. That's why he needs me. I'm smarter than he is. Although I must admit he's one fantastic judge of character. So, I have to think that this Sam guy is worth waiting for."

"I'll make sure I tell him when I see him," said Koy. " I'll be sure to mention that this Eyespellian and his wife told me that he was a great guy and we are meant for each other. He'll especially like the part about being a good father. That ought to about crystallize things. In fact I think we'll get married next Wednesday and I would like you two to be Best Man and Matron of Honor. How about it?"

"Not a chance," said Jo, "but we do expect an invitation and I'd say a lot sooner than you think."

"Wow, you're serious and I believe you. Do you do Tarot cards?"

"Nah, they just slow me down."

"You know what, I believe that too," said Koy laughing out loud. "I am truly tickled. Sam is such a brilliant idiot and I have such a crush on him. I'll tell you who else is one heck of a guy, and that's his friend Jack. The three of us were inseparable in college. And Jack's wife, fantastic person."

"So you see," chimed in Phillip, "there's a whole bunch of Mystic Management types running around loose. I agree with you about Jack too. He was a lot quieter than Sam, but lots of wheels turning there. Sam and Jack are exactly the type of CEOs that can begin to give Mystic Management enough mass to give the world a big shove. I see people like you, me, Jo, Sam, Jack, his wife from what you say, and Christian and his wife, Sally, shoving the world in the direction it needs to go. I might have been pretty angry during the time of madness but a lot of what's in those old manuscripts is as least as true today as it was then. The lack of community, for example, is more appalling today than it was then. Nice, you've got me on my soapbox instead of you telling us more about you."

"It's the reporter in me. And that's the truth; I have been into being a reporter since I was about two I think. My parents used to always tell me to stop interviewing them. I was evidently incorrigible around Christmas time trying to find out what they had gotten me. Just for the record, my parents are great people; I actually enjoy spending time with them. My brother, Albert, now there's a piece of work. He's three years older than I and not what a girl would dream of for a big brother. I seriously believe he's a criminal and just hasn't been caught yet. I don't have a lot of friends; I'm a bit of a loner and pretty much like it that way. I'm a loner but I don't get lonely if you know what I mean. I go to yoga classes, meditate on a daily basis, play the flute, and I love bowling if you can believe it. Anything else you would like to know?

"Just how did you come by the name Koy?"

"Phillip, have you been in my head?"

"Absolutely not, honest, why?"

"Well, my name is my fondest possession and I rarely talk about it. But I suppose you rarely talk about Eyespell either. My name defines me; it is my essence. It's of water and flows throughout my being. It's really hard to describe. My name pours forth my soul; it allows me to be here. Understand, my parents are some blend of French, Italian, Spanish, and a little German, and obviously a little dark-skinned something. They're not sure about that part. Anyway, I once asked them where 'Koy' came from and they simply shrugged their shoulders and said, 'From God we suppose.' When pressed they said they had no preconceived notion, no pun intended, of what to name me. They knew I was a girl and decided to wait until they saw me before trying to name me. Seems they both took one look and together said 'Koy.' Can you imagine that? Actually, you two probably can."

"Now that's a story," said Jo.

"Are you sure you're not from Eyespell?" said Phillip. "I am really touched by that. That must be what I've sensed in you, your name, your essence. Just wow, Ms. Koy Sosa, no middle name."

"No middle name," said Koy. "I think I'm ready for more Eyespell. Still in the mood."

"Still in the mood, even more so. By the way, do you now get how special you are?"

"Yes, I think I do. I am guessing that Eyespell didn't get out of the mess it was in despite the efforts in the Valley of the Blue Noon. That has got to be the most interesting name of a place I've ever heard, the Valley of the Blue Noon. Download me, Doc. Oops, hold on. Are you up for a little more gap filler first? Questions seem to sneak in when I'm not expecting them. This compressed mind-link stuff I think bends time a little whether I try to think linear or not."

"Right again. I have noticed the same thing with mind-link. Thoughts seem to show up whenever they feel like it, not necessarily attached to the subject at hand. Sometimes that can be really distracting. I'll be teaching a seminar with Christian, for example, and something Leo told me will just pop in and want resolution."

"Something Leo told you? There you go again; but I'm sure that's another, *another story*. I'm not even going to ask. But I am curious about how you got from Florida to DC after the accident and how you ended up a stock broker of all things? And if you could do all that why didn't you contact your family who I gather was in the DC/Northern Virginia area? I assume they hadn't died before you got back?"

"You've hit upon the most convoluted part of the story, at least in terms of the time of madness. I'm not sure where to start. While at the hospital right after the accident the psychiatrist who was assigned my case took a real liking to me. It was very unpsychiatrist-like. Instead of maintaining what would be considered a professional distance he wanted to make sure I didn't up end in the world totally void of any connections. To make a long story short, he did a bunch of testing and had a pretty good idea that I was the intelligent sort. He particularly saw my potential with numbers. Coincidentally, he had a cousin in DC doing the stock thing and, voila, so it came to pass. And, yes, my parents were still in the DC area, but the major gaps in my memory remained."

"You still didn't know you were Phillip Hansen?"

"Correct. It seems I remembered things I had learned. I had glimpses of people and places but nothing specific. In fact, anything that could connect me to any place or person that might help me identify who I was, was simply not in my consciousness. We even tried hypnosis, and nothing useful happened."

"So the psychiatrist really couldn't help much?"

"Well, not with his trade anyway. But like I said he befriended me and helped me get started without my identity. How rude of me, his name is John Telamanni. Nice Italian boy. Oh, that reminds me. Wanna hear a funny story in real time?"

"Oh no, not the psychiatrist and his mother story," popped in Jo. "It really is pretty funny. When John was trying to get Phillip here to settle into a new identity John told him the story about how his mother caused him a major identity crisis. He kiddingly told Phillip he was better off without parents, especially his mother. John said that alone could eliminate years of therapy. Before Phillip goes off on the psychiatrist's mother story he left out something rather important. When I met him he was not Phillip Hansen, a minor fact that my spirit guides forgot to tell me by the way. To get him back in the world he had had to take on a new name, get a new Social Security number, driver's license, and anything else he needed to claim to be a real person in our society. And this is where Phillip owes a real debt of gratitude to John. John helped Phillip though all of the bureaucratic hoops and even gave him $7,500 to get him up and running in the real world."

"That's amazing," said Koy. "I think John Telamanni should be included on that Mystic Management supporters list. Quite a shot of Karmic Kindness garnished with sprigs of Gentle Generosity and Ego

Empowerment. I've got to know, Phillip, what name did you take while waiting for your memory to return?"

A broad grin spread over Phillip's face. "Why Leo, of course, Leo Sosa."

"That's it!" screamed Koy. "Moose, drive me to the airport. That's not even possible; get out of town! And I even called you Leo earlier this evening. But Leo Sosa, how unbelievable. You picked a name that connected your past, Leo, and your future, Sosa."

"Let me tell you, when Sam called me and told me your name, well, that's why I went running to find Jo. Like she said, I never run. Maybe we haven't known each other forever in the linear sense, but do you get the feeling time has bent around us a bit?"

"I would like to meet Dr. Telamanni."

"And you will. But I've got to tell you that story he told me about his mother. In fact, John wrote it to me in a letter. It went something like this. Remember this is John speaking, not me."

A Matter of Misperception

Right around my thirtieth birthday, I mustered up enough courage to ask my mother why she used to spit at me when I was a child. I had finally developed enough self-esteem to ask this delicate question. And, I wanted to know if she realized what an awful thing spitting at me was. She was horrified, denying the whole thing.

I remember that when I was a child and my mother became angry with me, she would rapidly wave her hands back and forth in the air and follow me with quick, short steps from room to room. She would swear at me in Italian and then she would shake her finger at me with teeth clenched and lips tightly pursed. This struck terror in my heart. And then came the really scary part. Positioned within inches of my now trembling body, she would utter several guttural sounds, move her head jerkily forward, and just as her head snapped to a stop, a faint bit of saliva would shoot in my direction. What kind of an animal was I to cause my own mother to behave in such a barbaric way? To cause your very own mother to spit at you must mean you're despicable!

After a few sessions with my therapist, I confronted her again. She still denied it, emphatically saying she would never do such a thing. But this time, I really cornered her; I gave her specific examples and ran around the kitchen acting out the whole horrific scene. I screamed those awful utterances and, with all the nastiness I could muster, I spit at the imaginary child huddled in the corner. I did it twice, just for effect.

By this time, my mother was laughing uncontrollably. Frankly, I was appalled at her behavior. When she finally collected herself, she told me that I had just solved one of the greatest mysteries she'd had as a parent. She proceeded to explain that she never did understand why I would instantly shape up whenever she would hover over me and yell in Italian, "And you, and you, and you!"

"And you," in my mother's Italian, came out, "Et tu, et tu, et tu." Now, say "et tu" with any speed and gusto and a little tracer of saliva can't help but shoot straight out from between your pursed lips. What a misperception and what a relief; my mother was not a beast and I was not a worthless being.

Many puzzling and upsetting things happen to us on our journey toward self-fulfillment. Identity and positive self-esteem become more and more elusive. It is literally as if we keep falling through the real world, never quite landing in it. It's as if our reality is full of holes; we can't find solid ground. I wonder how many misconceptions and miscommunications are never explained and resolved? And I wonder what these do to our identity, self-esteem, and relationships? Perhaps we learn to fear and avoid others' expectations of us altogether in order to defray the cost of misperception. Often, by adulthood we learn to be totally alone.

"Now hold on a minute," said Koy. "You say that came from John?"

"Yeah, it was his way of trying to make me feel better that I was all alone and that parents can cause some real psychological trouble. After all, he was a psychiatrist and knew what big trouble mothers are."

"Hey," said Jo, "I object. I have been the perfect mother to both you and Christian. Sorry, I meant wife and mother."

"You know, one of these days, Mrs. Hansen, I'll get a step ahead of you. And when I do, look out is all I can say."

"You two are distracting me. I heard a couple of things in that little psychiatrist and mother episode that echoed some things you said in your dissertation on the real world and that holes in reality thing."

"Indeed. I like your mind; a bit like an elephant, you don't forget anything. Yes, I would think that John Telamanni has definitely influenced my thinking. Shouldn't we be getting back to Eyespell? I mean the Council of Elders hasn't even officially heard from Kathryn or the four who made it back. Their perceptions might be quite enlightening."

"Okay, I'm ready. Let's have the next installment."

CHAPTER 15

▼

PERCEPTIONS

The intention of holding a Full-Round had been to celebrate the return of the Eyespell Experiment participants. However, that initial intention was negated by the unexpected appearance and intensity of Earth-plane vibrational leakage. The Full-Round was abruptly cancelled as the Elders retreated into Oneness and planned the subsequent pilgrimage to the Valley of the Blue Noon led by Leo with his cadre of monks. Neither Kathryn nor the four returnees ever got the chance to share their perceptions of their Earth experiences with the Elders' Council. Now that the planetary cell-matrix was back in check, the Elders were anxious to hear from the returnees. While there would be no Full-Round to celebrate their return, Kathryn, Antonio, Melissa, Nancy, and Pete would at last each have an opportunity to share with the Council and with Eyespell the highlights of their time on Earth.

Anxiously waiting in the Council Chamber, Kathryn quickly moved forward and addressed the Council immediately upon their return, "With all due courtesy and respect to the Council and our four returnees, I would like to share my perceptions of the Eyespell Experiment with you *before* we address the specific Earth-lifetimes of Antonio, Melissa, Nancy, and Pete. I feel that my insight as Overseer of the Eyespell Experiment will help put our findings in perspective. Is that agreeable with everyone?"

Daniel, without hesitation said, "Your request makes sense, your experience is the logical starting place. I hope the rest of you can stand to wait to tell your tales. I know we can hardly wait to hear every detail. I suppose we could multiple-mind-link and get it done in one fell swoop, but that wouldn't be nearly as much fun. And, after our encounters with Earth-plane vibrational leakage, we are due some fun, don't you agree? I'm in the mood for a good old-fashioned story like the ones told when you were kids out in the desert with one of us on a learning expedition."

The group gave Daniel simultaneous and unanimous nods of agreement.

Kathryn began her part of the story by detailing several observations about incidents on Earth and her perceptions of the Eyespell Experiment overall. However, it was almost immediately noticeable that her manner was out-of-character, almost officious.

"The catalyst for the Eyespell Experiment was the observed hopelessness of Earth's American youth. We thought that five premature, self-induced deaths occurring simultaneously would communicate a message to Earth that something was drastically amiss. The Earth deaths of our five Eyespell Experiment participants on their twentieth Earth birthdays were designed to carry a dire message to the American people. The suicides were intended to be a warning that their society needed to take on the serious business of recognizing its emotional sickness, and to begin the healing process."

Kathryn continued, but in a clearly agitated tone. "None of us recognized the high numbers of teenage and young adult suicides on planet Earth, in the United States in particular. By the time our reentry window was reached, twenty years into the experiment, a mere four, one in New York, one in New Mexico, one in California, and one in Florida, all at the same age, went almost unnoticed and certainly were not perceived as related in any way. And, of course, the fifth suicide never happened, but that's another story. Here on Eyespell even if we detected the slightest depression of one of our loved ones, it would be enough to prompt a meeting of the Elders' Council. A *negative*, self-inflicted transition, like the ones we designed for Earth, is simply not in the realm of our Eyespellian reality. From our perspective, five such transitions on Eyespell would be outrageous and cataclysmic and would spark a planetary emergency. Actually, the concept of suicide is so unimaginable we can't realistically put it into an Eyespellian context. We had no idea what we were dealing with. Our reality blinded us to the possibility that on Earth five suicides would barely be noticed. And, in fact, they were barely noticed except for a brief notation in a couple of local newspapers, and not even that much occurred in Antonio's and Nancy's cases. The suicides did not produce any interest at all much less the intended wake-up call to impending social disaster. Pete had an obituary and Melissa's story was only so much rich-kid stuff in the society section of the *Boca Raton News*. No one really cared enough to even mention Antonio's death, and Nancy is still officially listed as missing; the mesa she jumped off was in a remote location and the authorities never did find a body."

With even more agitation, then agitation turning to anger, anger directed at the Elders' Council, Kathryn continued, "The Eyespell Experiment was a complete and total flop; it generated no significant interest on Earth. And, except for Melissa and Phillip, you know, the missing one, the five participants led totally separate lives; who would ever connect their suicides, even if they were looking? No one made any cognitive connection among the suicides. We failed to account for the lack of community among people on Earth and the geographical separation among our participants finished the job totally. The planet Earth does not have abilities that even approach the sharing aspect of total planet telepathy link. So, another failure of this mission was our blindness to the lack of community on Earth." Kathryn stopped to take a breath and pretty much scowled at the Elders then coolly stated, "CNN twenty-four hour news is the closest they come to community."

Pete chuckled at Kathryn's cleverness and found the sarcasm in her voice particularly reminiscent of Earth. He also found his reaction a bit disquieting and reminiscent of Earth. He wiggled uncomfortably in his chair and caught Leo's worrisome glance out of the corner of his eye.

Oblivious to her uncharacteristic Earth-like mimicking, negative behavior, Kathryn continued on. "Only something spectacularly horrifying would have gotten the kind of attention you were looking for. Maybe if the five were close friends and committed joint suicides, maybe then they would have received brief national attention, maybe; and then only if the method was truly brutal, savage or in some way bizarre enough to make it newsworthy. Anything less would simply be uninteresting and not particularly newsworthy."

Kathryn stood smug, indignant, again staring at the Elders. Before anyone could react she blurted out, "Then, of course, there is Phillip, who is missing altogether! As you well know, I was uncomfortable from the beginning and to appease me you sent me to Earth for a firsthand look. I wish I had been more assertive at the onset of this foolishness. There was never consensus on this issue, and as far as I am concerned that is a violation of the Mystic Management we supposedly hold so sacred!"

The members of the Elders' Council were having a great deal of difficulty processing what was going on. Except for Leo; he had seen it before in Nancy. The Elders found the situation impossible, not because of Kathryn's disagreement with aspects of the Eyespell Experiment, but because of her negative tone and defiant body language. Without Leo having to say anything the others finally realized that Kathryn's behavior was another manifestation of Earth-plane vibrational leakage. They could sense a slightly negative vibration in several of the light-corridors. Thank goodness the fluctuation lasted only a fraction of a fraction of a second and did not translate into the cell-matrix. The physical reality of the Council Chamber remained unchanged. Relying on activities while in Oneness to reinforce the light-corridors and the power of the pilgrimage to the Valley of the Blue Noon, the Elders stood fast against this new attack of Earth-plane vibrational leakage. But, something more needed to be done and done immediately to change Kathryn's psychological temperament and to balance her.

The Elders chose unconditional love, total acceptance of Kathryn as the best defense against Earth-plane vibrational leakage. She was to be embraced rather than feared. This was a totally new strategy; embracing the problem of Earth-plane vibrational leakage.

Daniel moved closer to Kathryn and, looking into her eyes, spoke in a caring and positive tone, "In spite of your concerns about the Eyespell project, Kathryn, as appointed Overseer you gave unselfishly to the accomplishment of your task. You gave unselfishly for twenty Earth-years. You collected precise, firsthand, and invaluable information about

Earth. You protected the participants and recorded every detail of their life circumstances on Earth. You even helped them manifest their suicides into successful reentry to Eyespell. In addition to the data specific to Antonio and the others, you also amassed a great deal of information about what was happening generally in the experiment zone. You were able to tap the mood of America in a generic sense. We would be very interested in your perceptions."

Kathryn, unaware of her recent inappropriate demeanor, seemed genuinely pleased with Daniel's query. She responded very positively to him, and, in an almost bubbly voice said, "I documented two recurring themes in American society: (1) the individual's search for inner identity, positive self-esteem, and community; and (2) the search for what was idiomatically called the *real world*. These two concepts seem inextricably intertwined, and represent the nucleus of much Earth literature and debate.

"My hypothesis is that the previous Earth generation, the one just before the arrival of our participants, had expended so much of its time and energy concentrating on their own identity and reality issues that they inadvertently produced the feeling of hopelessness in many of their offspring. Of course Antonio, Melissa, Nancy, Pete, and Phillip Earth-fused as part of that generation of offspring. The stage seemed to be perfectly set for the Eyespell Experiment."

Myana, the Elder of the Pink-Light-Corridor of Unconditional Love, chimed in, "What an incredible lack of connectedness and compassion to have instilled this hopelessness into an entire generation. You must have found it impossible at times to be so close to such intense feelings of isolation and hopelessness. We all owe you a great debt of gratitude for being our Earth eyes, ears, and heart." The Elders leaned forward and swept Kathryn Song into their collective aura in expression of the ultimate Eyespellian compliment.

So far, embracing Kathryn to dispel the Earth-plane vibrational leakage was working well. In fact, Kathryn thought to herself, "What a wonderful interaction, although it's odd; something feels unbalanced. It's almost as if I'm being manipulated, but that's ridiculous, Eyespellians would have no reason to manipulate. I wonder if Earth affected me more than I think?" Kathryn commented aloud, "Imagine the pain in the uncertainty of not knowing if what you do is meaningful and valued by others."

"What?" asked Daniel. "What are you referring to?"

"I'm sorry," said Kathryn, "I must have been off on some other topic in my head."

Trying to glean some overall meaning in everything that Kathryn had said, Nathan, keeper of the Green-Light-Corridor of Nature, removed the emerald crystal from its pouch, placed it around his neck on its rope of light and almost tearfully addressed the Council. "Earth's pain is overwhelming. The magnitude of inner conflict is debilitating. The distance between the psychology of individualism and the possibility of inclusive community rips at the spiritual stamina of the planet. It is no wonder we chose not to look on in passive observation. The Eyespell Experiment was necessary and I do not see it as a failure. We are an intuitive people; it is not so much what we know, but what we feel that makes the difference. I sense the beginning of a healing on the Earth as a result of our efforts and I feel strongly that those efforts will continue to play a central role in a new age of Mystic Management on planet Earth."

Myana came forth removing the Pink Tourmaline of Unconditional Love from its pouch, placing it around her neck in a gesture of that love. She added, "I am reminded of an image in the *Book of Dreams*, "The Identity Garden." It is one of my favorite image-writings. Perhaps we could focus together on that image and in unconditional love send some positive identity and community building energy to the Earth."

Leo stepped forward and asked that Pete, with his refreshed memory of Eyespell, be allowed to lead the group in image. Pete smiled and effortlessly retrieved the image of "The Garden of Identity" from his recent daydream at the Council opening just days before. The vibration of "The Garden of Identity" was sent toward the Earth in a loving and healing gesture. The purpose of the Eyespell Experiment and the unselfish motivations of the Eyespellians continued to unfold.

The Council was attentive to and compassionate toward the recurring themes of uncertain identity, confused reality, and lack of community. They were much saddened at Earth's seeming inability to deal effectively with such issues. "Telepathy link offers such an easy solution to the complex problem of aloneness," said Matthew. "The energy from the Red-Light-Corridor could go far in stimulating the nine-tenths of the brain that Earthlings simply can't or don't use." The Council members nodded in agreement.

The Council dismissed how Kathryn initially made them feel chastised and again the light-corridors maintained their positive skew. Leo thought for a moment and then, to even further accentuate the positive, said in his most accepting and warmest voice, "Kathryn, you have, indeed, picked up some wisdom during your Earth travels."

Still unaware that her earlier behavior toward the Council was out of the ordinary, she accepted the compliment, but with the same nagging thought more clearly formed, "They are patronizing me again, the bastards." Then she said aloud, "I think I have shared all I need to for now. Let's hear about Antonio's life on earth." Her tone clearly and purposefully usurped the more typical approach of turning the meeting back to Daniel and asking what he would like to do next.

Daniel, caught off guard by Kathryn's command-giving, simply nodded approval. It's not like she violated a law or anything; it was simply a matter of courtesy to defer such decisions to the head of the Council. All could sense Kathryn's pride at taking charge, and all had heard Kathryn's inner comment, "The bastards." Her telepathy link was wide open; an unlikely mistake. It was more Earth-plane vibrational leakage in still another guise. Shockingly, disruption of the cell-matrix was still averted.

Antonio was reluctant to begin his tale. He was a bit bewildered and taken aback by Kathryn's behavior. All remained quiet in the calm before the storm.

Antonio was encouraged by Matthew to share his Earth experience with the Council. As with Kathryn, mind-link would have been the quickest way to glean his thoughts. However, Eyespellians loved that good spoken story and the Council decided to keep things at the spoken level initiated at the onset of the meeting in spite of the ominous hint of things to come.

With a little more urging, Antonio began his story. "It is strange to look back upon my Earth life. It's like looking at someone or something else, like imaging with the *Book of Dreams*. The fact that I have Earth memories from birth to twenty years of age is absolutely bizarre. Being back here has not dulled those memories in the least. What's peculiar is that my Earth memories include absolutely no inklings of Kathryn or anything Eyespellian. It's hard to explain. When I think about my Earth-time, it does not include, I should say, it does not allow for thoughts of Eyespell superimposed on that time based on who I am now. I cannot think of my life on Earth as an Eyespellian looking back at an experience I had on Earth. I can only think of Earth from an Earthling's persepective. My memories of the Earth experience are a totally separate consciousness and, yet, somehow fused with my total being. I am Eyespellian, but have the experience of a totally separate life on another plane. The concept of life on more than one plane is not, in and of itself, unusual; it's the present moment inability to fuse the two memories that boggles my senses. Again, the best way to describe it is that I cannot think of Earth or my experience there from an Eyespellian perspective, I cannot think of Earth in my Eyespellian mind; Earth memories stand separate in my consciousness. I have no idea how my Earth life affects who I am now but I know that it does."

The Eldersix, especially Matthew, were very attentive to what Antonio was saying. "Antonio," said Matthew, "try to explain exactly what you mean by the memories won't blend, that they are separate in your consciousness."

"It's really a hard concept to get a handle on. I don't know what else to say, but I'll try again. There are several things to consider. Let's start with my Earth-time. During those twenty years I had no recollections of Eyespell. Then there's right now. I recall the twenty years and sense nothing Eyespellian in that part of my memory while at the same time it's all part of who I am now."

Daniel got to laughing, "My boy, this is truly a puzzle and I seem to be missing a piece or two. Try again for this old man."

"This is embarrassing. I haven't had this much trouble communicating since our lessons in the desert with Leo."

Melissa, Nancy, and Pete chimed in, "Go, Antonio!"

Pete continued, "Seriously, I think you're on to something here. I have many of the same feelings, but I can't get a grip on it exactly, either. Keep at it and we'll see if we can help out."

"Okay," agreed Antonio. "I wish Phillip were here; he was always the articulate one. Here goes again. It's like being two distinct people, Antonio the Eyespellian and Antonio the Earthling. It is not Antonio the Eyespellian simply remembering being on Earth for twenty years. It's as if my Earth-time has its own soul, a soul somehow now mixed with my Eyespellian essence."

This was an unanticipated surprise. It simply had been assumed the time on Earth would be nothing more than a memory, a collection of data. It had not occurred to anyone that those twenty years on Earth might represent a life separate from anything Eyespellian; in a sense, a life within a life. The impact in terms of Earth-plane vibrational leakage was becoming uncomfortably clear. The Earth experience was not a mere memory, but an integral part of Antonio's present reality. The question was no longer if there would be continued Earth-plane vibrational leakage, but what would the consequences be and to what extent. It was one thing to dissipate external leakage at some physical level; it would be like cleaning one's aura of negative vibrations. That risk had been assessed twenty years ago at the onset of the project. This was quite another matter; internal leakage, involving not just memories, but soul fusion. The returnees had brought permanently to Eyespell, as part of their very essence, a soul distinctly of Earth. There had been no way to anticipate these consequences.

Daniel immediately queried the other returning Eyespellians about their memory patterns and their sense of an Earth soul. Melissa, Nancy, and Pete confirmed that they were having the same sensations Antonio described. Kathryn was not. Her experience was that of an Eyespellian who simply spent twenty years in another place, on another planet. The distinguishing factor was that Kathryn did not Earth-fuse; she did not experience being born an Earthling. Not being Earth-fused, her propensity toward severe Earth-plane vibrational leakage was quite surprising. The assumption had been that Kathryn would be unaffected.

Matthew spoke to the Council, "I think I understand what has happened here. As you know, through the Red-Light-Corridor of Energy, the five Eyespellians were transformed into light energy and sent to Earth to be born. Our travelers arrived on the Earth as points of red light. In this form they each searched for and entered an unborn fetus just as it was dying of natural causes. Such a dying fetus perfectly matched the needs of our experiment. The Eyespellian point of light was to enter the fetus immediately upon the God-soul leaving. Our plan was that the body would be of Earth and the essence or soul would be that of Eyespell. At the end of twenty years, the soul would return to Eyespell through planned reentry, taking up residence in the bodies of our travelers as we see them before us today."

Matthew paused deep in thought and then continued, "I knew the moment our light energy fused with the first unborn child that we had somehow connected, forever, our destiny with that of planet Earth. When our point of light entered the first womb, the God-soul returned lest we overstep our cosmic bounds. I never mentioned this because I was not absolutely sure about the return of the God-soul until today. As Antonio began to describe his feelings and the dual memory within his psyche, my suspicions were confirmed. Antonio's and the others' Earth lives are integrated with their Eyespellian essence, not just in memory, but in soul. The God-soul returned and, in a sense, was superimposed on the Eyespellian essence; two souls coexisting. This commingling of the two souls is a truly extraordinary and unexpected outcome. In light of this revelation, even though Phillip has missed reentry, there is nothing to suggest that he is not still alive and well on the Earth-plane. Much of the Eyespell Experiment that has taken us by surprise is the doing of God and His Universal Law, rather than the inadequacy of our experiment's design. The question is, what are the lessons for Eyespell?"

The Council Chamber remained still for some time as each Elder merged with his or her crystal charge to get a better sense of what Matthew was saying. Nathan was the first to break the silence, "In keeping the Green-Light-Corridor, I maintain the physical balance of the planet and the harmony between the cell-matrix of the planet and the feelings-matrix of our people. The vibration within the emerald crystal is shifting. There will be natural disturbances on Eyespell. We need to go to the old books and relearn how to prepare ourselves for disharmony with nature."

Each Elder spoke of the potential dangers to his or her light-charge. There was talk of sickness, conflict, chaos, ignorance, and isolation. There was allusion to lethargy, hatred, and abject poverty. Such thoughts and such words had not been a part of Eyespell's reality for millennia. As their mind-links were open, the impact of what had just occurred in the Council Chamber quickly spread throughout the planet. The people of Eyespell were stunned at the grim prospects.

Daniel adjourned Council and called a meeting of the Full-Round, the Council of the Three Hundred Thirty-Seven. The planet was to prepare for total mind-link. The Full-Round would commence in three days and would open under the light of the third moon of Oneness to discuss what might become of their planet of the light-skew.

Antonio still had not finished telling his story. He and the other recently returned Eyespellians were again put on hold. The importance of the details of their Earth lives was overshadowed by the uncertainty of Eyespell's future in the face of Earth-plane vibrational leakage. The cycle of Earth-fusion and reentry to Eyespell was complete for four of the five participants in the Eyespell Experiment. The cycle of lightness into darkness for all Eyespellians was just beginning.

Phillip, the missing Eyespellian, was the only part of the circle not closed. The Council recognized that he was most probably still alive on Earth and could be the single strand of hope in the broken light-skew. If Eyespell was to move toward the dark-skew, perhaps Earth could move toward the light-skew. Perhaps some balance could be achieved on a Cosmic plane allowing both planets to ultimately rest in a place of comfort; Earth more in the light and Eyespell just a little in the dark. Perhaps Eyespell would not be destroyed by Earth-plane vibrational leakage, and perhaps Earth could become more like the planet of the light-skew.

The Eyespellians felt humbled by the Cosmos. While the Eyespell Experiment meant one thing to Eyespell, it meant quite another to God. Phillip's non-return shifted from being thought of as a devastating loss to actually being the crux of the Divine plan for Eyespell and Earth.

Chapter 16

▼

IN THE FAMILY ROOM ...

"Phillip, I really need to think on this one. I am going to need a minute to gather my wits. What you just shared is, well, it's Cosmic in scope. I can't take the chance of asking the wrong questions, of being trite. I need some time here. While I'm thinking, however, you could tell me how it is that you are privy to all of this? Best I can tell, you are still here, on the Earth that is."

"I told you that part of the story is coming. If you think for a minute, though, I bet you can guess at least part of it. Keep in mind that there is always the possibility that Jo and I share a psychosis of grand proportions and this is one big hoax."

"This is no hoax; I attended the seminar at the Governor's Club and that was quite real for my money."

"For your money; if I recall, you got in free."

"Oh yeah, I've got it! Those Eyespell people were pretty sure you were down here alive and well."

"Keep going."

"And they found a way to contact you using telepathy. Oh my gosh, the mind-link you have been using all night: It is not limited to the confines of this family room; it can link across space, between here and Eyespell! Right?"

"Smart girl. I call it the Eyespell Connection. The first go-round was not quite that simple but I promise to give you a mindful when we get to that part of the story, and we are getting really close. Is your mind cleared up on this most recent development, the soul thing?"

"Well, that took me by surprise. I guess I just never thought about how you all got here. Maybe I just assumed you flew in. Somehow, I never pictured these points of light carrying five Eyespellians, each entering an unborn fetus. I mean, that's way out there. A dying fetus at that. The souls leave and in pop Antonio, Melissa, Nancy, Pete, and you. Do you have any idea how strange that is?"

"Oh yeah, I think so."

"Damn, Phillip, do you have two souls?"

"Oh yeah, I think so."

"Jo, any more of that wonderful scotch?"

"Coming up."

"You have memories of Eyespell, I mean living there and all? You know, earlier when you were trying to explain that alien thing and how you were born here as well; is having two souls what you were getting at?"

"Sort of. The problem is I'm as confused as Antonio and the others, only I'm here instead of there. So I guess some of it is different."

"Well, what happens when you die? If you have two souls do they both go to the same place? Oh God, I have no idea what the hell I'm talking about. Jo, help me!"

"I'm coming, I'm coming. Here's your scotch, and yours, Phillip-Two-Souls, and mine. I can't wait to see where this goes. My theory is there is a good Phillip and a bad Phillip and that one soul will go to heaven and the other one, well to hell I suppose."

"Or the Domeshodar," said Phillip.

"Save me," said Koy, "that's another story, right?"

"No, it's just a place. I think this is great fun; you're not 'born again,' are you?"

"No, but you evidently are; literally."

"Clever."

"So what do you really think, Phillip?"

"Well, I honestly do feel at a bit of a loss to explain it, kind of like Antonio. I definitely don't feel schizophrenic or anything like that. I don't sense more than one of me. I am definitely whole; I just have more soul than most."

"Now who's being clever. So you really don't have an answer."

"Nope, but I finally figured out that I don't need one. Think about it. Eyespell plans this experiment and everything goes wrong. At least so far. And why does it go wrong? They overstepped their bounds and God stepped in and said 'not so fast.' "Cosmo" is in charge of souls, not Earthlings, not Eyespellians, and certainly not me. So, not to worry, when the time comes God will figure out what to do with my two souls, if that's what they are. I find it fascinating but not anything I need to resolve. Now had I gone into theology instead of psychology, I'd be in a heap a doo-doo."

"It must have been a humbling experience when Eyespell figured out their plans were usurped by God."

"Indeed, but once they saw the big picture ... well, that's another story."

"I am going to hurt you, Phillip Hansen."

"Strangulation is the preferred method," piped in Jo. "When you really think about it, you have been a pretty fragmented guy, Phillip. You went out of body in the hospital after the accident, out of your mind for years afterward, and now, you have two souls. It is a damn good thing the Cosmos sent me to keep you in one piece. And you know what, Koy, he is so put together at this point it amazes me. I'll take a little hand-holding credit but Cosmo has done some mighty work on this boy."

"Did I detect a compliment in there?" asked Phillip.

"Yep, and a very large one at that. Koy, obviously Phillip and I have discussed this aspect of things many times. We really don't know the answers; we do know that a Power beyond Earth and beyond Eyespell is at work here, has been at work since the inception of the Eyespell Experiment. We also know that when Cosmo works, the outcomes, while sometimes most difficult to reach, are always worth the journey. We feel that Earth and Eyespell are on such a journey and we're good with that. Enjoy the journey."

"Enjoy the journey, I like that," said Koy. "Well, where from here? I assume things are going to get pretty hairy for Eyespell before they arrive at the ultimate outcome."

"Sit back and let me share a bit more."

CHAPTER 17

▼

THE DOMESHODAR

Antonio awoke with a start. He was having another nightmare about the Earth-time. Of all the reentrants, his Earth experience was by far the most psychologically difficult. He still carried with him in vivid detail the Earth memories and feelings that had led to his suicide, his giving up against a walnut tree. Early on he felt excited about his Eyespellian home and to be back in his Eyespellian body. However, his feelings of despair returned; his feelings of hopelessness returned with renewed intensity a couple of months after reentry. The feelings were manifesting even in his physical appearance. Some days, Antonio looked almost like the gaunt field worker who had died on Earth. This appeared to be part of internal Earth-plane vibrational leakage initiated by the Earth-time memories and the issue of an Earth-soul.

Due to the connectedness of all things on Eyespell, Antonio's nightmares created havoc with the planetary cell-matrix. When he dreamed about the harshness of his Earth experience, it caused the same kind of environmental breakdowns experienced with Nancy, and the first signs of Earth-plane vibrational leakage, only worse. There were unexpected and severe thunder and lightning storms, small stress cracks in the planet's surface, minor landslides, and so on. These manifestations of Earth-plane vibrational leakage were particularly problematic in proximity to Antonio's physical being. Things got so bad that Antonio had to be isolated away from both Elaysia and the Valley of the Blue Noon. This isolation was another negative first for Eyespell.

It was crucial that a way be found to psychologically soothe Antonio. It seemed that due to the nature of the Earth vibration causing the discomfort, typical Eyespellian remedies simply did not work. Typical mind-link therapy proved almost useless. This was a unique problem for Eyespell and it demanded a unique solution.

It was finally decided that Antonio would best benefit from the combined vibrations of three of the Elders. The Elders with the crystal charges for Unconditional Love, Oneness, and Energy directed their attention toward Antonio. Myana with the Pink Crystal of Love, Gracina the Clear Crystal of Oneness, and Matthew the Red Crystal of Energy began to work with Antonio's vibrations. His pain and the planet's pain were, indeed, interconnected, and Antonio's healing was first and foremost a labor of unconditional love.

Antonio was summoned to the Council Chamber and was invited into the twenty-seventh ring with the Elders. Because of the seriousness of Antonio's condition, the risk of negatively tainted vibrations fragmenting the crystal charge was ignored. He was seated on a large velvety pillow and instructed to sit spine-straight and cross-legged in the traditional meditative position.

Myana stood facing Antonio and pointed the pink tourmaline crystal's saber light at his heart chakra area. Gracina stood at his back and to the left, pointing the white light at his head, taking in both the third eye and crown chakras. Matthew also stood at Antonio's back, equidistant and to the right of Gracina and directed the red rays of his crystal, like guy wires, touching Antonio's shoulders and knees, encircling several major and minor chakra points at once. The Elders formed a double pyramid of light around Antonio with one light point to the north and the other light point to the south. Antonio was literally suspended in the aura of pyramid-light.

The Elders did not probe Antonio's mind, but rather let him fall asleep within the healing rays of their crystals. They maintained the light around him and meditated, affirming "Antonio's Earth-time nightmares are healed by his mind's own inner workings." They repeated the affirmation over and over like a mantra. The Elders maintained their vigil and unobtrusively watched, repeating the affirmation as Antonio began to dream about his experiences on Earth.

Antonio shifted into peaceful sleep. Myana, Gracina, and Matthew maintained their watch until he awakened. He seemed in tune with the planet's cell-matrix and left the Council Chamber a much more settled Antonio than the young man of just a day ago.

The "Antonio Meditation" as it was later recorded in *The Book of Dreams,* became a new approach to healing on Eyespell. Its discovery was the first positive fallout of Earth-plane vibrational leakage. The original mediation and several spin-offs proved to be extremely potent remedies.

The Eyespell Experiment, while couched in the hopelessness of the youth of America and climaxing in four suicides, never intended to put any of the participants through the seemingly horrible existence Antonio had experienced on Earth. Viewing Antonio's Earth-time through mind-link, it became apparent that the Earth-fusion had gone awry. Eyespell had never thought that such a dark-skewed life would be in store for any of the Earth-fused souls. As Eyespellians they had no concrete perception of what suffering really was; suffering, as an idea in the abstract, caused no pain. Until the link with Antonio's nightmares, no one was aware of his plight and what suffering felt like in a place like Earth. Any hint at such suffering and the Eyespell Experiment would simply have been aborted and the participants somehow brought home before the planned reentry. While on Earth the participants had no direct mind-link to or from Eyespell. As a result, during the twenty Earth-years, the Elders had no clue as to what was really going on within the most private recesses of each participant's mind.

This brought up an extremely puzzling issue; why hadn't Kathryn reported the extreme despair Antonio had been feeling? Again, if the Council of Elders had known, perhaps early reentry would have been possible. At least they would have made every effort to somehow soothe the pain Antonio was feeling. The Elders needed to speak with Kathryn, review the Earth-lives of the other participants, and, most important, find out why Kathryn did not disclose Antonio's very real despair on Earth.

The Elders invited Kathryn to the Council Chamber. They expressed their curiosity about why she had not reported the negative aspects of Antonio's Earth-life in her mind-links. Leo began, "Kathryn, as you know, Myana, Gracina, and Matthew have worked closely with Antonio to help relieve some of his vibrational discomfort. In their dream-link review with him, many aspects of his Earth-life that we had been unaware of were brought to our attention. This was especially true with regard to his times of extreme difficulty and hardship. My question is, why don't any of your reports, verbal, written, or mind-linked, speak of the anguish Antonio went through on Earth?"

Kathryn looked bewildered, "I'm not sure what you mean, Leo."

"Let me recount two specific incidents for you. What about his being forced to leave home, and his sometimes going days without adequate nourishment?"

"I know nothing of this. And, certainly, if I did, it would be in my reports along with a suggestion to halt the Eyespell Experiment. As you know, I was not exactly in favor of the idea in the first place. If early reentry to Eyespell was deemed too risky, I could have rescued Antonio myself on Earth. In fact, I most certainly would have done just that. I could have had him come live with me on the pretense of saving a homeless child that no one wanted. I would not have needed to explain anything Eyespellian to Antonio until the reentry window appeared."

Leo knew Kathryn was telling the truth in spite of her somewhat edgy attitude. There had never been occasion to suspect any Eyespellian of not telling the truth. And yet, here was this mysterious inconsistency. Did Antonio suffer as he said? How did Kathryn not perceive all that took place? It simply did not add up.

"Kathryn, I apologize for putting you through this kind of conversation. I do not doubt your integrity; however, something is wrong. None of the written records you have provided, or the mental recollections you've shared about Antonio's Earth-time, parallel his experience as he himself recalls it. While you state that there was some hardship as a field worker and, certainly, much identity crisis, you indicate nothing of a lifetime of severe struggle. It's as if you're describing an altogether different life than the one Antonio himself describes."

Kathryn thought a few minutes about what Leo was saying and then asked, "May I review Antonio's nightmares? I would like to see the life he portrays versus the one I have recorded."

Leo was able to accommodate Kathryn's request easily, through an agreed upon mind-link with Matthew. Antonio's nightmares and the recent healing efforts led by Matthew, Gracina, and Myana were closely examined by Kathryn.

Finally, she broke mind-link and spoke, "What I just experienced through Matthew may help explain why there is such inconsistency between what I reported and what Antonio actually experienced on Earth. In reviewing Antonio's dream and life through Matthew, it seemed it was not the first time I'd seen the negative events. It was as if I remembered them simultaneous to reviewing the dream supposedly for the first time. I suspect our problem is one of Earth-time versus Eyespell-time. Time on Earth, as we know, is linear, whereas time on Eyespell is, well, simply time. When The Eyespell Experiment participants Earth-fused in the red light, and were born on the Earth, they were immersed in linear time for the predetermined twenty years of the experiment. The events of the twenty Earth-years appear linear and sequential in the participants' minds. For example, when Antonio recalls his Earth-time, his memory stretches from conception to age twenty. The events in his Earth life follow a specific sequence from beginning to end."

"I did not Earth-fuse," said Kathryn. "I went to Earth out-of-body and manifested my physical being once there. I did not, however, manifest in linear time. There is no guarantee that my recording or experiencing anything on Earth is represented in a linear fashion. It is possible that I have selected memories and events from Antonio's total soul life, regardless of where or when those events actually happened. Or it could be a matter of what Earth psychologists call selective perception and retention, seeing and hearing only what one wants to see and hear regardless of the reality of a situation. Maybe Antonio's experience was simply too painful for me to assimilate."

Kathryn continued, "While I certainly manifested in linear space, I evidently did not manifest in linear time. So, as I've said, my memories could be like random selections from a laser disk. Without a specific point of reference, there would be no way to tell past from present from future, or, for that matter, if the event actually existed in time at all, or was only a creation of the imagination."

Leo felt a sudden sense of urgency; he needed to talk to Melissa, Nancy, and Pete. He looked at Kathryn and said, "Maybe you were right all along; maybe we Eyespellians should mind Eyespell and leave the rest of the galaxies alone regardless of our well-meaning motives. In this Experiment we seem to have overlooked a great deal. I hope we have not put the others through such a difficult Earth-fusion due to our oversights."

Melissa arrived at the Council Chamber already telepathically informed of the concerns. Leo asked her to highlight some of her Earth-time experiences.

"Let me start in reverse, with my twentieth year," began Melissa. "I was in my junior year of college and I was a reporter for the school newspaper. Earth was a strange place in terms of learning; some of the dumbest people on the planet were actually in charge of learning. Forgive me for being judging. I realize it's a characteristic not becoming of an Eyespellian. But planet Earth is a true contradiction when it comes to education."

Leo interrupted long enough to compare what Melissa was saying with his notes from Kathryn dealing with the time period being discussed. Again, there was inconsistency. For example, there was no mention in Kathryn's report about Melissa being editor of the school newspaper, or her disdain of the educational process. It was also apparent that Earth-plane vibrational leakage was manifesting in Melissa's subtle enjoyment of her judging attitude about Earth's educators. This became even more obvious as she continued.

"Earthlings' learning, I noticed, becomes stagnated uncomfortably close to the time formal education begins. It's amazing. I'm certainly not opposed to formal education, but I think Earthlings would be substantially better off if they got their education without ever confronting an educator."

Melissa began to laugh hysterically at her own joke. It took every ounce of self-control for Leo not to ask her to leave the Council Chamber. She was contaminating the light-skew. Myana was able to soothe the imbalance with the comforting vibration of Unconditional Love. Leo was disturbed by his own momentary impatience and recognized, firsthand, the true potential danger of this Earth-plane vibrational leakage which came from so many directions at once.

Melissa gathered her wits about her and continued, "Anyway, in order to make my point about these dumb educators, I wrote two pieces in the school newspaper. They were great. So great that I almost got expelled, except that those same educators were forced to uphold my First Amendment rights, freedom of speech and freedom of the press. In other words I could say and write whatever I wanted. And I did!"

Melissa, looking totally smug, inappropriately got in Leo's face and continued, "The first piece was absolutely a kick. Earth folks like to categorize, label, prioritize and rank everything, even teachers; oh excuse me, professors. Teachers teach in the lower grades and professors teach in colleges. See what I mean, they categorize everything. Anyway, the academic types' thinking is so archaic. Not only was the term *teacher* relegated to the lower grades, and *professor* uplifted to the college and university level, but professors were ranked in an academic pecking order. I have to tell you, by the way, that the Earth term 'pecking order' is derived from observing the behavioral patterns of one of Earth's absolutely bottom-of-the-barrel, dumbest beasts, the chicken! I think it's just great irony that supposedly smart humans, college professors, measure their status from observing these dumbest of beasts. I'm sure some professors eat chickens; maybe we should eat professors!"

Melissa lost it again in a totally manic outburst of laughter. This time the Council was prepared and already had her bathed in the soothing rose ray of Unconditional Love. However, Melissa was becoming more sarcastic with every recollection.

She continued, "Professors are ranked in four primary categories. There is the Lecturer or Instructor at the bottom, then the Assistant Professor, then Associate Professor, and Full Professor at the tippity top. Well, I thought such a ranking was disgusting. In fact, I thought it was rank."

The Council was hardly able to contain Melissa this time. It was as if she was possessed. Even though she managed to gain enough composure to continue, the Eldersix had her sit in a sealed vibrational vacuum chamber, taking no chances that this level of leakage might further escape into the planet cell-matrix.

Melissa again broke into a laughing fit, this time stomping her feet and slapping her hands almost uncontrollably against the tops of her thighs. She then calmed slightly and picked her thoughts up in some random place only her mind was connected to and continued, "... well, that one really did it. Yes, sir, they were really buzzing in the halls. It's really incredible. Most of them had what is called a PhD degree, a Doctor of Philosophy, a very big deal in educational circles (how big a deal depended upon where you got your degree, of course). I hope you're taking notes, Leo; I think you'd fit right in!" Again she began to laugh hysterically.

Leo blushed a little. In everyone's recollection this was the first time an Elder had ever been insulted. It took every bit of energy from each light-corridor to keep the planet cell-matrix intact. It seemed necessary, however, to allow Melissa to continue.

"Anyway, talk about dumb. Some of those folks running around with PhDs, Doctors of Philosophy, never even took a philosophy course. How can you be a Doctor of Philosophy without a single course, not one credit, in philosophy? What about Doctors of Medicine and Doctors of Law? Do you suppose they ever took a medical course or a law course? Idiots, one and all! Why is it so? Why don't they call it what it is?"

Melissa was actually screaming at this point. The Elders were prepared to remove her from the Council Chamber, out-of-body, to the fourth moon of Eyespell where Myana could concentrate the vibration of Unconditional Love around Melissa. If she were to continue in this state, surely both she and the light-skew would be permanently damaged. The cell-matrix would probably just break apart and Eyespell with it.

"Just one more story!" screamed Melissa. "Let me tell you about the second article I wrote for the school newspaper and I'll go to the fourth moon of my own accord."

The Council was surprised at her ability to read their thoughts in her manic condition. She was fully aware of their plans to remove her to the fourth moon. Melissa sat down, exhausted, ankles crossed with the sides of her feet on the floor, her knees bent and off the ground. She looked more like a broken bunch of sticks than an Eyespellian. In a whisper of a voice, she said, "Never mind, just take me away."

Melissa collapsed. She was taken to the fourth moon, given over to Myana's charge for a total mind, body, spirit healing. The Council sat quietly for several minutes. Kathryn was stunned by Melissa's perception of America's educational climate. As in Antonio's case, however, this perception was nothing she had been aware of, and therefore nothing she could have reported back to Leo.

To no one's surprise, when Nancy talked with the Council of the Elders, there were discrepancies between her Earth-time experiences and Kathryn's records. In Nancy's case the Earth-plane vibrational leakage was the most severe. Antonio's leakage was focused in despair and for Melissa the focus was sarcasm. Nancy's primary problem was anger and this proved to be the most serious Earth-plane vibrational leakage Eyespell would face. Nancy's anger was neither sporadic nor manic, it was constant and deliberate. It approached evil, a vibration Eyespell was totally unfamiliar with and unprepared for. Nancy got into it right off.

"You know, you Elders, you Eyespellian Elders are not as unique as you might think. The Earth has its New Age and you better pay attention to the Earth's crystal charge, and the power of that charge to bring Eyespell its due for hoarding the light-skew. There are rituals on the planet Earth, Satanic rituals to name one type, the vibrations of which could cause this planet to crack in two! Eyespellian rainbows would be shredded into ribbons of black suffering. The blue sun would fall from the sky and the planet would be bathed in the hideous warmth of a deadly and silent radiation that would slowly turn skin to scrap heaps of burnt and crusted flesh. You would be forced out-of-body forever."

Nancy smiled an unnatural smile in a face that shifted almost imperceptibly, alternating between striking beauty and intense ugliness. The dome of the Council Chamber began to give off quick, sharp, cracking sounds as a warning that it might shatter into trillions of bits of molecular dust if the vibrational onslaught were to continue.

The Elders, taking Nancy's essence with them, moved out-of-body to the farthest reaches of the Pinar Galaxy. They came to rest on the outermost edge of the Domeshodar, a menacing black hole. Legend had it that the ancient Eyespellians, in the time of creation of the light-skew, cast out all evil, throwing it into this galactic hole.

The negative vibration near the perimeter of this place was too great for any Eyespellian to endure for very long. Daniel, keeper of the Yellow Crystal of Knowledge and Head of the Council, recognized the acute danger here on the fringe of Eyespell's galaxy. To save the other Elders and his beloved planet from the rapidly encroaching grip of the dark-skew, he grabbed Nancy's essence and dove into the center of the Domeshodar.

Shaken by this powerfully negative experience, the remaining five Elders materialized in the twenty-seventh ring of the Council Chamber. As distraught as they were, they still needed to continue to try to save Eyespell. They formed a prayer circle around the perimeter of the central ring, meditating on the spirit of the sixth and lost elder. They did not move for thirty-three days.

The cell-matrix of the planet was breaking apart as the Earth-plane vibrational leakage, sparked by Nancy's outburst in the Council Chamber, unleashed tinges of evil upon Eyespell. Pockets of devastation were swift and cataclysmic. Powerful, exploding volcanoes appeared out of nowhere. Floods of sand moved in rapid whirlpools sucking the landscape into the core of the planet. And lightning strikes fused the ground into crusted and blackened Earth-like moonscapes. Eyespellians fled the planet surface out-of-body. They stayed suspended in cavities of safe space high in the planet's aura wondering if they would ever be able to return.

Four hundred twenty-six physical bodies were lost in the destruction. The physical essences of these Eyespellians could be re-manifested, but only at a great energy cost in times already draining the light-skew. Matthew, Keeper of Energy and the Red-Light-Corridor, along with those in his charge, would play the instrumental role in the re-manifestation of the lost bodies. It was uncertain when this healing work might be possible.

There was great demand on the Council's energies in many areas simultaneously. There was the constant vigil of protecting the light-skew of the planet, the repairing of substantial breaks in the cell-matrix, and the healing of those with extreme vibrational discomfort, such as Antonio and Melissa. And there was Daniel; in the face of all of this, the Eldersix were reduced to five.

At noon on the last day of the five Elders' thirty-three day vigil, a beautiful clear diamond cut in the form of a double pyramid manifested at the exact center of the prayer circle. The crystal appeared to be floating about seven feet above the floor of the chamber, giving off a pure yellow light. Over the next several hours, the form of an Eyespellian manifested around the crystal. The full figure stood holding the diamond crystal high above his head with one point of the pyramid resting on and balanced within the center of the heels of his cupped hands. The Council acknowledged this being as the new Keeper of the Yellow-Light-Corridor. Pete emerged from the yellow aura. He was the fourth Eyespellian to have returned and was, indeed, the same entity who had donned a Raider's cap on the streets of New York City.

Pete spoke to the Council, "Greetings. I now keep the charge of the Yellow-Light-Corridor. I am soul-son of Daniel and take his place here by his choice. He must stay out-of-body to cleanse his spirit of the Domeshodar, a task of unknown duration. I know of Earth and I know of Eyespell."

The clear diamond crystal on its rope of yellow light lay glistening against Pete's chest. With him in the center ring the Council was again whole and would resume its vigil over Eyespell under Leo's direction as new head of the Eldersix.

CHAPTER 18

▼

IN THE FAMILY ROOM ...

Koy sat shaking her head. "Whew, Eyespell was really in trouble by the look of it. If I didn't already know it somehow came out of this, I would have to think, that's it, done, gone. And by just a few stray vibrations of probably less intensity than a good domestic argument. Well, maybe that's a bit of exaggeration."

"Actually, you're not that far off," said Jo. "I've had some disagreements with Phillip that would have produced at least two volcanoes and a mudslide."

"Eyespell didn't have mudslides," said Phillip. "But, I guess anything's possible with your hate look and sarcastic, uppity, snippety, bitchy, witch-woman temperament." He laughed and said, "That line alone, spoken seriously, would have been enough to blow half of Eyespell into the Domeshodar."

"Hey, where did you learn all of those mean words? I am incapable of a really good hate look and I'm not a sarcastic, uppity, snippety, bitchy, witch-woman. Wow, I really like the sound of that, sarcastic, uppity, snippety, bitchy, witch-woman. Never mind, I accept the compliment."

"You know, you two are really bad and I think Eyespell would have a real problem with both of you."

"Yeah, that's probably why they left me here," said Phillip with a smile. "Can you imagine a planet so fragile? Like you said, Koy, a good domestic argument would send stress cracks around the world of Eyespell. Imagine a good fist fight; maybe even a homicide or two, a little war. Can you imagine? When you think about it, the Earth-plane vibrational leakage actually experienced on Eyespell was almost nothing in the scope of things we see around here every day. The events in one good newscast would finish Eyespell for good."

"I can't wait to find out how they survived it. Things were going downhill pretty fast. By the way, that whole dissertation by Melissa on education; that sounded a lot like you. If fact, I think she could have written *The Parable of the Wheel*, you know about the old farts spinning on that wheel and all."

"For all I know she did write it and I picked it up as some Eyespellian bleed-through that I wasn't aware of at the time," said Phillip. "But, you're right; her little outburst sounded like it was heading right that way. She as much as called Leo an old fart; try integrating that into the light-skew. Melissa's dissertation is not the only one that started to ring familiar. I thought for sure they were going to try to use 'Joe Sent Me' on Antonio. It seemed like the perfect solution for getting rid of those nightmares about the Earth-time."

"You know, you're right," said Koy. "What do you know about the Domeshodar?"

"Very little at the moment," said Phillip, "but I have a feeling it will become a priority for me to find out more about it."

"What makes you say that?" asked Koy.

"Just a strong intuitive feeling. Every time I hear the word I feel like I'm reaching for something. I feel like I have a responsibility there. And, that's not another story."

"And why is that?"

"It's not another story because it hasn't happened yet."

"I'm not touching that one, Dr. Hansen."

"Me either," said Phillip. "So, should we mind-link back to our story and find out how Eyespell gets out of the horrible mess they're in?"

"Let's do it."

CHAPTER 19

▼

THE GATHERING OF LIGHT

As the fourth moon of Eyespell rose, the predetermined time for the Full-Round had come. The Council Chamber was full, the Eldersix were in the center circle, and the entire population of Eyespell was in mind-link, preparing to conduct the planetary business of survival and preservation of the light-skew. The light-skew had been intact since the first recorded Full-Round over ten thousand years ago. The meeting of the Full-Round was typically a celebration of the light-skew, not an attempt to preserve it. The encroaching and ever more powerful force of the dark-skew was threatening Eyespell's very existence. The question was whether or not Eyespell could gather enough light to overcome the seemingly inevitable darkness.

Loss of the light-skew was actually a possibility. It was the first time that movement toward homeostasis, the balance of light and dark, had become an Eyespellian reality. Since the return of Kathryn and the four, evidence of homeostasis was undeniable. Eyespell was put on notice that there would be unprecedented and unwanted change. Until now light versus dark, good versus evil, had only been hypothetical abstractions carried down by the Elders in the recounting of legends. The concepts of juxtaposition of light and dark and homeostasis were the subjects of scary midnight stories shared by teenagers while on pilgrimage in the desert during no-moon.

Leo addressed the Full-Round. "Because of the seriousness of our situation, there will be no opening ceremony and no display of lights. All of our light energy must be conserved for the business at hand. Eyespell is changing and not in a manner that is desired or apparently within our control. We are moving into unknown territory. This is a frightening prospect. Fear of the unknown is an inner conflict, and Earthlings frequently find themselves immersed in such conflict. Fear has been virtually non-existent on Eyespell, until now."

Leo continued, "First and foremost we cannot respond to Earth-plane vibrational leakage in anger, regardless of how negative the impact of that vibration might be on our planet. Our task is to constructively deal with the unknown; we need to understand and deal with the effects of homeostasis on our planet. Exactly how balance will permanently affect the light-skew and the cell-matrix is unknown to us. So far the impact of the leakage has been disruption in nature and in the states of mind of those closest to the Eyespell Experiment. We have experienced thunderstorms, earthquakes, dissension, anger, and sarcasm. We have actually experienced the loss of physical bodies. Do we have the capability of dealing with these new and undesired realities? Are we capable of changing or have we developed such a need to maintain the status quo that we will perish?

"The purpose of this unique Full-Round is to develop those strategies needed to reverse the effects of the leakage brought on by the outcome of the Eyespell Experiment. If that is not possible, we hope to at least mitigate its effects and to understand the realities of light-balance for Eyespell. Indeed, the key is for us to understand and embrace balance."

Nathan followed up with, "The movement toward homeostasis must be slowed enough to prevent the pendulum of light from swinging too far into the dark zone, the dark-skew. It is the dark-skew that maintains the vibrations of sickness, conflict, chaos, ignorance, isolation, lethargy, hatred, and poverty. Some of these factors, potentially lethal to our way of life, already have been felt on Eyespell. The Green-Light-Corridor is particularly sensitive. I am unable to maintain our natural environment as we have known it. The nature of Eyespell is shifting dramatically even as we speak."

Nathan's words trailed off. Eyespell continued to display a disharmonious and hostile natural environment, a side of nature totally unfamiliar to Eyespellians. The planetary cell-matrix seemed to be breaking apart in spots as the initially small stress cracks in the planet's surface widened into giant fissures. In these days of approaching homeostasis, anomalous natural occurrences became more and more frequent. Nathan hoped to harness the collective energy of the Full-Round to keep the planet from regressing to a totally primitive natural state.

Eyespell's natural beauty was unparalleled in all of creation. From outer space the pastel planet shone against a galaxy of star clusters. Its vast desert sands glowed a soft pink against the rays of a blue sun. These same sand oceans reflected a soft blue, and sometimes a deep aquamarine, in the light of a yellow sun. A myriad of colors converged on the hillsides and mountains, leaving trails of pastel rainbows. What the daylight did not dazzle by two suns, the night sky outlined under the colored lights of four moons.

And then there was the aliveness of the planetary cell-matrix itself. The cell-matrix was united with the color affinity of each Eyespellian, individually, and all Eyespellians, collectively. All of this culminated in a shimmering and ever-changing aura of thought-colors superimposed upon the sun-colored sands, rainbow mountains and moonlit horizons. This fusion of mind and nature produced hues in infinite harmony. A glimpse of Eyespell from space was, in and of itself, mystical and compelling.

As Eyespell moved on its new and dangerous path there remained, in the heart of every Eyespellian, the hope that something this beautiful in the universe would not simply disappear. As an ancient nature continued to awaken, the fate of the planet was none too clear. There were dreadful thunderstorms with lightning strikes, dangerously high sand tides, ground tremors, landslides, and a host of other natural disturbances. The most dramatic upheaval occurred in the desert outside of Elaysia. It rained so heavily that flash floods flowed over the Blue Desert sands and into the crater-like Valley of the Blue Noon. In the immediate aftermath, only the tower tip stood out of the water, needle-like, at the center of a huge lake. The holy place was now inaccessible in the traditional manner.

Those gathered in the amphitheater began the desperate job of trying to reverse the planetary condition. Rather than preserve light, Leo changed his mind and directed that the light-corridors be opened in a majestic attempt to accentuate the light-skew. This light show was perhaps more glorious than any before. The Elders and others in the Council Chamber wore monk's garb, and it was pronounced a holy time. Eyespellians everywhere were in touch with the vibration of the three hundred thirty-seven in the gathering of light. The earlier decision to deprive the Full-Round of its light show was reversed with the recognition that nothing could be held back in this desperate attempt.

The immediate task was to slow nature down. Nathan, centered in the twenty-seventh ring and at absolute-middle within the chamber, held the Emerald Crystal of Nature cupped in his hands high above his head with the points of the pyramid facing up and down. The remainder of the three hundred thirty-seven, and, in turn, the entire populace of Eyespell, including those souls in birth/death transition, color-visioned in consonance with the green hues of Nathan's crystal.

Never before had a single color-strand achieved such potency in the dimension of Eyespellian reality-creating. A globe of light began to emanate outward from Nathan's cupped hands. The globe slowly turned, elongated, and reformed as a larger sphere. It increased its physical dimension while in constant cyclical motion. The entire amphitheater became immersed in the globe's penetrating light. Within hours, all of Elaysia and the closest desert areas were enveloped in the emerald green. Ultimately, the entire planet and its aura, including the four moons, were within the crystal's one-color of nature.

The erratic behavior of a nature gone wild slowed. The pull toward homeostasis also slowed. While the cell-matrix continued to change and even fragment in pockets of time and place, the extreme natural disasters of the dark-skew were, for the present, averted. Eyespell continued its planetary healing process under the guidance of the emerald vibration for the equivalent of forty Earth-years.

Time is not linear on Eyespell; it is a multi-dimensional measurement. Describing an instant versus an eternity becomes tricky business when trying to measure peoples' actions against places and events. During the nature-healing, the Elders maintained their vigil in the twenty-seventh ring of the council chamber for the entire forty years. From a time-linear perspective this would be an impossible strategy whereas in non-linear time it was just one of many possibilities.

During the Elders' emerald immersion, Eyespellians everywhere attended to the cell-matrix and consciously "thought" energy toward healing the environment, calming nature, and ensuring the permanence of the light-skew.

The physical fabric of the planet was one thing, its psychological and spiritual well-being were quite another. Leo focused his attention toward Kathryn, Antonio, Melissa, Nancy, and Pete to deal with the psychological impact of Earth-plane vibrational leakage. He took them to a protected oasis deep in the Blue Desert. With the exception of Peter, who was now an Elder, they were still the locus of Earth-plane vibrational leakage and the starting point of many light-skew disturbances. Close and constant check on them helped keep a pulse on the planet's mental condition. When one of them behaved uncharacteristically of Eyespell, Leo telepathically alerted the other Elders and they would, in turn, divert a quantum of Elder-energy to momentarily still the vibrational leakage. It would do little good to abate the scourges of nature if the people of Eyespell were to suffer a global psychosis.

An amazing thing happened during this time of turmoil. As the emerald sphere expanded its dimensional boundaries and enveloped the entire Eyespellian domain, there were continual and soaring energy releases something akin to sunspots. At the apex of one of these energy releases, Myana and Gracina reached with their spirits into the universe far beyond Eyespell. As their soaring spirits were returning from the vastness, they brushed past the aura of Earth. For a fraction of an instant, they sensed a familiar life-force, the life-force of an Eyespellian. There could be only one conclusion - Phillip, the missing Eyespellian, was alive and on Earth.

With intense feelings of exhilaration, hope, unconditional love, compassion, and oneness, Myana and Gracina put their energies together attempting to contact Phillip on the planet Earth. They were almost immediately successful in their task. They identified themselves to the Cosmos as "Elders of the Light" and then, using their crystals as transmitters, called out to the mind of Phillip Hansen. They hoped to reach him while his mind was quiet in meditation or sleep. Within a matter of hours, they sensed a response clearly of Phillip's vibration. And, within a few hours after that, they sensed a second, and unexpected, response, a response clearly Eyespellian but not of Phillip.

They pressed toward the Council Chamber with the astonishing news. There was not one Eyespellian on planet Earth, there were two!

CHAPTER 20

▼

IN THE FAMILY ROOM ...

"So that's part of the rest of the story. What do you think, Koy?"

"I think it's truly incredible that Eyespell found you and Christian at the same time. That must have been mind blowing for everybody involved."

"You should have been there," added Jo. "Remember I told you how excited Phillip got when he talked to you that first time and he came running to find me? Well, he about went nuts when he felt Eyespell touch him that first time and for real. He was jumping up and down, laughing, and yelling how he was not crazy after all."

"Right," said Phillip. "And you felt obligated to point out just how nuts I was behaving and said you weren't so sure about the crazy thing. It was a terrible blow; all this time you had been assuring me I was not crazy and that Eyespell really did exist. And, poof, at the moment of truth you tell me I'm nuts."

"That's my job," said Jo. "I need to keep you in line. And, Koy, he's hopping around acting like a madman and damned if he doesn't get a phone call from Christian telling him something really weird just happened. I thought Phillip was going to fly through roof and be done with it. He absolutely could not contain himself. It was actually pretty funny listening to him on the phone trying to convince Christian that it was okay; that he, Christian that is, wasn't nuts. He had told Christian this would happen some day and this was the day. Of course, what Christian didn't know is that he was the absolute end-all proof for his father that he, Phillip that is, wasn't nuts. Phillip figured they couldn't both be crazy. Now there was that time in the attic with the old manuscripts and all that, but there really wasn't any tangible proof until that day when Eyespell found them both. And let me tell you, things really began to roll from there, but that's the rest of Phillip's story and I wouldn't think of stealing it."

"I can't imagine what it's been like in the Hansen household over the years."

"Trust me, Koy, it's been very cool, very cool indeed. The kinds of things stories are made of, but you'll never print it," said Phillip.

"Where would I possibly start? Let me see, I met this guy at a seminar who had a very cute son, but it turned out they were both aliens. Well, actually, the son was only part alien, but they really weren't sure. Then one day the people from their home planet contacted them and everybody lived happily ever after. Is that about right, do you think?"

"I like you better by the second," said Jo.

"Me too," said Phillip.

"I am chomping at the bit to find out what happens from here. How is it that Eyespell had never contacted you before this? You were having memories of Eyespell on your own and seemed quite aware of Eyespell as your home. But, there was always a small piece of you that wasn't sure. There was no proof. Christian's phone call that day must have been a major event in your life."

"Oh, it was. And why there had been no direct contact before that time is still confusing to me and to my buddy, Leo. Oh, yes, we've had many a conversation since that first glorious day. Once the spell was broken, like Jo said, things really began to roll. But I'm getting ahead of myself. Anyway, we, meaning all of us involved, don't know why no direct link was established before that time. I later found out that Kathryn spent an untold amount of time trying to reach me. Nothing. The Elders tried individually and in mind-link. Nothing. My guess is that the time was simply not right. You see, there was much more happening that neither Earth nor Eyespell had any control over. There was Cosmo out there orchestrating a goodly amount of the goings-on. I hope God doesn't mind me calling Him or Her Cosmo. Somehow Cosmo seems homier and fits better in our family room conversation. But it had to be God; there is just no other answer that works."

"Just think of it, Phillip, being at the center of some Divine Intervention. How special."

"I truly know how special it is. I know because it feels so ordinary, kind of like that end table next to the couch. It's just there."

"It's going to be awfully hard for me to explain how I gleaned so much astonishing information from a couple of end tables in Waterford, Virginia, on a beautiful spring evening. Both of you amaze me. You are so calm about all of this. You take it in stride. You don't even act as if it's that big a deal."

"It's the biggest deal around," said Jo very quietly. "If you really think about everything you've heard this evening, it's impossible to process, at least intellectually. But, Koy, you don't seem to be having that much trouble. What does that tell you?"

Koy sat without saying anything for a bit, then offered, "I'm the third end table in the room."

"You got it," said Jo and Phillip at the same time.

"Tell me the rest of the story," said Koy. "Oh, wait a sec, I had another thought. The fear of the unknown that Leo was talking about is a lot like the Kookamonga Effect you wrote about. You know, your son on the sidewalk taking apart that bearded iris. In fact, Leo even said that the fear of the unknown was an Earth thing. What I'm getting at, well, it makes me wonder if Eyespell was having bleed-through from you without realizing it."

"Interesting idea, Koy," said Jo.

"Jo, do you think it's possible that Eyespell was picking up some of my stuff? I certainly was picking up some of theirs without realizing exactly what was going on," said Phillip.

Jo answered, "Hey, anything's possible in this scenario. I could definitely see where your thoughts would transmit to Eyespell. The difference, of course, is they wouldn't think anything unusual was happening. Without paying close attention, for example, Leo would read your thoughts as just another opinion coming out of the collective consciousness of Eyespell. He certainly wouldn't think he was going crazy or anything like that."

"Hmm, I'll have to chew on that a bit. Very interesting," said Phillip.

"Phillip, I had another thought," said Koy.

"Yes?"

"I was thinking that given the level of confusion and chaos wreaked by Earth-plane vibrational leakage, don't you think it odd that there was absolutely no violence among the people of Eyespell? Nancy seemed the hardest hit and even she did not turn to violence. It seems that, on a personal level, a bit of nastiness and sarcasm was as bad as it got," said Koy, puzzled.

"That's true," Phillip answered, "but Daniel had to be pretty worried that there was more to it. After all he jumped into the Domeshodar with Nancy. That seems like a pretty drastic reaction to a little mouthing off."

"Exactly my point, Phillip. I think Daniel thought violence was a possibility, the next iteration of Earth-plane vibrational leakage. I, too, thought Daniel overreacted based on what was actually happening in the moment. But he seemed absolutely sure about what needed to be done."

"Violence as the next iteration of Earth-plane vibrational leakage. I never thought of it in those terms exactly. And what would be the iteration after that, and after that? I could see the values of the entire civilization crumbling. Eyespell might survive, but at what cost? What a scary proposition," worried Phillip.

"The absence of violence is actually even more amazing when you study the whole situation," said Koy. "Just look at what was happening to the physical planet itself. All kinds of nasty and unprecedented disturbances. And how did the people of Eyespell react? They were scared as hell and being violently tossed about by a totally chaotic planetary cell-matrix. Think about it, Phillip, a few hundred Eyespellians died, or, in Eyespellian terms, lost their physical essence. So what did the people do? Did they go crazy and start killing, looting, and destroying whatever was left? Did they lash out at the Cosmos? No, Eyespell's collective reaction was to work together in Oneness to solve the problem. Now that's impressive; that's a very enlightened culture in my opinion, a culture that could not be easily dispatched by a few negative vibrations!"

"You know, Koy, I get the impression that you understand the Eyespellian spirit better than I do," said Phillip. "You are so right in what you say. I don't think I have ever expressed, in words, the resilience of the Eyespellian spirit. Maybe I never understood it this well before. Are you sure you're an Earthling, Ms. Sosa?"

"I was when I got here, but, at this point, like Jo says, anything is possible in this scenario. So, anything else, or shall we go back to Eyespell?"

"Let's go back to Eyespell," agreed Phillip, "and, on my part, with a whole new appreciation for everything else that happens. Actually, this next part of the story is extremely exciting. My "hearing" from Gracina was quite a confirmation, but to have Christian back it up with a description of his own contact was exciting beyond description. I could not imagine where it was going to go from there. And there's further explanation of the time of madness and how Eyespell etched itself into my reality. Can you handle it?"

"Now what do you think?" asked Koy.

"I like to ask stupid questions so the moose and the dog can keep up. So, let's see where this goes. Oh, wait a sec! This might be as good a time as any to clear up a few things about death and religion on Eyespell."

"What about politics? Never mind," chuckled Koy. "I can't imagine Eyespellians stooping to anything even remotely deemed political. Telepathy and mind-link would take the dishonesty and gamesmanship out of politics."

"Yes, and therein destroying the whole point of political activity," laughed Phillip. "But, there's still death and religion. And, I'm not quite sure where to begin the explanation. First off, the terms death and religion are technically misnomers. Well, you'll see what I mean as I try to unravel this for you.

"On Eyespell, religion is personified by Oneness, the White Moon, the White Light Corridor and its Keeper, Gracina. The White Light Corridor permeates all of Eyespell, the planet and its peoples. It is the Religion of Oneness, Oneness with the Life Force, with God. There are no sects, factions, or any other dividing lines distinguishing different aspects of Oneness. There is simply Oneness. There are no churches or regularly scheduled ceremonies. There are, however, holy places and times of meditation. For example, there is The Valley of the Blue Noon, Elaysia itself and, as you will see later in our story, another incredible holy place. Eyespellians are always connected with God, and even more intensely during times of meditation such as a Full Round, or a manifesting through one or more of the light corridors. Religion, if one chooses to call it that, is a constant awareness of God."

"It sounds more like spirituality than religion," reflected Koy.

"That's how I see it; it's semantics," responded Phillip. "Now, on Eyespell, death is a bit more difficult to conceptualize. On Earth we are born, we die, and, well we don't know exactly what happens after death. There are many religious dogmas and they don't all agree on the after-death details. Some have even decided that death is simply the end, nothing follows. Moreover, regardless of your beliefs, the Earth concept of death ends a linear progression that begins at birth. In a sense Earthlings begin to die the moment they are born. Not a very cheery prospect put that way."

"Not cheery is an understatement," contributed Jo.

"And the difference on Eyespell is what?" asked Koy.

Phillip continued, "On Eyespell there are, what we might call, transitions. The key is that life-energy cannot be minimized or destroyed. Life-energy can, however, change or transition from one place to another; it can change its form even, but not the energy itself. Furthermore, as we have discussed, time on Eyespell is not linear. There is no progressive birth-to-death time line. Instead, time can curve back on itself in warped instants-in-time."

"Curve back on itself?" asked Koy, perplexed.

"This is the hard part to conceptualize," responded Phillip. "While there may be the appearance of a linear life, there is the ever present possibility of time curving back and forth."

"Well, that certainly clears it up," laughed Koy.

"Jo, can you help me here?" asked Phillip.

"Would it be fair to say that Eyespellians can simultaneously experience past, present, and future in brief instants-in-time?" offered Jo.

"Yes," said Phillip. "When the time line bends, an Eyespellian can experience many instants in time seemingly at once. It's kind of like a computer appearing to multi-task when in reality it's doing only one thing at a time but very quickly, in mere billionths of a second."

"That sounds dizzying and very uncomfortable," said Koy, moving her head in slow, wide circles.

"No, actually it works quite comfortably," said Phillip. "Think back on the youngsters in the desert on Eyespell talking with Leo. If you recall, the reason given for their highly sophisticated language skills posing no problem, even at their very young ages, was the existence of the telepathy link. Well, that's not the whole story. Those youngsters were experiencing multiple instants-in-time as the time line bent back on itself."

"That helps," said Koy.

"Here's a conundrum for you," said Phillip. "Ask yourself how old the Eyespell Experiment participants were when they left Eyespell? Then ask how old they were when they returned. Apparently they were the same age when they returned as they were when they left. Yet, they were born on the Earth and spent twenty years on Earth."

"Can't be!" hollered Koy.

"Oh yes it can," said Phillip calmly. "Basically the participants left and returned in one of those instants-of-time. The reentry window everyone was so concerned about was simply one of those multiple instants-in-time."

Koy thought for a minute and said, "So, in a sense, anyone could be any age, young or old, alive or dead, all at the same time."

"More or less," said Phillip. "Eyespellians transition from birth to death and beyond, and yet always remain part of the collective consciousness in a non-linear time mode. They never die in the same sense as people die on Earth."

Jo offered, "Maybe it's like a video game where characters literally pop in and out of existence. Even when you lose one it can come back at the next level."

"Jo, that's not nice," said Phillip. "It sounds like you are comparing Eyespellians to the Mario Brothers."

"Okay," said Koy, with her hands over her face. "In the words of Popeye the Sailor, 'I can takes so much but I can't takes no more.' So on with your story and let's get back to Eyespell, Dr. Hansen."

CHAPTER 21

▼

THE EYESPELL CONNECTION

Phillip was in his study, leaning back in his desk chair, admiring his curio cabinet collection. Per usual, he found himself drawn to the beautiful chunk of rose quartz, its *pinkness* filling his consciousness. On this particular day his reverie was interrupted by a mysterious woman's voice calling to him. He knew instantly and with every fiber of his being that someone from his home, Eyespell, was making contact with him. She identified herself as "Gracina of the Light." This voice was different from those in the past; it was specific; it was undeniable. When Christian called and told him that he too had heard a voice definitely from outside himself, a voice identified as "Gracina of the Light," there was no doubt in Phillip's mind that the first verifiable contact with Eyespell had been made.

It took very little to convince Christian what was going on with Eyespell. He was busting to immediately hop a plane from Rochester, New York, where he lived with his family, to Virginia. Phillip laughed at his son's obvious urgency to get together. There was no holding Christian back; he planned to arrive at Dulles International at three o'clock the next afternoon to talk about Eyespell, only this time for real.

Phillip hung up the phone and in his excitement dashed for the study. He felt compelled to meditate. He now had confirmation from Christian that Eyespell existed. While he had always relied on Jo to help him maintain his faith, he was absolutely high with this new validation. As he approached the study door it dawned on him in speeded-up time that he had just swept past Jo in the hallway. Her laughter was just catching up with his brain and her voice trailed off in his head, "And I suppose you'll be off to Eyespell, Dr. Hansen."

He yelled out the study door, "Do you wanna come?"

"It's too far and I don't have a thing to wear," came the tongue-in-cheek reply.

Although Phillip had made his way to the study intending to reconnect with Gracina through meditation, he was too hyper to deal with anything demanding such focused attention. His brain was filled with mind chatter and could not be quieted. He had learned years ago that the soul would quiet the mind of its own accord when the time was right. Nonetheless, he felt like a little kid anticipating his new toy, still wrapped and under the Christmas tree.

He kicked back onto the study sofa and thought about conversations he had had with his inner child. The first dreams of another time and place had come spontaneously, shortly after his accident along the interstate in Florida. Memories of Eyespell gradually evolved. His first true belief in Eyespell and his Eyespellian identity came to him through conversations with his inner child, a child he was introduced to during therapy sometime after Florida. Most of those early inner-child talks hinted that Eyespell was more than part of a passing vision. The child within revealed, at any given time, only that which Phillip seemed capable of assimilating. More often than not, this inner child pushed the outer man to his limits of understanding.

With the help of his inner child, his dreams and memories of Eyespell ultimately became a significant part of a higher reality. Even though Phillip sensed everything about Eyespell to be true, there was no tangible proof of it. He still had nagging doubts left over from his time of madness.

As always, Jo was there to help him through these moments of doubt. While the evidence of Eyespell was no more tangible for her than for him, her arguments in favor of a higher reality that included

Eyespell were convincing. Jo would often meditate with Phillip, sharing the vibrations of her higher self with him. After such a meditation, he was always sure about Eyespell's existence and his strong tie to the pink planet floating in the galaxies of his mind. Jo always restored his faith.

At some point the dreams about Eyespell changed; they were unlike the old memories. And they were more than dreams, there were conversations and those conversations did not appear to be from within. The voice was from without, from somewhere, someone, outside himself. The voice came to him in waking moments, not just dreams. This was both confirming and frightening. The voices were a confirmation of Eyespell or, perhaps, a confirmation that he was psychotic.

Phillip recalled that during his time of madness, things Eyespellian were both comforting and confusing to him. The comfort came during periods of meditation when he would become one with the child. He often envisioned Eyespell through the child and the higher self. During these meditations, as the memories of Eyespell unfolded, the predominant feeling was one of extreme peacefulness. It was a lot like the feeling of being immersed in that white light at the end of the tunnel. His anxieties were momentarily soothed and the possibility of his ever having another panic attack seemed remote. "God was in his heaven and all was right with the world."

Confusion almost always came directly on the heels of such comforting peace. Phillip's logical side always tried to make sense out of the Eyespell insights, feelings, and memories revealed in meditation. He tried to understand things that should have been allowed to stand on their own merit. When in his logical mode, Phillip was left hopelessly incapable of believing his feelings or convincing himself that Eyespell was anything more than delusion; it was simply part of his worsening madness.

Phillip's concern for his mental stability became even more intensified when visions of Eyespell began to occur during full consciousness. Sometimes, when he was caught up in the beauty of a natural setting, for example, he would spontaneously recollect something about Eyespell. His mind might be peacefully immersed in the beauty of a scene and the child would slyly throw in a vision or two; he would catch Phillip "unawares." Much later, Phillip came to call these times of spontaneous revelation, "child-chatter."

As he scrunched his body even farther into the study sofa, he recalled one child-chatter evening in particular. He had left his office for the small parking lot by way of a path. There was no sidewalk, only pine needles, mulch, and leaves set between old railroad ties. The path was framed by thick ground cover, a couple of big trees forming a canopy of branches above, and, at one end, a bunch of piled up coral rock that had a man-made waterfall in mind.

It was dark by the time he started along the path and there was slightly more than a drizzle coming down. A large spotlight nailed to the biggest tree illuminated the slanting rain. About halfway into his journey, Phillip sensed a single movement, a single frame taken by the reflex of an eye. There was a breath inhaled that captured some different reality, something just out of sight. That fraction of an instant pierced his very center and then it was gone, and Phillip was almost one step farther along the pathway.

He looked back, somewhat perplexed, curious, almost onto something. And then, with another reflex of an eye, Phillip envisioned himself standing in the middle of a cool afternoon desert, basking in the light of two suns. And in yet another reflex, with a blue sun still in after-image, Phillip found himself staring at four glorious moons and a galaxy of unfamiliar stars in spiraling array. And then all of it was gone and, again, he was almost one step farther along the pathway.

This is how Eyespell had been revealed, in puzzle form, with small pieces of memory set in place to become part of Phillip's consciousness. It is no wonder that he sometimes questioned his sanity.

Phillip's mind returned to the study as he stretched his body slowly and deliberately like a cat, one stretched-out foot barely touching the far end of the sofa. He got to thinking about how the time of madness had seemed to last forever. Once the anxieties had started they remained a focal point of his life for quite a long time. His anxieties caused him to do some strange things.

At one point Phillip had insisted on moving with Jo and two-year-old Christian back to Florida where all the craziness began. They locked up the old Waterford house and headed for Boca Raton. He hoped to find his answers in this place from his past. He had taken a job as Visiting Professor of Psychology with a small private college.

The return to Florida marked a period of intensive inner searching. Phillip had made great strides in his personal awareness during this time and had all but dispelled the madness. Somewhere in all of this he finally began to acknowledge and internalize his own expertise as a therapist and teacher. Even though convinced he was not going crazy, Phillip still faced an interesting psychological dilemma – he continued having lucid visions of Eyespell. His inner quest intensified. He was prepared to follow his feelings and acknowledge them as truth, especially his feelings about Eyespell.

Phillip turned on his side and this time stretched an arm over his head and around the curved arm of the couch. He sighed a long sigh. It was already two in the morning, Waterford-time. His mind wandered off again, this time to one momentous day when things Earthly and things Eyespellian had finally begun to fall consciously together.

"It must have been over thirty years ago by now," thought Phillip. "I remember that day as if it were yesterday. I wasn't exactly depressed; I was just a little off to the side, experiencing that not-quite-here feeling. I remember watching myself from somewhere else that morning; I remember watching and wondering what was real, what was relevant."

Phillip stretched forward as if to get closer to his reverie. "There was the weather; it was beautiful and surrounded me. There were the birds whistling and chattering at the feeder and the orchids blossoming in the lanai. There was the little brown mouse that wandered by each morning to eat yesterday's hibiscus flowers then-fallen and scattered among the deco bark and round chattahoochie stepping stones. And, of course, there was The Mo, the fluffy, white family cat who mindlessly watched the whole scene from between the vertical blind slats and the frame of the sliding glass door. It was clear to me that all of this was relevant."

Phillip sat up and planted both feet squarely on the study floor, elbows on his knees and hands clasped around the top of his head as he thought, "I remember leaving The Mo by the window. I got in my car and headed for work. My certainties about what might be relevant began to fade almost immediately. I noticed that I was still tired from yesterday's work; my finances were in shambles; Jo was unhappy about being in Florida; and the anti-Christ, guised in the garb of the terrible twos, had moved into Christian's body. By the time I reached my office, I was less cognizant of that same beautiful weather, a golden rain tree, the huge banyan, and the small lake, beyond and to my left. It was no longer clear to me what was relevant."

Phillip stood up and began to pace in front of the study couch. His thoughts were very agitating. "By the time I walked into my office and opened the desk drawer to collect my notes for that morning's lectures, I was totally uncentered. I was separated from the very things in nature that just a little while earlier I knew to be relevant. I remember desperately trying to center myself and grasp the meaning of what I did for a living."

Phillip stopped his pacing and stood at the window, transfixed by his thoughts remembered, "I needed to sit under the trees by the lake and feel the day, the blossoms, the creatures, the Earth. I needed to be like an Ancient One, elbows in the grass, sharing with my students. I needed to transcend the moment in a myriad of colors, feelings, and emotions. I needed to be mystical."

Phillip spun around, and facing his imagined self on the sofa, almost yelled, "And there it was! My Eyespellian self had been fully recognized for the very first time. Yes, there it was, that which I called the renaissance in my soul."

Phillip crossed his arms and hung one hand over each shoulder as if hugging himself, "Indeed, the renaissance in my soul is still the creation of my own reality from past, present, and future memories. It is my ability to transcend self-image and present circumstance, moving to a higher plane. This renaissance in my soul explains why I sometimes feel the monastery walls at my back when working in the garden. The sweat on my brow belongs, perhaps, to a medieval, or perhaps Eyespellian, monk. Sometimes, the sound of raindrops beating down on the brim of a baseball cap, or ice clinking in a glass, jerks me into an unconscious awareness. At other times, scenes in old movies or pictures of distant places bring back bittersweet memories of experiences that I've never consciously had. And that is the renaissance in my soul that I discovered one day at a small Florida college."

Phillip, still hugging himself, stretched his neck like a turtle popping his head out from under his shell and peered at the couch to make sure his imagined self was still paying attention. In a sudden gesture he let go of his shoulders, shook his head and buried his face in his hands as he recalled what he had actually done that day even in the light of his incredible self-discovery. He had let his logic get the best of him, and he had actually taught his classes in their classrooms. Phillip winced as he could hear his own voice droning on in lecture as if he were there right now. He was able to recapture the feeling of utter despair that had surged up when he first realized that he had chosen the wrong reality once again. He had chosen the collective aloneness of a sterile classroom. He had bypassed the oneness of nature; he had forfeited the connectedness with Eyespell in the face of logic. He had given up being mystical; he had not chosen a piece of the Eyespell puzzle that day.

Phillip literally jumped onto the sofa and came crashing down on his imaginary self, ecstatic that he never made that infamous error of logic over connectedness again. From that day forward, Phillip had made the "Eyespell teachings" his secret reality, and had followed them. And now, some thirty years later, Eyespell is reality – reality also confirmed by his son.

Phillip was still too excited to meditate and by now too overtired to sleep. Dropping back onto the study sofa his head filled with positive and exciting thoughts, he had a sense of childlike hopefulness. Keenly aware of the positive and exciting feelings continuing to well up inside of him, he thought, "I was not always so optimistic and hopeful; hope was a hard-learned lesson for me." Phillip stretched out flat on the study couch and began to drift off in spite of his excitement. "Christian should be here in just a few hours; I can hardly wait. I think we're in for a magnificent adventure." Phillip smiled at his childlike presence of mind. "I love who I am now. I am so full of hope. I'll never forget that day years ago when I learned about the choice between hope and despair in the ice cream parlor; the ice cream parlor, can you imagine? Christian was still a toddler and I recall my state of mind then so vividly. I remember as if it were yesterday."

Christian and I were in the ice cream parlor having lunch. A young father came in with his much younger son of about two, two-and-a-half, tops. The little one was somewhat duck-like with his almost-people-walk. He was following his giant dad, eyes bug-like as only a small child's can be in anticipation of an ice cream treat.

As they were leaving, I noticed that the child's face was particularly beautiful in his joy and innocence. And then, I thought to myself, "How cruel life is, young one. Someday you will watch a child such as yourself and, like me, now grown, you will think what a cruel joke life is."

In my chosen thoughts, the child's eyes, buggy with excitement, seemed to turn instantly sunken with desperation and lost hope. That moment was one of the singularly most unpleasant of my entire life. Imagine, with a thought, a mood, the instantaneous loss of hope, I was able to turn the pure innocence and excitement of a child into menacing darkness in my mind, the beautiful rose into a flowerless stem of painful thorns. I turned lunch into the rubble of my life.

Across the table from me, Christian's lips began to move and I almost simultaneously heard him say, "i-cream," pointing toward the counter. I think the request startled me; I didn't know there was any ice cream left.

Phillip fell asleep still thinking about that long ago day's lesson in the ice cream parlor. His last thought before dozing off was, "There is hope in despair and despair in hope. The choice is in our control, in our thoughts, and all in that reflex of an eye."

After falling into a shallow sleep, Phillip saw Gracina's face in a dream and remembered her as one of the Eldersix of Eyespell. The Eyespell puzzle was nearing completion.

The alarm went off and startled Phillip toward the morning coffee that he could smell brewing in the kitchen. Jo was sitting at the kitchen table doing the daily crossword puzzle.

"You're just in time," she said, with a big smile and a big hug. "What was the name of the movie that won the academy award six years ago? It's on the tip of my tongue, but I just can't get it. It was about that business guy from Pakistan who was supposed to save the world. Remember, we watched the DVD and you and Christian spent the next two days arguing about the plausibility of the plot. And if memory serves me correctly you lost that argument."

"Yes, yes, I remember well. But I remember everything except the title. You know, the memories of Eyespell are incredibly vivid since Christian called yesterday. They're not memories at all actually, they're real communication."

"Yes, and Christian will be along this afternoon and the two of you will be heading off to some holy place to meditate together."

"How could you possibly know all that?" Phillip asked.

"While you may be from Eyespell and different, my husband, I too have my dreams and my memories and my meditations. When Gracina of the Light called to you, I heard her as well. Think hard, what's the name of that fool movie?"

Phillip thought that Jo was probably the only woman on the planet that he could be married to, managing to be one step behind her most of the time. "Since you seem to know more about what's happening than I do, any thoughts on where Christian and I are supposed to go or what, exactly, we're supposed to do?"

"I thought you'd never ask. I have it all in writing for you. Last evening I had quite a long session with my spirit guides. And I can't wait to see Christian, it's been too long."

Phillip finished his coffee, took the papers Jo had prepared for him, and went out into the garden to study them. The aroma of wet honeysuckle was still fresh in the air. It had to be Phillip's favorite smell and reason enough to settle in the Virginia countryside.

He squeezed behind the table of the big redwood glider with the bright green-and-white canopy and cushions and sat. He pulled his wire-rimmed glasses out of his shirt pocket and began to read the beautifully handwritten papers. Phillip was fascinated. A slight breeze came up before he realized that what Jo had given him to read was inscribed in a handwriting unrecognized by him, and it was on a sort of metallic paper that did not move with the wind. This "paper" was not of Earth! Another piece of the puzzle aligned. This paper and its message were of Eyespell and manifested here through channel. Phillip began to read.

> Gracina of the Light put these thoughts and instructions into the cosmic mind. I have picked them up and, in turn, pass them along to you, Jo Hansen. It has been long since we last spoke, my lady. It would appear that your husband and your son have important work to accomplish on the Earth-plane. Their destinies are at hand and, indeed, the destiny of your entire planet. And that of the planet Eyespell.

Phillip continued to read, his mind virtually reeling with the limitless possibilities.

> Dressed in the plain brown garb of the monk, make your way to the Red Rock country surrounding Sedona, Arizona. Specifically, go to the base of that which is called Cathedral Rock where the vibration is female and the color is yellow. Be there at full moon in full meditation and await our vibration. Bring only your son.

Phillip put the metallic-like pages in his pocket and made his way back to the house. He had no inkling where he might locate monk's clothing and he was not all too sure he liked the idea. He chuckled to himself, realizing that this was no time to let logic or practicality get the best of him. He had had little sleep the night before and decided a good nap would be in order before picking Christian up at the airport. He figured if he left the house at two or so, he would have plenty of time to meet the three-thirty flight.

Phillip awakened to the familiar sound of a car pulling into the gravel driveway. Just as he was thinking about getting annoyed at such an unexpected intrusion, he realized that it was already five-thirty and it was his car pulling up with Jo at the wheel and Christian beside her. He rushed outside to meet them.

"Good grief, Jo, why didn't you wake me?" He smiled and worked his way around to giving them both big hugs. "I've got too much to do to be getting senile and oversleeping, missing people at airports."

Christian was ecstatic to see his father. "Well, where do you suspect we are off to, Dad?"

"According to your mother's spirit guides, we have to make our way to Sedona, Arizona's Red Rock Country, land of the positive vortexes. We are supposed to arrive at Cathedral Rock on the night of the full moon wearing, of all things, monk's garb. How's that for mystery?"

Christian did not seem surprised. He unzipped his soft-sided suitcase and pulled out two monk's robes in the drabbest brown one could imagine. "Will these do?"

Phillip just shook his head. "Now how in the heck ... what?"

"It was really strange. After we spoke on the phone yesterday, I fell sound asleep. I had a dream that Mom was inscribing a very important note, a channeled note. I didn't consciously remember anything about it. But, when I got up this morning to get ready to go to the airport, I had a strong intuitive feeling that I should leave early and stop to see a monk at the monastery near town. It was funny. He met me at the entrance as if he knew I'd be coming. He introduced himself as Brother Andre, handed me two robes, and gave me his blessings. He was crying; 'tears of joy,' he said."

Phillip Hansen was sure of one thing. They were not in this alone. "We have three days to get to Sedona for the full moon. We should leave for Phoenix day after tomorrow."

"There is one other thing, Dad, the crystal. We need to wait here for it to come our way. Brother Andre told me that we could expect a large, beautiful golden crystal in the shape of a double pyramid, pointed on both ends. He said just to wait for its arrival."

Neither Christian nor his father made a habit of arguing with the Cosmos. They were content to wait for the anticipated crystal the monk had said would arrive. They had a great dinner, a garlic pasta dish Jo was famous for, and spent the rest of the evening speculating about the "Eyespell Connection," as Christian dubbed it.

The next afternoon at about four-thirty, a small van pulled into the Waterford driveway. A stocky man of about seventy-five worked his way laboriously out from behind the wheel. He slid the side door open and removed a package from the back seat. He finally reached the front door and used the knocker instead of the doorbell. Phillip answered the door.

"My heavens! Jo, Christian, it's our old friend John Beechmont. John, how are you? We haven't laid eyes on you in ages. Come in, come in, sit down. What in the world brings you to our doorstep this glorious day?"

"Phillip, you have always been a mystery. I think you are waiting for this." He produced the package he had taken from the back seat.

Phillip took the package and opened it carefully. Wrapped in a silken scarf was an opaque, golden topaz, cut into a double pyramid, pointed on each end. The stone looked flawless, about 2 inches at the center and about 3 inches from point-to-point, best Phillip could tell.

He looked at the crystal and then back at the man who had handed it to him. "And where on Earth did you find such a treasure?"

"In a vault at the Smithsonian. This stone has never been on display. It was brought to me by an old man of at least a hundred years. Let's see, it must have been right around the turn of the century; yes, long time ago. He showed up in the gallery right around closing one Friday afternoon. He insisted on seeing me privately in my office. He took the crystal from an old leather pouch tied at his waist. Of course, I could only guess at its enormous value and was shocked to see it in the possession of this old man.

"He looked me straight in the eye and said that this crystal had been 'manifested' for a man named Phillip Hansen, and that I should give it to him; I would know when the time was right, he said I would know the exact time.

"I was enthralled, staring at the flawless stone. When I looked up, it was as if the old man had simply vanished into thin air. I searched for a good fifteen minutes and he was nowhere to be found. I even called security.

"I met you for the first time almost five years after that incident and here I am; it's time. Last night I had a dream about the old man. He told me to bring you the crystal today. Understand its value, Phillip; I could have retired simply by selling this crystal the day after it came into my possession. Use it well and God bless you."

John stayed for a quick cup of tea with the three Hansens, then worked his way back behind the wheel of the van and was gone. As he left, he was crying; "tears of joy" he hollered from behind the wheel.

Christian hurried to the phone and called the airline, making reservations for the next day. He and his father were scheduled to arrive in Phoenix at three-thirty. This would put them in Sedona hopefully no later than five-thirty by the time they retrieved their luggage and rented a car.

The flight to Phoenix was uneventful as was the drive to Sedona. Upon arrival in town it was simple enough to find a vortex map depicting the exact location of Cathedral Rock. Rather than trust either of their map reading skills in the dark, however, they paid out thirty dollars to a local and followed her down an obscure dirt road to a small parking area adjacent to the site. By that time it was dusk and the full moon would be rising in, what would prove to be, a clear-as-glass night sky.

Father and son donned their monk's robes, feeling odd to say the least, and in awe picked up the beautiful golden crystal. Through a second channeled message to Jo it was made clear that they were to wear nothing but the monk's robes and sandals and to bring nothing but the crystal. This message was manifested, like the first, on that same metallic material.

They made their way down a small embankment and across a dry streambed. The climb to Cathedral Rock was gradual and, while there was no specific pathway, the route was easy to follow under the light of the full moon. After about ten or fifteen minutes, they were at the base of the rock. There were outcropped ledges of red sandstone all along the perimeter. They skirted the ledges wherever possible, and climbed them only if the walk around and up seemed too long. In any event, they never had to climb more than six or eight feet before reaching the next rocky plateau. The sound of red sandstone rocks falling and breaking under their sandaled footsteps was almost musical. The vibrations of this place were filling their consciousness. Energy surrounded them. The full moon was hanging in the sky as if awaiting its next direction from the conductor of the Cosmos.

Finally the two "monks" reached the solid tower of rock protruding from the desert floor. They looked up wondering where they might possibly go from there. Further climbing was more than either of them was prepared to do. Then Phillip remembered, "In full moon and full meditation," and he intuitively knew they had arrived at their destination. He shared this with Christian and they sat cross-legged at the base of the tower. They simultaneously broke into a long, single-toned chant and achieved a deep meditative state within minutes. Bathed in the full moon's light and in the aura of Cathedral Rock, father and son shared the same cosmic space as if they were one mind. Phillip and Christian Hansen had achieved total telepathy link.

While in this state of oneness, they were hailed by Gracina and escorted in "vision" to the Valley of the Blue Noon. The tower in the middle of the crater-like valley was almost identical in shape and proportion to the center spire of Cathedral Rock. With the vision of the twin towers, the two pilgrims immediately understood the connection between this holy place on the Earth and that holy place on Eyespell.

Phillip placed the golden topaz against the heels of his pressed-together palms and stretched his arms high above his head as if in an offering to a higher power. The two Earth-bound Eyespellians were lifted out-of-body to the pinnacle of Cathedral Rock.

At first light, father and son "awakened" from their meditation, still cross-legged at the base of the spire. Without speaking, they made their way down and back across the streambed to the parked car. Christian was the first to consciously realize that they had been communicating the entire time. They were still in telepathy link with each other and with Eyespell. The "Eyespell Connection" had become reality.

CHAPTER 22

▼

IN THE FAMILY ROOM ...

"Fantastic," said Koy. "You know how every story has a best part? Well, that has got to be it! I loved it, especially the parts where Christian showed up with the monk's robes and then that guy showed up later with the crystal. Too cool. Do you think the old man who delivered the crystal to, oh, what's his name?"

"John, John Beechmont," said Phillip.

"Yeah, do you think the old man who gave him the crystal was from Eyespell?"

"Not a chance," said Phillip. "You're slipping, Ms. Sosa."

"You mean I'm wrong?" Koy feigned a hurt, frowny look.

"Remember our earlier conversation about this being bigger than either Earth or Eyespell? You know, the three end tables in the room here."

"Oh, how lame of me!" exclaimed Koy. "Of course, the old man was not from Eyespell. He had to be a messenger from Cosmo."

"Now you've got it. And that was not the only crystal delivered that day."

"I know, but 'that's another story.' But I'd bet money Eyespell got one too.'

"And the young lady with the long, dark hair wins."

"How about more coffee and cheesecake, is that a good prize?" asked Jo. "I can tell by the starved look on Phillip's face that he's up for it. How about you, skinny?"

"Sounds great," chimed in Koy and Phillip.

"Hey, Jo, do you really think I'm too skinny?"

"I said skinny, not too skinny. There's a difference you know," quipped Jo. "Come on, let's go make another pot of coffee and cut some cake. Come along, we'll give Phillip five minutes with his thoughts."

On the way to the kitchen Jo said, "This part of the story is also my favorite. For one thing, my perfect son Christian starts to play a major role from here on. And you know how mothers can be. But more than that, my heart used to ache for Phillip when his belief in the Eyespell thing fluctuated. He would get so depressed and out of sorts. He really did think there was something very wrong with him. And, when he was at his worst, he thought I was just humoring him about Eyespell. I would assure him that he was okay and that Eyespell probably existed just as he imagined it. He would say, 'Yeah right; how would you know?' I was in a tough spot. While my guides told me all about saving Phillip from despair and suicide, they made it clear that he had to come to the reality of Eyespell on his own. While I could give him my assurances I could never tell him the whole story, that Cosmo told me Eyespell really did exist. When Phillip shared his memories, dreams, and the voices, it was easy for me to piece things together. I believed in Eyespell way before he did even without Cosmo telling me anything. You know the old saying 'Cosmo works in mysterious ways?' Let me tell you, this was one of those mysteries."

"I don't see how you did it. No matter how much you love somebody, it's really tough when they are not being totally rational. For example, I bet you weren't too pleased about moving to Florida so Phillip could find some of the answers he was looking for."

"Not pleased at all; that's about when Cosmo and his buddies had me at the end of my rope. You're right, as much as I loved Phillip it was impossible at times. His anxiety was the absolute worst. It would come on like gangbusters for no apparent reason and then disappear for an equally unapparent reason. Trust me, even I thought he was nuts at times; not really, but it would have been easier. You can help nutty people. What do you do for a guy as bright and sane as Phillip? You know how Eyespell was falling apart because of Earth-plane vibrational leakage? Well, that's how Phillip's personality was. He was like the planet Eyespell, full of stress cracks and volcanoes. It was horrible. And his suffering was very real, that was the saddest part."

"It does seem, though," said Koy, "that he did find some answers back in Florida."

"That's true enough and except for the mold, the bugs, the humidity, and the old farts in Albertson's grocery store, I came to like Florida in some ways. But, thank God Phillip had taken only a temporary teaching position. When he found his answers, or all that he was going to find, we came back to this house. Actually, Christian and I came back a few months before Phillip. I knew he was going to be okay when he shared his insight about teaching and what was relevant, and his insight about hope. He came to understand that it was his choice. Nothing was being done to him. He had the choice of following his spirit and intuition, and he had the choice between hope and despair. While he still had doubts, he was a whole lot more peaceful within himself. He decided to be a hopeful Eyespellian and the hell with whether he could prove it or not. Eyespell simply felt good. I was never so grateful as I was for those insights he gained in hell; excuse me, I mean Florida."

"So you really think trading off mold and mildew for a good old Virginia ice storm was a good deal?" asked Koy. I'm not sure I like either; I was thinking Santa Barbara. And the good news is if I save up for the next four-hundred-thirty-six years I would be able to afford a small garage in Santa Barbara and that's not counting inflation. Oh yeah, and I probably won't live that long. Other than that ... "

"You could move to Eyespell; it's my understanding that housing is free. You could get Leo to whip you up a condo on the beach."

"Now that works."

"Stick around, Christian and I will take you to Death Valley with us."

"Death Valley; not crowded, but hot, kind of ugly. I'm sure I'd enjoy the company, but no thanks."

"It's not crowded, hot, or ugly in the future; trust me."

"Not you too; I suppose that's another story."

"Indeed it is; indeed it is," agreed Jo. "Coffee's ready; shall we join Phillip and moose Joseph?"

"I didn't think you two were coming back," said Phillip.

"We missed you and wanted to hear more," said Koy.

"And there is definitely more," said Phillip. "What was really amazing was coming away from Cathedral Rock as two Eyespellians in telepathy link. That was truly amazing. It left no room for doubt whether Eyespell was real or not. We left Cathedral Rock as changed people, that's for sure. Of course, it was nothing as spectacular as our second visit."

Koy cut him off. "But that's another story. Between you and your wife over there, I am going to need very intensive therapy to get rid of Hansen-plane vibrational leakage and that's the truth." They all had a good laugh.

"She didn't tell you any secrets in the kitchen, did she?"

"No, nothing secret, honest. Here's to fresh coffee, another piece of cheesecake, and another chunk of the story."

"If you're ready, Miss. You asked earlier about how I came to know about Mystic Management. Christian and Eyespell told me. This is my favorite part of the story."

CHAPTER 23

▼

THE MYSTIC MANAGER

It had been three weeks since Christian had returned home to Rochester from Sedona. He was sitting on the back patio waiting for the noise of the distant freight train to clear the air and the sound of the dusk-crickets to return. Between the kids' tub-splashing squeals and the growls of their mother being a huge water monster, he could barely hear the droning sounds of the TV pouring through the open window. Smiling, he thought, "My world is totally different now. A month ago life seemed comparatively simple. There is no question that my life began to change with the initial revelations about Eyespell. Those old manuscripts of Dad's and the leather-bound notebook describing scattered details of the Eyespell Experiment were indeed fascinating. However, prior to Arizona, the idea of being half-Eyespellian could be taken with a grain of salt. Now I am forced to consider the literal truth of the matter. This growing reality places everything in a new light. There is more to be done in this life of mine than I had ever suspected."

Christian was the CEO of Used Water Works, Inc., whose primary business was water recycling. The corporation was environmentally aware, socially responsible and on the cutting edge of a technology central to planetary growth and survival into the next century. Its vision statement was simple and to the point, "Used water works for mankind." Christian and his company were successful by any American corporate standard, and on a path he had first envisioned when he was only a college sophomore.

With the Eyespell connection now a reality, Christian's life took new and unexpected turns. He could communicate with his father at will, just by thinking. He was in steady contact with Eyespell, primarily through lucid dreams, and he, more often than not, knew exactly what the people around him were thinking. His ability to predict complex business trends increased markedly. With the Eyespell connection a reality, Christian had a mission, a heightened sense of purpose, a forthright insistence upon changing things, making them better. He had always thought of himself as a visionary, and he was extremely comfortable in that role, especially now.

He recalled from his father's old manuscript several statements about a new model of how things should be, a new paradigm. There were powerful statements about how the old paradigm kills, how Earth must change in order to survive. He sometimes imagined himself as spokesperson for just such a new paradigm, and felt that he would achieve, and use, a position of corporate power to "save the world!" To say he felt a certainty of purpose would be understatement. The whole scenario reminded him of that movie that won best picture a few years ago, the one about the Pakistani business leader. He never could remember the name of it, but its leadership concept was huge.

Christian was still on the back patio as dusk turned to darkness. The TV was still droning on with no audience and the tub squeals had turned to before-bed quiet time. He was writing a few remarks on the inside front page of his dream journal, "The first inklings of my new calling came to me in dreams that began almost immediately after my experience at Cathedral Rock. The dreams were most often didactic, dreams with a message. The messages were often hidden in typical dream confusion and dream magic. I sometimes felt as though I were reviewing bits and pieces of someone else's dream.

"Parts of dreams seemed as though they belonged elsewhere. Other times there were long narrative interludes without any visuals at all, as if someone were whispering a story inside my head. Other times I would dream lucidly, actually interacting with the dream plot at a conscious level. My dreaming would go back and forth among the elements of narrative, typical dream stuff, and conscious interaction. I knew it was important to meticulously record each dream in this journal. I wanted to study them and to be able to interpret them carefully. At times I was not quite sure where the lessons began or ended. In any case, I wanted to share each dream with Dad in exacting detail when I saw him. Our newly developed telepathy skills are sometimes fraught with a bit of mental static."

With darkness imminent Christian put the journal down and thought about that first dream of less than three weeks ago. He had read this journal entry so many times and had pondered each word to the point where he could repeat it by heart. The first dream was of particular interest. He recorded it in three distinct parts for easier interpretation; the dream images and messages did not flow logically, shifting from place to place and subject to subject. This first dream is entitled *Myth Building*. The narration at the beginning of the dream was a kind of warning for Christian not to get a swelled head with all the notoriety that was likely to accompany the pursuit of his new mission. As he sat in the dark, eyes closed, he could picture his steady black-ink-handwriting against the buff-colored and light-blue-lined pages of his journal. He sat back enveloped in the newly fallen darkness and reviewed that first dream in every detail.

The First Dream - Myth Building - Part I

I dreamed about a man who daydreamed a lot about being famous. He had the silly habit of daydreaming just before bed. A great deal of dream time and dream energy was spent wondering how he would actually handle his newfound notoriety. He wondered just how clever he would be on the talk shows. He could picture the host of the show laughing the way hosts do when they've been had and they're "hading" you back. The man wondered about the money. How much would he have? He dreamed about everything he could buy and every place he could go.

The thought of spending the summer at an A-frame in the mountains was wonderful. However, he started to worry about practical things spoiling the whole adventure he had only begun to create. He worried about being gone to the mountains all summer. He thought, "Who will take care of the two cockatiels, Woody and Cheeks? What about Lucky, the lost parrot who landed in the mahogany tree out front last spring? And then there were the three cats. Who would mow the lawn and weed the shrubbery beds? Good grief, the fish tank would probably have to be drained and the fish relocated. What if there was a bad storm, who'd secure the house? And, besides that, who'd take care of the pool? And, what's the use having a pool anyway if I'm going to be gone all summer?" By the time the man finished with this line of thinking, the daydream of being famous just wasn't worth it. Overwhelmed by the details, the man picked himself up, went to bed, and had a night dream about a mystic manager.

The First Dream - Myth Building - Part II

In a dream-workplace there was a mystic manager who modeled kindness and generosity. This corporate environment was psychologically healthy, an environment flowing with feelings of common purpose and community. This was an extraordinary and unorthodox corporation. Its existence was prophetic and signaled a paradigm shift. There was emphasis on long-term goals versus short-term profits, sustainability versus maximized profits, teams and individuals working toward common goals versus quick profits, ethical and legal action versus legal-loophole-profits, socially responsible behavior versus irresponsibly gained profits, loyalty to employees versus downsizing, and unparalleled service to customers versus buyer-beware-profits. There was nothing new in concept here. It was the implementation of all these ideas within one corporation that was exceptional and paradigm-shifting. The mystic manager re-established, remade, and remodeled the old notions. The rigidity of the chain of command was replaced by the flexibility of teamwork and group-centered leadership and all of this directed toward sustainable communities. The fabric of economics was challenged.

There was a *globalness* about this time and place of the mystic manager. The changes in this corporation would stretch to their potential, explode, and recreate themselves into massive and permanent shifts, impacting the total business environment. Each thing, each change, each small shift was recognized as part of the larger whole; it changed the global environment of business. And, ultimately, what happened in this business environment reflected in education, reflected in government, and reflected in the society as a whole. Mystic Management was the new frontier of community building.

Business was the springboard to other areas. Business technology was being used to plan, direct, organize, and evaluate the community of humankind, the consummate organization. Business textbooks began to map out entire sections on Community Building Strategy. The mystic manager understood that what happens in one person reflects in another person, and another person, and another person. The mystic manager understood that community could be built by capturing and molding just one fuzzy piece of the human hologram.

The First Dream - Myth Building - Part III

The dream stuff stretched and I had that jolting, falling sensation. I came down hard on a linoleum floor next to an old maple kitchen table. I grazed the table as I fell and a small book landed in my lap: *The Mystic Manager: Qualities and Characteristics*. I had become a part of the dream; I was no longer a passive observer.

Still amidst that stretchy dream stuff, I opened the book. The dedication was simple: "Toward an effort to move from the traditional business world's concept of the P*R*O*F*I*T of exploitation, to the new business community's concept of the P*R*O*P*H*E*T of sustainability, toward the acceptance, dissemination and implementation of Mystic Management on the Earth."

I was stimulated by the juxtaposition of "profit" and "prophet." I recognized this as the crux of the new paradigm; this was the shift toward the new model of sustainability. With the book still open to the dedication, I thought about what this might mean. Maybe a Mystic Management would look at nature in a new way. Maybe a tree could be appreciated for its value as a living thing rather than its value as a resource. Maybe the mystic manager leaves the tree alone and develops a new technology altogether. Maybe Mystic Management goes beyond sustainability toward a new dimension of physical reality creating.

At this point myriad thoughts whispered in my head as if spoken through the very fibers of my imagination. "Imagine such a shift of vision," said the soft female voice. "Imagine a conversion of energy from the economics of industrialization to the synergy of mind, body, and spirit linked in a globally conscious system. Imagine the ultimate information system beginning as a single strand of cosmic stuff pushing against imagination to create the reality of a collective togetherness, a collective consciousness. Imagine such a reality for the Earth." The inner whisper trailed off and my consciousness again focused on Mystic Management.

I could sense that the leadership of Mystic Management would set the systems and sub-systems of all things into a totally compatible order. This would represent a shift to a management-for-sustainability where economic systems would operate in harmony

with environmental systems. It would be a movement
from the false magic of the myth of inexhaustibility to
the mature reality of nurturing for perpetuity. Mystic
Management leadership would seek the constant
harvest, the long-term solutions.

Christian focused away from the dream journal pages running
through his head. The night air had turned chilly and he abandoned
the patio for the comfort of his favorite living room chair, stopping
on his way to tuck in the kids. His thoughts were still with that first
dream, "That dream with hints of Mystic Management is dramatic. I
need to pursue the dream of Mystic Management. I need to make that
dream a reality." He envisioned himself as the mystic manager, and
Used Water Works as the mystic corporation. UWW would become
the corporate role model for a society poised and ready for positive and
dramatic change.

Christian was thinking he ought to give his Dad a call to discuss
this Mystic Management business in detail. Phillip's voice immediately
popped into his head, "Why use the phone, son?"

"Good grief, Dad, you startled me," thought Christian. "I am
definitely not used to this mind-link stuff. Have you been listening in
the whole time?"

"Of course not. Your telepathy link opened just this minute.
Anyway, what's up?"

"I've been reviewing that first Myth Building dream again, and I
think it's time to do something with that Mystic Management stuff. I
have a very strong feeling that it's time for me to take action, to become
the Mystic Manager, if you will."

"Well," said Phillip, "perhaps we should get together and develop
a blueprint. I know your mother is anxious to see you and the family.
I don't have anything going on for the next few days, the weather is
great and we're really in the mood for a drive. If we leave here tomorrow
morning around ten o'clock, we can be on your doorstep by six-thirty
or so. Ask Sally what she thinks of our coming."

Without getting up from his chair, Christian yelled in the direction
of the kitchen, "Sally! Sally! I've got Dad inside my head and he wants
to know if it would be okay if he and Mom came tomorrow for a few
days? Dad and I need to do some brainstorming."

Sally stuck her head around the corner so she could eyeball Christian and said, "The kids will be thrilled; I think it's a great idea. I suppose using the phone so your mom and I could get in on the conversation would too common for you Eyespellian types." Before Sally stopped laughing the phone rang. She and Jo finalized the plans while Christian and Phillip finished up with their Mystic Management business for the evening.

Christian went to bed that night with that "visions of sugar plums" feeling. He could hardly wait for his parents' arrival the next evening. He finally fell asleep hoping for a prophetic dream to add to the materials that he and Phillip would be synthesizing in less than twenty-four hours. Christian was not disappointed. He awoke about four in the morning to carefully record the dream he labeled *Systemic Change*.

The Second Dream - Systemic Change

My garden was in serious trouble. Several of my favorite plants were being attacked by insects. The insects were sucking the life out of the flowers, bushes and trees. I referred to my gardening encyclopedia and under the heading of "systemic insecticide," I read, "Systemic insecticides are those that are applied to the leaves or soil, are absorbed and circulated within the plant, killing harmful sucking pests."

How interesting, I thought, "With the application of a systemic, the plant itself becomes the cure for its own disease. The insects, detecting no change, feed themselves into oblivion."

The dream stuff stretched and I turned from the gardening book and found myself, bigger-than-life-size, atop the Used Water Works headquarters building with a huge sprinkling can filled with some unknown and powerful-smelling concoction. I carefully angled the can slightly backward and toward myself so as not to accidentally sprinkle the rooftop. As I gingerly approached the edge of the building's roof, I leaned out a little, looked down, and saw what must have been a one-story-high, brown glass bottle.

The bottle was lying on its side, cap off, and label up. An ever so slight breeze brought that same powerful sprinkling can odor from the uncapped neck of the bottle to my nostrils. I stretched a little farther in order to read the label. Across the top, in heavy black print, I could make out the words, "Systemic Change."

Before proceeding, I carefully scrutinized the rest of the label. There was a warning printed in red script on the very bottom, "Harmful or fatal if absorbed through the left side of the brain; keep away from all logic." The middle portion of the label contained what I was looking for, instructions on what to do atop a corporate building with a very large sprinkling can of Systemic Change.

Momentarily distracted, I looked up. In that fraction of a second, the dream stuff changed again and I found myself normal size, sitting under a tree, and having a very lucid conversation about organizational and societal change with someone who identified herself as the Mystic Manager.

She said, "A major error in dealing with problems of organizational change is to disregard the systemic properties of the organization and to confuse individual change with modifications in organizational variables."

I gently squeezed the end of my chin between by thumb and the side of my pointer-finger and said in my most academic tone, "I think I know what you are getting at. If the insects recognized that the plant was different once treated with the systemic insecticide, they simply would not eat it. They could continue to live on the plant, to coexist with the plant; they would merely have to stop sucking the life out of it."

As I looked up to get a reaction to my brilliant insight, the dream stuff shifted and I again stretched bigger than life, finding myself, sprinkling can in hand, back atop the UWW headquarters building. I tipped

the can, soaking the rooftop, sides, interior, and grounds
of the corporate headquarters with Systemic Change. I
then held the can high over my head and soaked myself
in a shower of that same "concepticide."

By the time Christian finished recording his dream, he was ecstatic
and wanted to shake the whole family awake to share his excitement.
He barely managed to contain himself as he ran from the bedroom and
silently slid across the shiny kitchen floor in his bare socks. "I wish Dad
was here now."

"I am," came the soft reply.

"There you've gone and done it again; you've scared me half to
death. I still don't get what, exactly, turns this telepathy thing on or off.
Anyway, what can I possibly do to calm my speeding mind until you get
here? I just had the most amazingly prophetic dream. I've just soaked
myself and corporate headquarters of Used Water Works in something
called Systemic Change Concepticide."

"Now there's a turn of a word. It sounds like something an Eyespellian
would say." Phillip laughed aloud, "Concepticide, how terribly clever.
I'm sure you'll share all the details with me, but I already know what
it is we have to do."

Christian plopped down on a large floor pillow and just blurted out,
"And what's that, oh brilliant one?"

"We simply have to figure out what's in that concepticide. See you
tomorrow, actually later today. I've got another forty-five minutes of
sleep coming and I'm going to grab it before it gets away. Speaking of
getting away, to calm your mind just let it wander, don't try to tame it.
What would you do if you were appointed mystic manager of the world
starting tomorrow? Good night and I love you."

"You too, see you for dinner." Christian clasped his hands behind
his head and thought, "Mystic Manager of the World, let me see."

All manner of things came to Christian as he let his mind wander in
search of Mystic Management puzzle pieces. There was the role of Used
Water Works. Christian was certain that under Mystic Management
leadership it would become the ultimate cutting edge company and
transcend current technology, introducing a new era of environmentally
perfect wastewater reclamation. World concern about water shortages
and water pollution would come to an end. The world water well would

become unpoisoned, and a non-economics would evolve around an unlimited water resource. His vision was that this new system and its accompanying social implications would trigger community building as a focal point on the planet Earth. The availability and utilization of recycled water resources would be the takeoff point of a new economic paradigm compatible with the planet and its peoples; recycled water would literally be Earth's concepticide.

The critical puzzle pieces would revolve around the tenets of Mystic Management, tenets that he and his father had not yet fleshed out. Christian imagined that his campaign for Mystic Management needed to get underway immediately. He pictured conducting meetings and issuing company-wide memoranda to inform every employee of UWW, from Chairman of the Board to janitor, about the new paradigm. He imagined a flurry of activity and open discussions of issues of creativity, sustainability, and the constant harvest. All ideas would be solicited to assure the success of this new long-term world-view. He would be so bold as to openly solicit ideas to save the planet. And he would even recommend that a two-day period be set aside for all employees in the corporation to brainstorm, brainstorm, brainstorm. He would prescribe a forum where the organizational hierarchy was irrelevant, a forum where all ideas were welcome and necessary to the process. His intent would be to make sure that every employee be empowered in the new Mystic Management. Community building and compassion for the entire world would begin with UWW.

Christian imagined awesome results. The people, ideas, and energy focused behind his positive leadership would spark like a laser, a laser warming up to project a piece of the human hologram. The dream stuff that he had been faithfully recording would begin to stretch into the real world, and corporate America would be on the pathway to community building. Mystic Management would be projected onto the fabric of society.

Christian pictured himself sharing and communicating his vision of Mystic Management for the remainder of his life lest it fall by the wayside as fad with little or no long-term durability. He would become the exemplary model of the new management. He would gradually widen his sphere of influence; he would give talks to community organizations, church groups, colleges and universities, and corporate groups around the country and around the world. He would in every way possible bring the concept of Mystic Management into the public eye. He even hoped to do a talk show or two, only unlike the poor fellow in his dream he would not let his newfound notoriety spoil the daydream. And what a daydream it was, a virtual storm within his brain. He had to laugh at his unbridled idealism. What was even funnier is that he believed it!

Still on the floor pillow Christian dozed off into another dream, a dream symbolizing his mounting passion for Mystic Management. He took on an increased certainty of purpose that in itself was mystical.

The Third Dream - Colors of the Hologram

The Mystic Manager was lying in an open field, gazing into the pale blue backdrop sky. She saw the red, white, and blue; the streets paved with gold; the yellow brick road; the *Scarlet Letter*; the graying of America; black power; purple mountains' majesty and amber waves of grain.

She saw the colors of America come into focus as her vision expanded beyond the borders of a manifest destiny. She saw the colors of America in an instantaneous panorama as she *looked to the sky from the Earth*.

Christian awakened and, as was his habit, immediately recorded his dream. This dream reminded him of a passage in his father's old attic manuscript. The excerpt was entitled "Planetaryvision." It began, "And in the real world, a man *looked to the Earth from the sky* and he saw the colors of the whole Earth in an instantaneous panorama from outer space." The reference was to an American astronaut reflecting upon his feelings from space during an Apollo Mission. "Community already exists," thought Christian, "we just have to be able to see it." He dropped back to sleep, pen still in hand.

While UWW would ultimately make its physical presence known in Death Valley, its brain, headquarters, operated from Rochester, NY. Today Christian planned to do his work from his Rochester, NY, home; UWW headquarters would survive a day without him. He took the day off gathering all of his materials and thoughts in anticipation of his father's arrival. Six-thirty finally came and his parents pulled into the driveway right on schedule. Making few bones about their desire to get on with their work, Christian and Phillip were almost immediately dismissed with some healthy kidding and finger shaking by Jo, Sally, and the kids. Sally said, "We're going out to dinner and to a movie; you two get to go to the study with no dinner. Because we love you, we might bring something back for you. If you really get to starving, there's plenty of good stuff in the fridge." There were kisses all around and within minutes Christian and Phillip were busy trying to figure out what was in that bottle of Systemic Change Concepticide.

They decided to do their Mystic Management work in the study. It was a very peaceful room on the second floor. It overlooked a steep backyard hill going up perhaps two stories higher than the house itself. You felt you could almost reach out the window and touch the hemlocks, pines, and spruces that climbed the steep bank. Inside, the furnishings were organic, made exclusively from naturally fallen pine logs hewn into intricate and unique designs. There were cushions to ease the body and many pastel fabrics and drawings placed around the room to ease the mind. There was a ficus tree in one corner trying to reach the heights of the cathedral ceiling with huge beams, matte-finished steel plates and lag bolts holding the whole thing up. On a table near the ficus was a small dish fountain, bringing the sound of gently falling water into the room. And there were two curio cabinets filled with crystal balls of every imaginable color and size. One cabinet held a huge, pink rose quartz ball as its central focus; the other held a huge blue and green fluorite ball as its central focus; Eyespell and Earth.

Phillip and Christian sat at the round table near the window overlooking the hill and yard. Phillip reached into his briefcase, pulled out a stack of materials and gently placed them on the table. Christian went over to the desk, grabbed a different stack of papers and his dream journal, and added them to the already substantial pile on the table. "Well, that looks like everything," said Christian, "my dream journal and notes, your old manuscripts, journals, and other writings. Where do we start?"

Phillip reached into his briefcase again, this time bringing out a silken pouch. "Let's begin with a brief meditation." Carefully opening the pouch, Phillip said, "This is the topaz we used at Cathedral Rock during our first mind-link with Eyespell. Perhaps if we get things started, our Eyespellian colleagues will join us." Phillip gently placed the golden topaz double-pyramid on one of its sides in the center of the table. Both he and Christian sat in silent meditation for several minutes. The entire room seemed to take on the golden glow of the topaz as the two men let their spirits wander the galaxies toward Eyespell.

"Are we ready to begin, Dad?"

"Yep. I can feel the energies flowing."

About then, both Phillip and Christian heard a resounding "yes" within their psyches. They were in link with each other and with Eyespell. The inner voices said, "Begin your work and we will interject where appropriate. As is the Eyespellian way, your creative thoughts are most important and we would not presume to dictate their exact direction. By the conclusion of this psychic-conference-call you will have workable definitions of the six Principles of Mystic Management."

Phillip smiled and said, "Our Eyespellian faculties still amaze me. I really had to laugh last night when Christian found himself confused about how to turn his telepathy link on and off. Seems you folks from Eyespell just did the same thing to me. I didn't honestly expect a direct link with Eyespell this evening. Somehow I thought Cathedral Rock was a unique experience perhaps to be followed up by some later visit to the same site. While I may have expected some insight from Eyespell, I would not have suspected a direct telepathy link from Eyespell to study. Just for the sake of comfort though, could we use the spoken word along with our telepathy link?"

"Hmm, Dr. Hansen, suffering from a bit of the Kookamonga Effect, are we?" asked Leo.

"Absolutely," said Phillip. "And I think it's cheating to use my own psychology against me; don't you think so, Christian?"

"Not at all, Dad. It's quite enjoyable to see you behind the eight ball with somebody else besides Mom."

"You've got a smart boy there," said Leo.

"Smart ass is more like it," said Phillip, laughing.

"You two have no idea how typically Eyespellian you are. Fact is, here on Eyespell we love a good spoken conversation or story in spite of our telepathic capabilities. So, let's have a good talk."

"Leo, I am just this minute remembering that you were my teacher on Eyespell!" said Phillip. "I loved those lessons in the desert. I can't say

I recall exactly what they were, but I remember loving them. I would be willing to bet some of it had to do with Mystic Management."

Christian kiddingly said, "All of that was before my time, I don't remember a thing."

"You'd be amazed what your soul remembers," played in Christian's head as if sung into his consciousness by several people, by a church choir.

"Wow, how many are on this 'call', Leo?"

"A bunch of us: the entire Elders' Council and a couple hundred others right here in the Council Chamber. And our links are open, so who knows who else is listening in. Now get to work, you two," said Leo, laughing.

"Dad, the one thing that impresses me the most about our contact with Eyespell is how good the interactions always feel. There is never an unkind word or thought. I never feel chastised or criticized, nor in any way am I made to feel uncomfortable or stupid. I mean here we are in contact with hundreds; it's a brand new experience for us, and yet I feel totally a part of it and in no way inferior just because it's a new experience. And I have no concern that I might make a mistake and be made to feel foolish."

"That's true. In my time of madness I remember thinking I was going completely crazy, yet my contact with Eyespellian images was always soothing and kind; they always abated my feelings of despair and panic. I'm not sure I ever pieced it together quite so clearly or consciously before. The bottom line is that my dignity has never been violated by anything Eyespellian, whether we're talking about our experience at Cathedral Rock or my just holding the rose quartz specimen from my curio cabinet and thinking about the pink planet."

"Maybe that's the starting place for finding out what's in that systemic-change *concepticide*," said Phillip. "One major ingredient must have to do with respect, dignity, compassion, and kindness. In any management scheme there should be no room for disrespecting others, belittling anyone, or being unkind. It seems to me that any unkindness would likely come back to haunt the perpetrator in the long run. Certainly if not in this life, then in the next. I've always believed that 'what goes around comes around,' it's a karma thing."

Leo piped in, "I can't believe how close you have come to a Mystic Management tenet we hold dear. We call it 'Karmic Kindness: What goes around comes around *and kindness is the only way*.' You've hit it exactly on the head. Of the six primary Mystic Management principles, Karmic Kindness is number four."

"Dad, do you want to record this or would you like me to?"

"You do it, your dream journal is far prettier than this beat-up old leather one." Phillip looked across the table at his son. At that exact moment, he felt great hope for Earth's future.

"Okay then, principle number four, Karmic Kindness: 'What goes around comes around and kindness is the only way.' I have a really nagging question: How do you suppose we could ever presume to convince managers, supervisors, leaders, or business types at any level to be kind?"

"We can't dictate kindness if that's what you mean, but we can, you can, provide the example, the model. Remember your dream, Christian. It takes just one piece of the human hologram to create that which you seek. And already we have six pieces: you, me, Sally, Jo and your children. And I sense there will be significant others very soon. Let's get the message out there and see what happens."

"If I might add something here," said Leo. "On Eyespell, thoughts and light create reality. That's what we're all about and that's what you're all about. The Eyespell Experiment was no accident. The energy of the two of you on Earth adds unique possibilities. Look at the example you might provide; don't forget, you are of Eyespell and you are of Earth."

"Well then, let's open our minds and get creative," said Christian.

"Creative, now there's a word that keeps popping up," added Phillip.

Christian immediately expanded on the idea. "Last night when I let my mind wander, trying to quiet my excitement a little, the significance of creativity kept coming into my thoughts. In my imaginary mystic managing, creativity held a place of critical importance. Not only were all ideas welcome, but necessary. And that meant all ideas, all the time, and from anybody willing to contribute. In fact, as I pictured the new Used Water Works paradigm, I realized that creativity was a primary trait in everything we did."

"What I like about what you're saying is that there is an implied community aspect to the creativity you propose. It seems as though everyone is involved in some way in the process of management. It seems to be a collaborative effort," said Phillip.

Leo interrupted, "Not surprisingly, you've done it again; you've hit another Mystic Management principle right on. The principle is Collaborative Creativity, and it is the first tenet. It promotes a style that examines all ideas. Everybody's ideas are welcome all the time."

Christian, wincing a little, said, "As a manager in the real world, hypotheticals aside, I balk at this notion the more I think about it. It's a wonderful idea in theory, but I'm afraid it could put us out of business in practice. While kindness might have personal costs and demand a bit of psychological realignment, this creativity notion could become so time consuming that productivity would suffer beyond salvation. After all, time is money and this process could easily get out of hand. I even thought in my mind wanderings of last evening about having a two-day brainstorming session. That was only two days, and yet the cost would probably be prohibitive. How could you possibly make creativity work all the time and involve all people?"

Both Christian and Phillip sat silent, listening to lots of mind-chatter. The Eyespellians seemed to be talking all at once, making it difficult to interpret in any meaningful way. Finally Matthew spoke, "You've certainly set off a debate here. By the way, I'm Matthew, one of the Elders. Seems everybody has an opinion about what you're saying, Christian; it's quite lively and delightful. We have tremendous latitude here on Eyespell on the issue of creativity and how much time it might take; we do not have an economic system based on tradeoffs among limited or scarce resources. We do not juxtapose time and dollars against performance. In fact, it would be fair to say we don't consider the economics of anything, ever. We do not have money and we do have unlimited time within which to accomplish anything we desire. We literally combine thought and light to produce whatever physical reality we want."

"And I thought I was creative," quipped Christian.

Phillip sat squinting as if in bright sunlight, shaking his head slowly up and down deep in thought. He finally said, "We can't give up on this collaborative creativity idea. It's too important; I think we need to put the concept out there. We need to encourage everyone to incorporate their natural creativity into their work at all times. While I may be an Eyespellian, I've spent many years on this planet and I know it's important to go as far as you can with an idea. I've learned to 'push the envelope' as my colleagues are so fond of saying. This is where new paradigms live, at the edge, away from that which is logical and practical based on current practice. Significant change begins as a matter of faith, not logic. We certainly don't want to put you out of business, Christian, but what can we do to avoid that while still promoting creativity? You can and should brainstorm about how to best enliven and incorporate Collaborative Creativity into daily work. What would have to be different to allow this concept into your daily business routine?"

"I think I see what you mean," said Christian, "do what you can. Don't say 'no' to an idea; say 'yes, we can accomplish this much within our constraints.' If I can't afford two days of creativity go for two minutes or whatever is allowable given the constraints. We need to learn to trade off more effectively. If value is placed on creativity and, therefore, the ideas of every person in the organization are considered, then that is the starting place. If creativity is perceived to have little or no value, it will never be considered part of the optimum mix of viable alternatives. This is exciting."

"So, how can we write it down?" asked Phillip. "Try this. 'The first tenet of Mystic Management is Collaborative Creativity, which means placing value on creativity and welcoming and considering creative ideas from all members of the organization. Collaborative Creativity acknowledges and supports creativity within appropriate time and dollar constraints. And, creativity must be allowed at least some amount of time no matter what the constraints are."

"It sounds a little clumsy, but I've got it down in my journal. We can clean it up later, Dad. So, what's next? So far our Systemic Change Concepticide has two ingredients: Karmic Kindness and Collaborative Creativity. And now we should add a teaspoonful of, of what?"

"Perhaps a teaspoonful of smart aleck?" chimed in Leo.

"He's always been a problem child," said Phillip laughing aloud.

"And you, Phillip, the perfect child. Do you realize you are almost half-a-century late for dinner?" Everyone had a healthy laugh. Leo continued, "I find your conclusion extremely interesting. I cannot remember ever having to compromise or settle for a portion of anything. We are accustomed to reaching consensus and then creating what we've decided upon. While you are trying to define Mystic Management for the Earth, I need to think about new strategies for solving the problems evolving on Eyespell as a result of our intimate contact with you and the aftermath of the Eyespell Experiment."

"I don't understand, what problems?" asked Christian.

"I honestly don't mean to put you off, but I think we should concentrate right now on finishing up the Mystic Management principles. I can assure you that both you and your father are, and will continue to be, in the thick of Eyespellian matters, now and in the future. But, that's another story. I think we should concentrate on getting the Mystic Management principles into a useful construct so you can begin the work you saw in your dreams. Now that we are able to connect so easily, we can deal with the issues I was alluding to. Does that work okay for you? I really don't want you to feel put off."

Christian's reaction was immediate, "I trust you enough, Leo, to let things unfold in their natural course. Which brings up the next point I was thinking about, trust. How often is there trust among individuals in organizations today? How often is there a mutual respect for the unique talents and abilities of every member of the organization? There needs to be a shared management and group-centered leadership. In my experience, position means power and power means autocratic direction-giving, often with total disregard for the welfare and needs of the individuals being directed. Too often there is lip service paid to the idea of empowerment; it looks good on paper and makes for a good vision statement. The reality of empowering others, however, is far too threatening for most executives. It signals to them loss of control, loss of power, and most assuredly a perceived loss of profits. They feel that people are our most important resource as long as the idea isn't carried too far, as long as people aren't actually empowered. I'm afraid there's too much ego in our leaders."

"The ability to trust others is important up, down, and across the organizational hierarchy," said Phillip. "Such trust and empowerment works in all directions. For example, you are trusting that Leo will let things unfold as appropriate, and he is trusting that you have something intelligent to say about the principles we are trying to define. There is not an unhealthy questioning of motives. The assumption is that we are all working toward the same goal, and that it's in the best interest of all of us to get there, to achieve that goal."

"Exactly," said Leo. "What you are getting at is the Mystic Management tenet we call Ego Empowerment. It also speaks to our ruling by consensus. The orientation is mutually-directed rather than self-directed or other-directed. It is the second tenet."

"I hate playing the devil's advocate," said Christian, "but here again I see a problem. I don't think you'd get much open disagreement with the idea of empowering employees. There's a lot of conversation out there about the benefits and virtues of empowered employees. Besides, it sounds silly to be against it, you would sound like a tyrant. So everybody says they're for empowerment. The human resource is the most important, right? Look at companies that embrace the management strategies of customer service, continuous improvement, and employee empowerment. Customer service is costly, but essential. Continuous improvement saves money and improves quality. Employee empowerment is costly, time-consuming, and threatening to the autocrats. The typical outcome is to dump that part of the system. What you are left with is customer service and continuous improvement in a downsized, autocratic, stress-producing, inhumane system. 'Do more with less' is not the same as empowering employees. This is a deadly paradigm."

"So, Christian, tell us how you really feel," said Phillip, with a smile.

"Good grief, I sound as crazed as some of those old manuscripts lying there on the table. I'm beginning to sound like you did forty years ago, Dad."

"It's nice to know we get worked up about the same things. So, what are you going to write down in that journal of yours?"

"Let's see, the second tenet of Mystic Management is Ego Empowerment, the ability to honestly respect and value the unique talents of every person in the organization. Ego Empowerment demands a legitimate shared management and group-centered leadership. Delegation is not synonymous with downsizing."

"We're not doing too badly," said Phillip. "So far the only concept that will put you out of business is unbridled creativity; oh yeah, and unmitigated decision by consensus. I agree that delegation is not synonymous with downsizing. Besides, less downsizing is, while expensive, still within the range of sustainability and reasonable profits. It's just not a profit maximizing strategy. I think corporations simply need a little encouragement from a self-confident leadership."

"Yes, indeed," agreed Phillip. "Self-confidence would go a long way in reducing dependency on authority, power, or any other potential misuse of position. I think it's up to top management, all management for that matter; actually it's up to everybody in the organization to go the extra step to encourage others. Giving others encouragement is a wonderful way to dispel one's own insecurities. And of course it's a positive circle: giving, encouragement, feelings of security, more giving, more encouragement, more security, and so on and so on. It would be like Karmic Kindness on steroids. Does anyone have a name for it?"

"I do," said Leo. "We call it Gentle Generosity."

"Okay then," said Phillip. "That bottle of Systemic Change Concepticide now has four ingredients. Let me recap, no pun intended." Phillip hung his head in mock shame at his horrible joke. "All right, all right, I'm sorry."

"You know, Phillip, a terrible joke like that sent via mind-link can cause our whole planet over here to mind-crash. You should really be more considerate," chuckled Leo.

"Anyway, the four we've discovered so far include: Collaborative Creativity, Ego Empowerment, Gentle Generosity and Karmic Kindness. Leo, we are assuming that the order in which we've come up with the principles has not posed a problem. Are we giving each tenet its proper due?"

"Absolutely, the order of discovery is no problem. It's the process that's important. There are two others yet to describe."

"Got it," said Christian. "It always fascinates me how good ideas are so interrelated. It's as if everything were just one thing. It's the whole system/sub-systems thing."

"And there you have captured the sixth principle: Systems Sensitivity. All things are, indeed, interconnected, and what happens in one part ultimately affects all other parts. What were you thinking, Phillip?" asked Leo.

"Oh, just that that's how change occurs. Progress, whether it be technological, psychological, or spiritual for that matter, is one thing linked to another in an infinite series, an infinite continuum. No matter where you impact the continuum, all the rest of it vibrates. It might be like taking past, present, and future and hooking them together. One would always lead to the other in some non-linear expression of oneness."

"Okay, I'm writing this down," said Christian. "Collaborative Creativity, Ego Empowerment, Gentle Generosity, Karmic Kindness, Systems Sensitivity, and one more. I fear we are doing this the hard way, but we are doing it. Is this the way, Leo?"

"Any way that gets the job done is the way. There is no rule suggesting that there is one best way to do anything. There might be a thousand ways, all valuable. How do you feel about what's going on, Christian?"

"I feel fine, we are getting there. In fact I feel great and appreciate that you are not simply dictating the Mystic Management principles and expecting me to follow them with none of my personal energy invested. You seem to have great tolerance for multiple styles. I sense here the last principle we are looking for. And what do we call it, Leo?"

"Inclusive Integrity: there is no one best style that covers all situations all the time. What's important is achieving the goal."

Phillip popped in, "So how does our complete list of ingredients read?"

"Try this," said Christian, putting the finishing touches on his journal entry. "The six tenets of Mystic Management are: (1) Collaborative Creativity, (2) Ego Empowerment, (3) Gentle Generosity, (4) Karmic Kindness, (5) Inclusive Integrity, and (6) Systems Sensitivity."

The glow from the golden topaz faded and the study returned to its more earthly hue. "They're gone," said Phillip, "Let's raid the refrigerator."

CHAPTER 24

▼

IN THE FAMILY ROOM …

"Systemic concepticide," mused Koy. "I think that's a high point. I might have to change my mind about my favorite part of the story, but for now I'll stick with that part where you guys really hear Eyespell for the first time, the first proof that it's all real. Well, I can certainly see where the Governor's Club seminar came from. You actually came up with the Principles of Management from Eyespell."

"Not totally," said Phillip. "Christian and I had to put an Earth twist on them. Could you imagine talking about the light-skew and light-corridors to a group of CEOs? I think we got about as far-out as we could keeping the name Mystic Management."

"You've got that right. I remember reading about Mystic Management before the thing at the Governor's Club ever happened. You know, when I was just Koy Sosa, my old stupid, simplistic self. You have really complicated my life, Phillip. Anyway, way back then, what, a few weeks ago? I had my doubts about Mystic Management. Now I'm sure I am going to spend most of my energy trying to convince the rest of the planet that this Mystic Management stuff is the real McCoy. I'm not at all sure how I am going to do that, but I will figure it out."

"I'm sure you will, star reporter. Actually, you have already figured it out. I'd say that piece, "Reflections on Mystic Management," is a pretty good start. Christian and I can take care of the CEOs of the world. It's the rest of the planet that you have to convince."

"Excuse me! Did you say the rest of the planet?"

"Somebody has to do it and you're perfect for the job. All you have to do is write and write and write and get your stuff mediaized."

"Phillip, 'mediaized'? You are making up words and we're right here in your family room with Jo, Eric, and the moose."

"And Christian," added Phillip.

"And Christian? And where might he be, under the couch? Not that Eyespellian thing, telepathy, mind-link? He's been here all along?"

"Well, this Eyespell thing is a pretty complicated story. I couldn't tell it all by myself now, could I?"

"Koy, Phillip refers to his path to remembering Eyespell as the time of madness," said Jo. "And it very well may have been madness for him. But, trust me, for the rest of us mere mortals *this* is the time of madness. They do this all the time. I'll be talking to Phillip and he'll answer me by telling me what Christian said or thinks. I hope to hell he turns that mind-link thing off when we're in bed!"

"Christian says we're not perverts, you know."

"See what I mean?" said Jo.

"I give up," quipped Koy, "but have you decided I'm supposed to convert the world to Mystic Management? *Media-ize?*"

"You're too young to remember," instructed Phillip, "but Marshall McLuhan said 'the message is the media.' "

"Actually, Phillip, he said the 'medium was the message.' I may be a youngster, but I have read a thing or two."

"Well then, you know exactly what to do. Write, write, write and get your words in every possible medium: newspapers, books, talk shows on radio and television. I think a Superbowl ad would be marvelous. You could use those drunk talking frogs with the long tongues, or whatever. You could give out coupons: 'get a free aura washing at mysticmanagement.com.' You could put banners in and on buses, slap-up posters on plywood construction walls along busy sidewalks. You could produce T-shirts and the soon-to-be-infamous Mystic Management bumper sticker: 'Shift happens.' You could even put ads in movie theaters to be shown before the shows start. And, of course, there is television, television, television. Well, what do you think, Koy Sosa, star reporter and mouthpiece for Mystic Management?"

"Jo, can you help me here?"

"You can come for Christmas dinner, would that do it?"

"Done, when do I start?"

"After I leave," said Phillip, "I fully expect that you and Christian will know what to do. Of course, you'll always be able to get in touch, and, yes, that's another story. But now we've reached the end of this one."

CHAPTER 25

▼

ON THE CAMPAIGN TRAIL

It was six years after Christian, Phillip, and their Eyespellian colleagues had first formulated the Mystic Management principles for and on Earth. Christian's success as CEO of Used Water Works was nothing less than spectacular. He was charismatic in his ability to preach and practice the six tenets he first scribbled down in his journal; he truly "walked the talk."

While he had not previously thought about a political career, Christian's involvement in that realm did seem an appropriate step in deploying Mystic Management on a wider scale. His nomination acceptance speech focused on the commitment he had made to uphold and spread the Mystic Management tenets worldwide.

Christian was running for a U. S. Senate seat in New York State. And he was sure to win. The world vision was changing. There was movement away from a nationalistic, monocultural perspective to a multicultural perspective. There was the positive impact of Mystic Management and what Christian's father called "planetaryvision." Planetaryvision is the broad vision of the world as an interconnected whole, not only in physical attributes, but in peoples and cultures. Distinct individual differences become something to celebrate.

"Dad, it's me, Christian. Stop what you're doing for a minute. Hi, Koy. I'm sure you are picking this up because you are in mind-link with Dad. Well, I'm here too as you discovered awhile ago. So, hello and I'm so excited that you're getting the whole story. Dad probably already told you that other than our close family circle, no one has been privy to the Eyespell connection."

"Anyway, the reason I am interrupting is that something is amiss here. Dad, I think we have one of those mind-links gone a bit goofy. First of all, about the last thing on my agenda would be to get into politics. And, besides that, notice the time: it says six years after we started the Mystic Management thing. Well, that's in the future.

"Koy, as if things weren't confusing enough, sometimes the mind-link jumbles the time as well as the facts of a situation. It's almost as if the mind-link pulls stuff out of the collective unconscious at random. It can be pretty funny really. Unless you don't notice what's happening and then it's not funny at all. In fact, one of the reasons the Eyespell Experiment went a bit awry was that the communications got jumbled up now and again, and neither Leo nor Kathryn realized what was happening. Anyway, I think we should play this link through and see what happens. I have a feeling it will be pretty good comic relief. Here comes the political speech I supposedly deliver sometime in the future. Let's listen to what I have to say. Are you with me, Dad?"

"Yep, I'm here, and Koy and Mom are listening in as well. The speech you have never delivered is coming in loud and clear.

> Ladies and Gentlemen, it takes but one fragment of the hologram to reconstruct the total image. We are here today to gather fragments of community to project through our laser. So let's focus our thinking on the history of American ideals. Let's focus on that combination of myth and milieu that defines our reality as Americans.
>
> We Americans have a propensity for forging into the virgin land, and very nearly destroying everything in our path on the way to achieving our high-minded goals! The themes of timelessness, sacredness, and rebirth through nature have taken many forms in the art, literature, politics, and business philosophies of

America. But somewhere in our desire for greatness we became corrupt! The purity we seek can be delivered to posterity only if an unadulterated tie with nature can be maintained. And somewhere in the past while seeking this purity, we instead delivered corruptness, as the untamed and limitless expanse of the American wilderness of the nineteenth century offered itself as a sacrificial ground for our unbridled greed!

What happened after industry ate up the land? Where is the sustained nature? Now the land is polluted; we have fouled our own nest. We must become one with our environment instead of haphazardly dominating it. We must celebrate the new frontier with new community achieved through Mystic Management and a mystic leadership. And I offer you the promise of both. Thank you.

"Good grief, Christian, that sounds like something you'd say."

"Actually, Dad, it sounds exactly like your old manuscripts."

"I'll be damned if it isn't! I knew some of those lines looked familiar. That line about sacrificial ground and unbridled greed definitely struck a chord. But I wrote that years ago. I can't believe it made its way into our mind-link tonight. It's like it was just plucked out of the collective unconscious and presented as fact. Well, I hope you win the Senate race, son."

"Oh, God help us, me a U. S. Senator. And running on your platform. Listen to the rest of it. I suspect it's one of your diatribes on education. Here it comes."

It is imperative that we, once and for all, liberate education. Traditional education kills creativity and domesticates students. In order to be viable, education must be dialogical; there must be the exchange of opinions and ideas among all involved in the process. Effective education must also reflect community and empower the individuals within that community to think for themselves.

"Sometimes your verbiage is insufferable, Dad."

"You know, I think I agree with you. The main thing is we need to continue to serve as role models for Mystic Management. We need to continue to spread the new paradigm and, of course, that's where you come in, Ms. Sosa. With the help of people like yourself maybe we can give the Earth a shove in the right direction. Mystic Management is still only a molecule adrift among all other possibilities. It is imperative for that molecule to permanently bond to the fabric of the Earth's social matrix.

"Earth needs to openly embrace the principles of Mystic Management to establish the basis for a cell-matrix, bonding Earth and her inhabitants. The most important characteristics underlying the possibility of Earth achieving this cell-matrix are compassion and unconditional self-love. And this is where our connection to Eyespell can really make a difference. Myana and her Pink-Light-Corridor need to shine upon the Earth."

"I can do that," interjected Myana.

"Myana, you're here?"

"We're all here Phillip. We needed to listen to make sure you told poor Ms. Sosa the whole story. And you have done an admirable job, I must say. Oh, and some of the confusion with this part of the mind-link story, Koy, is our fault. There are you guys in the family room, Christian at his house, and we Eyespellians all open to channel so to speak. That leaves a lot of room for interference as well as distortion of linear time.

"But I do think Phillip is right about compassion and unconditional love. I have noticed from our observations that love is a difficult concept on earth. It seems to take many avenues and almost none of them unconditional. A very big stumbling block is self-love and one must love oneself before one can truly love others. One of Earth's love avenues, if I can put it that way, is that Earthlings are better at loving at a distance than up close. Distance allows little contact and no responsibility for those we claim to feel loving toward. Loving in the abstract is less challenging than loving in a firsthand, personal way. Consequently, those of Earth have serious problems with unconditional self-love. Self-love seems achievable only by starting outward from a global perspective and then working inward to the self. Unconditional self-love is the innermost circle of the system, the smallest sub-system, the most personal. It is the locomotive roundhouse connecting meaning and identity in the physical world, the psychological world, and the spiritual world. In this context, unconditional self-love is also the outermost circle of the system and the most global. It is the stuff that spirals in and out of all living molecules; it is the building block of the planetary cell-matrix."

"Myana, you're as bad as my father with your verbiage," said Christian. "You full-blooded Eyespellians are pretty hard to follow sometimes. I see that planet Earth, through Mystic Management, is beginning to spiral outward into the transcultural and inward into a self-assured identity. The outward is the easier task. It seems that the further an Earth being moves away from self, the easier it becomes to love unconditionally. Love for its own sake has never been simple to achieve within the typical Earth vibration. Unconditional love is of the light-skew."

"That was very impressive, Christian, and definitely much clearer than what Myana said. But I am afraid even your half-Eyespellian nature isn't doing much better at clearing this up. I think Koy's eyes just rolled up into her head. I think she is praying for escape."

"As Myana, Elder of Eyespell, and Keeper of the Pink-Light-Corridor, I am determined to make my point in plain Earthling."

"Wow, an elder with a sense of humor. Sorry, it's just that it's usually my son who makes the smart remarks; I tend to be more adult and respectful."

"Maybe Kathryn was right all along; we should have left Earth alone and certainly shouldn't have spent any time looking for you, Dr. Phillip Hansen, star psychologist. That was for you, Koy," Myana said, laughing. "Anyway, I think I have the explanation we are looking for. On Earth, it appears that one can more easily and without expectations, take up the cause of an unknown child in a third world country, than the cause of a child across town, than the cause of a distant relative's child, than the cause of a sister's child, than the cause of a sister, than the cause of one's own child, and, most difficult of all, the cause of one's own inner child. It seems that the closer to self one gets, the more conditional the love; the more likely there are rules and expectations. 'I will do this if you won't do that'; 'I'll help if you promise to or not to ...'"

"Hurray for Myana," chimed in Christian, "except the sentence was too long and *than* was in it too many times. One thing I am pretty sure of is that people seem to be secretly terrified that something awful lurks inside them, something that might surface at any moment. This fear often leads to vibrations of things such as anger, hurt, pain, anxiety, guilt, worry, depression, and other symptoms of lost identity and poor self-concept. These inner feelings, whether manifested in any action or not, certainly make unconditional self-love a trying task. Trust me, I know. It's only recently that I have been able to sense my Eyespellian heritage. While I've been fortunate to have Mom and Dad as coaches, I've not always been so sure of myself or so able to love myself unconditionally."

Phillip was pensive. After a few moments he said, "Living on the Earth is like living in a vibrational cesspool. The trick is to survive life within the cesspool without becoming an integral part of its contents. The time of madness was my deepest immersion in the dark-skew; I was in the deepest part of the cesspool. If it wasn't for your mother, Christian, I don't know what would have become of me. Unfortunately, the dark-skew has its share of followers. There are those who have, indeed, willingly become an integral part of the cesspool. Many on Earth vehemently oppose the concepts of Mystic Management. In fact, I came across a pamphlet just yesterday launching devastating attacks against the new paradigm."

"Was that the one called 'Mystic Nonsense?' asked Christian.

"Yes, where did you see it?"

"It has been widely distributed, believe me. That pamphlet is quite a piece of propaganda. I hope this type of opposition doesn't slow the fruition of our efforts. In this case, the vibration smacks of mixed-message humor and black satire. It's just clever enough to confuse those who may be on the fence.

What's really disconcerting is that we are personally attacked. Our Mystic Management message is reduced to Pollyanna nonsense. Our opponents say that paradigms like Mystic Management will cost people their livelihoods, and maybe even their lives. You know how we say the old paradigm kills; well, they say the new paradigm kills."

"A loving message is deemed a dangerous thing to some people," Myana softly stated. "Could you mind-scan the pamphlet for me? You've got me curious."

"Allow me," said Phillip. "It's more like a speech than a pamphlet. Maybe even more like a sermon."

Mystic Management or Mystic Nonsense?

I believe that forces of good and evil battle all around us. I further believe that positive thoughts draw good vibrations and negative thoughts draw evil vibrations. And, most importantly, I believe that each of us is responsible for the vibrations we create and the energies those vibrations potentially unleash into our shared life space.

The most significant concept I will ever share with you is this: I believe that internal disharmony is the most subtle and widespread form of evil. I believe that individual internal disharmony is the springboard from which mild dissatisfaction can escalate toward severe warring among the peoples of this planet.

And, I believe this new Mystic Management philosophy you've been hearing about has the potential to create just such disharmony. I believe it is a bunch of nonsense. I believe a paradigm like Mystic Management will cost you your jobs and your lifestyles just for starters. It is quick to tell you what to give up, but not so quick to replace your loss with anything but a bunch of well-sounding words.

I speak the truth, out-of-mouth, or is that, out-of-body; oh so sorry. This Mystic Management stuff causes a lot of heavy thinking and therefore, a lot of potential disharmony. For example, we are forced to think about things that might produce guilt. And then, even if we end up doing the right thing, whatever that may be, we do it out of that guilt. This costs us a great deal of mental energy and produces a lot of that internal disharmony I was talking about. Why should the right thing feel so bad? And before long, nobody is happy, nobody is laughing. We all sit around wishing we could bring the old ways back. And how often have each of us thought that?

Now, these insights did not come to me easily. I think the Hansens and their Mystic Management are just silly. Maybe they should call it The 'Star Light, Star Bright' School of Management Thought. Before you know it, they'll be telling us that all you have to do is wish it, and, poof, there it is! My, my, how convenient. What shall I create today? Kind of stupid, don't you think?

Myana said, "Some brilliant half-truths if do say do. Can't do much about that. Indeed, the greatest truth in what your clever opponent says is that 'the subtlest form of evil is internal disharmony.' Such disharmony would, for sure, block unconditional self-love. It is amazing how one thing always seems to eventually connect to everything else. The circle must be pure or it ultimately contaminates itself. But, you know what, I think despite efforts like "Mystic Management or Mystic Nonsense," the concepts of the Mystic Management will flourish and the Earth will be moving more toward the light-skew. Nothing can change that transforming night at Cathedral Rock when Earth and Eyespell connected. Our two planets are in undeniable vibrational crossover. We can never forget that there is a Higher Power at work here, a Power determined to save both of our planets."

* * * * * * * *

With no warning, the mind-link took on a totally different vibration. The message that came through very clearly to all was, "It is time to meet again at the Valley of the Blue Noon and at Cathedral Rock. My children, Phillip and Christian on Earth, and Leo and Peter on Eyespell, should began making preparations for a journey into the meadow."

CHAPTER 26

▼

IN THE FAMILY ROOM ...

"Oh my," said Phillip. "Seems like the rest of the story is yet to come. Was that the most amazing vibration you have ever felt? I think we should sit here for a few minutes and let it completely wash over us."

Phillip, Koy, and Jo sat in peaceful contemplation for a long while, Finally, Koy spoke up, "Oh my, is right. That was amazing. When you first started that last mind-link I felt so disappointed that Christian would go into politics."

"You? I about died," said Jo. "I was going to immediately disown him as a traitor to the Hansen teachings. As his mother, I was going to give him a good spanking."

"That sounds a bit kinky, my dear wife, but I think I would have helped you. I couldn't believe it when Christian chimed in and said 'no way.' He picked up on the mind-link distortion faster than I did."

"By the way," said Koy, "At first I had no idea Christian was with us, much less Eyespell."

"Mind-link can be funny that way," said Phillip. "Of course, I knew Christian was there but didn't realize Eyespell was listening in until Myana said something. Isn't her vibration something else?"

"I'd say," said Koy. "It seems that tonight I have become part of the Eyespell connection. Can't say I would have predicted that on my way here. Jo, are you in on this telepathy thing too?"

"Only in the same way that you are. I can receive a mind-link just like you can, but I can't interact with the link; I do not have telepathic powers. My spiritual stuff is different from Phillip's or Christian's. Actually you are very much like me in the way your spirit works. You just aren't consciously tuned in yet. Anyway, that last segment was quite something. It sure ended up different than it started. That part about the greatest form of evil being internal disharmony was very provocative. It was really close to another conversation that Phillip and Myana had awhile back about unconditional love. That was the other thing; that circle of love, with far away being easy and self-love the hardest. It took a minute, but the conclusion was very interesting. There's no question that unconditional self-love is sometimes very difficult to achieve, and that it's sometimes easier to love people at a distance, people we may not even know."

"Anyway, I still think this is the story you will never print, Ms. Sosa," said Phillip.

"We'll see, Dr. Hansen, we'll see."

"Let's call it a night," said Jo. "I think I need some alone time. I don't ever recall Cosmo visiting our home before and I need to recapture that vibration."

"Good plan," said Phillip. "Koy, see you in the morning."

"What an evening. This reporter spent a few hours in the family room of Dr. and Mrs. Phillip Hansen. Besides the Hansens, their dog Eric and a toy stuffed moose named Joseph, Cosmo stopped by for a minute. You may be right, this may be the story I will never print. Goodnight."

PART III

UNION

CHAPTER 27

▼

THE MEADOW

By the light of Earth's July full moon, and in monk's garb for a second time, Phillip and Christian made their way up the flank of Cathedral Rock. At the base of the central rock spire, they sat cross-legged, facing each other with knees touching. With the golden topaz between them, supported by the tips of their twenty fingers they fell into a deep meditative state.

By the light of Eyespell's Full Moon of Oneness, Peter and Leo made their way to the tower of rock in the center of the Valley of the Blue Noon. At the base of the central rock spire, they sat cross-legged, facing each other, knees touching. With the golden topaz between them, supported by the tips of their twenty fingers, they fell into a deep meditative state.

At Cathedral Rock the golden crystal's light expanded to embrace both father and son within a chamber of yellow light. At the Valley of the Blue Noon the golden crystal's light expanded to embrace both Elders within a chamber of yellow light.

The topaz light continued to expand in the two holy places as the four remained in deep meditative states. As the light further expanded, Earth and Eyespell achieved connection through an interstellar corridor of space and time. The four pilgrims, two from Earth and two from

Eyespell, moved through the corridor from opposite directions at faster-than-light speed to a place that sat exactly between the vibrations of the two planets.

As their minds reached outward, they saw a million-faceted mirrored ball spinning against the dance floor of infinite space. The colors of the universe reflected in the ball's silvered mirrors. As if on cue, the dance-floor ball exploded into a trillion dots of cosmic color, reforming into a beam of brilliant yellow-white light stretching far ahead of each pair of travelers. Their journey continued along the beam from opposite directions as if falling through a tunnel toward an incredible white light. Phillip recognized this as the same tunnel and light of his near-death experience just prior to his time of madness.

Within what seemed mere seconds from the onset of their journey, the four pilgrims in simple monk's garb spilled out from the tunnel onto the soft carpet of a lush green alpine-like meadow. There were two mountain streams appearing pencil thin against the larger perspective of the surrounding meadow. They were flowing down gentle slopes from opposite directions, cascading over moss-covered, rounded boulders. The melodic sound of water, making its way over the rounded rocks, soothed and invigorated. The wind almost imperceptibly sang in the uppermost reaches of the stately trees at the meadow's perimeter.

The four pilgrims walked to the edge of the meadow and stood on a ledge of neatly layered rock just above where the two streams merged. The crystal clear waters cascaded gently into a shimmering pool below them. Still awestruck by their journey and the beauty of their reached destination, no one moved or spoke. After several minutes, the four embraced and cried soft tears, tears of joy. It was as if Eyespell and Earth had joined like the streams meeting above the pool, as the four pilgrims embraced two separate but united worlds.

The yellow-white light they traveled upon intensified, as golden light specks drenched the meadow and its visitors like a spring morning's shower. Bathed in this light shower, the four pilgrims felt peacefulness and unconditional love. Language could only begin to pay tribute to the intensity of feeling.

A Figure of Light manifested before them and picked up the two golden topaz crystals lying on the ground before the four travelers. He gently merged them and reshaped them into a single perfect sphere. The sphere was placed in a small moss-covered cave of rock only slightly larger than its circumference. Just above the cave the two streams, for a distance separated, merged again and danced over the ledge of rock in a small waterfall shielding the cave entrance with a shimmering veil of water.

The Figure of Light sat among the four and spoke these words into their consciousness, "Welcome into the love and the light. The golden sphere is the symbol of the perfect manifestation of Divine Order. It is the coming of the spirit. The energy and essence of the four of you together in this place makes it possible for you to carry the vibrations of the meadow ten-thousandfold to Earth and ten-thousandfold to Eyespell."

"Earth and Eyespell come together in this meadow like the two streams. And, like the two streams, they merge as one. In this merging the continued evolution of both planets is assured. Eyespell will be of the light and Earth will be of the water. Light and water are of Eyespell and Earth." The Figure of Light touched their souls once again, leaving them bathed in spirit.

Peter, Leo, Phillip and Christian stayed in this holy meadow between Eyespell and Earth for ninety-nine days. The destinies of Earth and Eyespell were forever connected in visions of light and water, manifested in a meadow between two worlds.

CHAPTER 28

▼

THE ELDERNINE

Eyespell's cell-matrix finally stabilized and the planet once again moved in harmony with the light-skew, only now a light-skew not so fragile as to be destructively intolerant of vibrations unlike itself. Eyespell underwent major shifts and embraced rather than avoided Earth-plane vibrational leakage. Eyespell began to create a new reality, a reality meshing the vibrations of Earth and Eyespell.

It became increasingly evident that the dangers lie not in Earth-plane vibrational leakage, but in how it was perceived and dealt with. Earth vibrations never had the capability of destroying Eyespell, only Eyespellians were capable of destroying the planet and its light-skew. The problems arose through their own manifested terror of homeostasis, balance. The fear of Earth-plane vibrational leakage and its consequential negative impact was an Eyespellian-created reality. Although unintentional, the negative impact of Earth-plane vibrational leakage was, like everything else on Eyespell, manifested by the Eyespellians themselves. With the acceptance of Earth-plane vibrations, balance between the dark-skew and the light-skew was allowed to create a more inclusive reality.

Upon their return from the meadow, Peter and Leo brought this philosophy of inclusiveness as the solution to the planet's dilemma. The golden sphere shaped by the Being of Light symbolized inclusiveness through a melding of Earth and Eyespell. Leo visioned this new course for Eyespell, and through planetary mind-link, visioned the meeting in the meadow, the four pilgrims, and their encounter with the Being of Light. What happened in the meadow was brought ten-thousandfold to Eyespell. It did not take long for Earth-plane vibrational leakage to be reduced to the category of "different" rather than "dangerous"; something to embrace rather than to shrink from.

Under Leo and Peter's direction the Elders held several Full-Rounds expanding upon this new "Philosophy of Opposites." The objective was for this new philosophy to become integrated into Eyespell's collective consciousness and planetary cell-matrix. Because Eyespell was a culture of consensus, there was much discussion during the Full-Rounds. It was essential that each Eyespellian found right action through free choice. Expansion of Eyespell's consciousness could not be achieved through directives from the Council of Elders. Ultimately, the Philosophy of Opposites was incorporated with Mystic Management and new ideas and approaches began to expand the connotation of Inclusive Integrity. The Philosophy of Opposites specifically added an element of openness toward outside influences. Eyespell had always been loving and inclusive, but only within its own framework. Eyespell was capable, willing, and even eager to give of itself to the universe, and thus to the Eyespell Experiment. It was a compassionate planet. But Eyespell's framework did not include receiving back from the universe except from a Power even more of the light-skew than Eyespell itself. Embracing opposites or even differences was not part of what Eyespellians did. Coming to a philosophy that was *receiving* as well as *giving* was initially no easy task for the Eyespellian consciousness.

Ultimately, in an endeavor to embrace opposites, the vibrations of Earth were so completely absorbed that they manifested as new and darker colors of the Eyespellian rainbow. This new assemblage of colors in the deep indigo-to-purple-to-violet became part of Leo's crystal charge and the Blue-Light-Corridor. The pastel beauty of the planet was actually enhanced with the addition of this planned, understood, and appropriate contrast. The encounter with the Being of Light and the insights gleaned through His compassion and love were deemed so extraordinary that a new page entitled "Meadow Spirit" was added to

The Book of Dreams. What happened in the meadow was nothing less than a crossroads in Eyespellian evolution.

Mystic Management espoused, valued, and celebrated differences as never before. With this adjusted psyche and acceptance of even extreme opposites, Eyespell was for the first time truly secure in a multifaceted Universe, a dynamic giving-and-taking universe. Acknowledgment of Earth as a sister planet on its own pathway of the light-skew gave Eyespellians the ability to effectively deal with and dispel all fear of the dark-skew. As comfort with Earth vibrations increased and work with the new color configurations amplified, what was just awhile ago dubbed Earth-plane vibrational leakage, was now the basis not only for new colors in the Eyespellian rainbow, but also the basis for the formation of an entirely new light-corridor. The first hint of this phenomenon was the appearance in the Eyespellian consciousness of a glorious, deep purple amethyst crystal on a rope of light. This was unprecedented and magnificent. And who would be its keeper?

Antonio, Melissa, and Peter, with their Earth-fused memories, were tremendous assets in the conversion to balance and the expansion of the light-skew. It was still strange to think that Peter, now one of the Eldersix, had been Pete, NYC juvenile delinquent. However, it was just this type of fusion that made the psychological shift possible on Eyespell. Probably the most valuable and difficult lesson for Eyespell, and a prime reason for its continued vision of embracing differences, was the loss of Nancy and Daniel in the Domeshodar. All were convinced that such a loss could have been averted with their new, more balanced vision. Perhaps, with the new joining of Earth and Eyespell, even this grievous loss might yet have a positive resolution. With Daniel somewhere off-world and out-of-body for an indefinite period, cleansing his spirit of the Domeshodar, and Nancy still deep in the Domeshodar, there certainly existed a formidable challenge. But just maybe the Domeshodar might be a far less threatening place now with Earth-plane vibrational leakage as an ally.

****

As a very special birthday celebration and after having completed his role in the Earth's transition to Mystic Management, Phillip Hansen manifested permanently to Eyespell. He would not have been able to maintain his life force on planet Earth for much longer, and he was not yet ready to end his current incarnation. A new reentry window was created for him on Eyespell. On Earth it appeared that Phillip died peacefully in his sleep. It would have been difficult to leave Jo and Christian behind were it not for his telepathy link. They were literally never more than a thought away.

The missing Eyespellian had finally returned home several years after the original reentry window had closed on the Eyespell Experiment. He found himself naked under the fourth and most beautiful moon of Eyespell. The moon shone a bright pink across the white desert sands as if in his honor. Phillip's aging, Earthling frame had already tightened into the pleasant anatomy of the typical Eyespellian. It did not take long to become one with the planetary cell-matrix; he could feel it in every molecule of his being.

A light breeze swept over his limbs and carried a barely perceptible voice between its undulating currents, "I'm coming, I'm coming, I'm coming." Phillip instantly sensed the voice as Leo's. He looked up and caught a glimpse of Leo almost bounding over the evening-lit sands with a small bundle between his hands.

He stopped just short of Phillip, almost running him down in his excitement. He threw the bundle in the air and grasped him in a crushing bear hug. "You are the fifth one back! So many years late, but back nonetheless. I believe I've just thrown your clothes away. I think I'm excited." The sands shifted ever so slightly under their feet as the cell-matrix positively and excitedly responded to the long overdue reunion.

Phillip gathered up the bundle, spilled out the contents, and got dressed. With pure mischief in his eyes he said, "This may be the first time I've ever seen an Elder leaping through the sand. With so many years to plan it, you would think you could have hit my reentry a little closer."

"Yes, you would think. But, alas my son, just like the first time, you were the problem, not me. I almost had a fit when I reached the reentry point and you weren't there! My agitation probably caused a thunderstorm or two. I think I even used a little profanity, something I learned from you during your Earth-time. I was exactly where I was supposed to be, three dunes to the north. But you landed here. Just a flicker of a thought about the light tunnel that broke your telepathy link last time, and wham, you were three dunes off on reentry. That'll make an Elder leap!"

Phillip could barely stop laughing at Leo's feigned indignation. Finally he managed to say, "It feels so good here. I haven't laughed so hard in over a hundred years. The only comparable feelings on Earth are my love for Jo and Christian. I am even now in touch with them. I have obviously avoided any reentry trauma; everything seems in perfect working order."

"Wonderful. Bring your mind-friends and join us for the party. Everything is set."

"So where is this party?"

"Exactly three dunes to the north where I believe you were supposed to be in the first place."

Phillip's homecoming to Eyespell was nothing less than spectacular. There was light bending just-for-the-fun-of-it, rainbow making, and other games of the light-skew. The initial bouts of Earth-plane vibrational leakage bent on destroying Eyespell were gone and the planet cell-matrix felt whole with the return of this adventurer.

Phillip took up residence in Elaysia and almost immediately turned his psychic attention to issues of Eyespell's expanded Blue-Light-Corridor and what might be done about the still uncertain destinies of Daniel and Nancy. Perhaps his prolonged stay on Earth would allow him to intervene in a way impossible for any other Eyespellian. Phillip and Leo spent much time together, hypothesizing about what might be done and when. They often discussed the beautiful golden sphere and its having been left in the meadow to assure Eyespell's and Earth's joint destinies. They wondered if another visit to this meadow might hold the solution to Daniel and Nancy's problem. They shared their thoughts openly and there were exciting debates as to where the place of the yellow light might actually be in physical space, assuming, of course, that it had a physical reality. And that was the subject of even more exciting debate, was the meadow a real place? Things were quite normal on Eyespell; debate was lively and time was of no consequence.

And then it happened. In the midst of particularly lively planetary bantering about the exact whereabouts of the meadow, the deep amethyst crystal recently brought into Eyespellian awareness manifested in physical reality. It materialized hanging from its rope of light around the neck of none other than Phillip Hansen. The Eldersix instantly became the Elderseven with Phillip taking charge of the newly formed Purple-Light-Corridor. This was the coming of the spirit.

A Full-Round was immediately called and for the first time on Eyespell a Full-Round opened with the laser show from seven light-corridors coming from seven crystals in the twenty-seventh ring of the Council Chamber. And with this opening came other new things to Eyespell. The three hundred thirty-seven in the Council Chamber became three hundred thirty-eight. The planetary cell-matrix physically expanded to host a beautiful purple desert with its shifting sands of color in every hue of purple. A fifth and violet moon appeared in the night sky. And most amazing of all, new souls arrived on Eyespell as purple points of light. In-body, their cheeks shone ever so subtly with the beautiful purple tones of the spirit. The whole had become greater than the sum of its parts. There was, indeed, a cosmic synergy on Eyespell. The spirit of Eyespell filled the Pinar Galaxy.

Phillip took up his crystal charge and led his new soul mates into the purple desert for their first pilgrimage. They totaled two hundred twelve. Their robes were a deep purple and on each sleeve was the insignia of two planets in overlapping arcs, one distinctly blue and one distinctly pink. The area where the two planets overlapped was a purple-plum tone. The symbolism was of Earth and of Eyespell.

This first pilgrimage was both celebratory and solemn in its purpose. The celebration was one of new souls, a new light-corridor, and a new Elder's leadership. The immensity of this level of change on Eyespell was staggering even to the Eyespellian imagination. This was the first time the reality of Eyespell came from both inside and outside of the Eyespellian consciousness; it was a giving and a receiving. Eyespell had become an open system. Something else was different here. Eyespellian reality had always been predictable; it was, after all, created by consensus. This new reality, this expansion, was different. The manifestations of recent days did not appear to be totally controlled by Eyespell. The seeming contradiction was that the created reality of the Purple-Light-Corridor was both one of consensus and one of surprise. The physical manifestation of the amethyst crystal light charge was, in itself, a cosmic surprise. While Eyespellians had always been pleased with their creations, they had not been surprised by them. Moreover, the expansion of the planet's size and the fifth moon in the night sky seemed beyond the reality-creating abilities of mere Eyespellians or, at least they had never consciously thought to create anything of such magnitude. With the arrival of the souls of the Purple-Light-Corridor on planet Eyespell, all doubt about whether there was outside influence was erased. Eyespellians were certain this was not their creation. This was of the One Infinite Creator, this was of God.

This pilgrimage of the two hundred twelve to the purple desert was not the typical Eyespellian pilgrimage. The Elder leading such a happening always had a certainty of purpose and direction. Phillip was as an infant in his role as the Seventh Elder of Eyespell. He was not even clear where, exactly, out from Elaysia the purple desert was. It was even less clear what, exactly, it would be like in its topography or its vibration. For all practical purposes, except for a brief light show at the last Full-Round, no one on Eyespell had had any experience with the Purple-Light-Corridor. In spite of this uncharacteristic backdrop there was no fear of the unknown on Eyespell, simply quiet, focused, and yet childlike expectation.

After walking five days north and past the Valley of the Blue Noon, the party of two hundred twelve found themselves at the fringe of the purple desert. As they stood looking out for the first time over the multi-purple-hued dunes, dark colored sands washed over their feet in small waves of greeting. The colors in their cheeks sparkled in consonance with the gently tumbling grains of sand as they fell back into the desert. Phillip removed his crystal from its pouch and held it high above his head as the two hundred twelve introduced themselves to their new landscape. The party moved a short distance onto the purple sands and gathered into a prayer circle. This was a circle of joy, celebration, and welcomed new beginnings. It was in stark contrast to the circle of foreboding Leo had hastily formed to protect the Eyespell Experiment returnees from the first tremors of Earth-plane vibrational leakage in what seemed just a moment ago. Phillip now stood at the center of the circle and with his amethyst crystal pointed toward the heavens, opened the Purple-Light-Corridor and formally presented this new place to all of Eyespell. The purple vibration was now officially part of Eyespellian reality. After much rejoicing, the corridor was closed and the pilgrims set about the more solemn aspect of their first pilgrimage into the purple desert.

Phillip addressed the children of the Purple-Skew. "It has been a wonderful celebration of new life on Eyespell, both symbolically and literally. We are of the spirit. When I was on planet Earth and moved through the tunnel of near death, I saw a tribesman running and yelling "We are of the spirit, we are of the spirit, we are of the spirit!" The experience was profound. Even though it seemed totally disconnected from my conscious thoughts, I somehow knew that the tribesman was announcing the 'coming of the spirit.' I could feel his excitement. In the meadow somewhere apart from both Eyespell and Earth, the Being of Light used those same words. I thought that the coming of the spirit meant that the Being of Light would connect Earth and Eyespell in a cosmic dance. I had no inkling of this time and this place. I had no inkling of the destiny I now feel for us. I know that through the power of this light-corridor, the Purple-Light-Corridor, we can retrieve Daniel from out-of-body and save Nancy from the depths of the Domeshodar. We can make Eyespell truly whole again."

Each pilgrim spoke softly into Phillip's mind, "Let us begin."

Phillip knew intuitively to journey farther due north into the heart of the purple desert where he would find the place they sought to begin their work. This time he moved with the absolute certainty of an Elder leading a holy pilgrimage. The monks packed away their beautiful purple robes and donned the brown garb of serious business on Eyespell. They moved across the purple sands chanting, drenched in the light of the violet full moon.

At daybreak they came upon a succession of steep dunes leading upward like a giant stairway. At the top of the seventeenth dune the desert sands gave way to a concave carved bowl of lavender stone. The bowl sloped down to a huge cave entrance. Phillip knew this to be the place they were seeking. He led the pilgrims into the mouth of the cave. The vibration was reminiscent of the Valley of the Blue Noon as this too was a holy place. Whereas the valley of the Blue Noon stretched up and out from the landscape, the Cave of Purple Dawn, as it came to be called, leapt into the desert floor. The inside of the cave was lit as if by invisible candles, and shone mirror-like crystals of all shades of amethyst lining its walls and ceiling.

The pilgrims moved to its innermost sanctum and formed a tight 'ball of monk' part in-body and part out-of-body to become one with each other and the Purple Dawn surroundings. At the very core of the ball, Phillip pressed his crystal to his solar plexus and the two hundred twelve monks began to spin slowly in place in a counterclockwise direction. The Purple-Light-Corridor burst open creating an intense stream of deep purple, almost black, light from the Cave of the Purple Dawn to the Domeshodar. The energy force produced by this incredible burst of spirit pierced the blackness of the hole and snatched Nancy's essence, returning it to Eyespell filled with purple light. Nancy became one again with her body and awoke as if from a long sleep. She found herself in the cave surrounded by the absolute love of her soul mates. She glowed a deep purple.

Phillip was the first to speak. "Nancy, do you know where you are?"

Her reply was quick. "Know where I am? Of course, and you, Phillip, I see you finally made it home." Her broad smile and loving eyes did not speak of a woman whose vibrations, not long ago, threatened to destroy an entire planet. She hugged Phillip for a long time and in due course made physical contact with each Eyespellian in the cave, and mental contact with the entire planet of Eyespellians. She remembered nothing of the Domeshodar except that she had been there. The pilgrims, now numbering two hundred thirteen, left the cave.

Phillip's incredible excitement about Nancy's return was only slightly dampened by the failure to bring Daniel back to Eyespell. He thought to himself, "I'm sure we will succeed next time."

"What do you mean next time?" The booming voice reverberated around the cave's opening and seemed to mightily bounce off the concave floor and into everyone's head.

Phillip and the others looked around but in the glare of the yellow sun high over the desert could not see anyone. Nonetheless, Phillip could feel the strong vibrations that went with the ever-so-strong voice. And then, from out of the shadow of a giant bristle cone tree growing out of the rock, stepped a tall, very black man. Around his neck hung, from a rope of light, a pitch-black smoky quartz crystal. All of Eyespell recognized the vibration of this man; it was Daniel. The Elderseven were now Eight.

"Yes, I am Daniel and you have brought me home, Phillip Hansen, or should I say Elder Phillip Hansen?"

Phillip was unable to speak. He approached Daniel and put his hands around the black crystal hanging at his chest. He was astounded at what he felt.

Daniel laughed a booming laugh. "Curious, isn't it? Mine is the Crystal of the No-Light-Corridor. All of Eyespell's light-corridors are my no-light-skew. I am the black pigment in the white paint. Mine is the crystal charge that will give Eyespell ultimate balance and ultimate protection. I complete the circle from Gracina's White-Light-Corridor to this, the No-Light-Corridor. There is so much power in my blackness that I manage this charge alone. I will remain the only one like me on Eyespell. My return is the ultimate gift of the two things Eyespell has feared, Earth-plane vibrational leakage and the Domeshodar."

Phillip hugged Daniel and all of Eyespell welcomed him home. The only thing Phillip managed to say was, "So what do you think of this purple desert?" All had a good laugh at Phillip the Elder's inability to verbally express his incredulous amazement at the events in the purple desert and the Cave of the Purple Dawn.

It wasn't long before Eyespell got back down to the business of debating the all-illusive whereabouts of the meadow. But they had time.

****

Earth's new vision took on physical as well as psychological expression. Within a mere quarter of a century after Phillip and Christian returned to Earth from the meadow, Mystic Management had permeated almost every major corporation, government, and educational institution across the planet. Subsequent to his father's return to Eyespell, Christian Hansen carried on the work of Mystic Management and was instrumental in the planet's sustained movement toward the light-skew. Christian vigorously pursued his objectives for UWW, Used Water Works. His objective was to infuse the Mystic Management philosophy on a local and a global level through UWW's example.

Jo Hansen, showing only about a third of her age, stubbornly insisted upon remaining on the Earth-plane. She said that she had much left to do and her time to manifest elsewhere had not yet come. Whenever Christian became too insistent upon her leaving the Earth-plane for, perhaps Eyespell, Jo was quick to remind her son of his own "getting older" status. On Earth, unlike on Eyespell, there was not yet general acknowledgment of the existence of a sister planet moving in concert with a cosmic plan. While the acceptance of divine help had always been within the scope of the Earth psyche, the concept of extraterrestrials helping the Earth move toward the light-skew was not yet a part of most people's thinking.

Capitalizing on Christian Hansen's Eyespellian heritage, the Elders used sustained mind-link to bring the Mystic Management teachings of the Council directly to the Earth-plane. These times of sustained link were dubbed Earth Summits. They were planned gatherings drawing large crowds, and typically "awakened" many already enlightened souls on planet Earth. The continual movement toward the light-skew was greatly enhanced by these sessions and was most noticeable in the slow metamorphosis toward a planetary cell-matrix. The connection between the aliveness of the planet and its inhabitants was undeniably apparent. For the first time people of Earth noticed the relationship between feelings and physical reality. It became obvious that the planet's physical/geological well-being was tied to its inhabitants' psychological well-being. A harmony espoused by the lofty ideals of Mystic Management seemed appropriate for keeping the Earth intact. Compassionate community-building was central to the Earth's conscious move toward sustainability and the focus of this newly recognized relationship between people and planet.

****

Ultimately, the conflicts between disciplines such as economics and ecology dissipated as the Constant Harvest Philosophy replaced the myth of inexhaustibility. This fresh direction for Earth evolved through its water conservation technology, the benchmark for which was set by Christian's leadership in Used Water Works. UWW developed crystalline city-structures that evolved out of their visionary water resource technologies. And with the advent of the first crystalline cities, the basis for Kensian economic thought became almost instantly outmoded. New strategies were in order, strategies steadfastly bound to the long-term survival of planet Earth.

The groundwork for this transformation had existed since the late twentieth century, beginning with the biosphere experiments in the New Mexico desert. UWW's conception of crystal-like city structures that combined water conservation technology, a new economic paradigm of "prophets not profits," Mystic Management, and an environmentally-alive cityscape, would become the new model of sustainability. This was the crossroads in Earth evolution much like the advent of the Purple-Light-Corridor was the crossroads that permanently shifted Eyespell's consciousness.

The first crystalline structure was built in Death Valley, California. It was based on the hexagonal properties of the quartz crystal replicated in huge double pyramids. Each was some two thousand feet across and ten stories high at its mid-point. The first crystal city contained twenty-seven clustered pyramids and three thousand thirty-nine permanent inhabitants.

Of course, Christian, his wife Sally, their two children and Christian's mother Jo were among the first citizens of the new crystal city. The city very quickly became a place of inclusive community. Several of the CEOs who had attended Christian's and Phillip's seminars on Mystic Management relocated their companies, their employees, and their families to the City of Light as it came to be known. Folks like John Beechmont, the fellow who had delivered the topaz to Phillip and Christian, and John Telamanni, Phillip's psychiatrist, retired to the city. Sam Simpson finally grew up and married Koy Sosa, the first Mayor of the City of Light and author of the bestselling book, *The Story I Said I'd Never Print*.

The inhabitants lived, played and worked within the crystal environments. The natural evolution from fragmentation to community put the world on notice that it could be done. The energy of the structure itself was healing and the relationships among the residents, and between the people and the planet, could be felt from every corner of the pyramid city. Within this city and among its inhabitants, the nature of community eventually enhanced communication skills to within a whisper of telepathy, mind-link, and cell-matrix as experienced on Eyespell. And this first city would become the template for all cities on Earth throughout the next millennia.

The water recycling technology of UWW formed the most critical infrastructure for these new cities. All water was captured, rejuvenated, and prepared for reuse. It was possible to capture ninety percent of the water on the first complete cycle alone. In economic terms, that meant if all of California used 35 million acre-feet of water per year, after the first year of recycling, some 31.5 million acre-feet of water could be available for reuse. Maintaining the same level of productivity in the second year would demand only 3.5 million acre-feet of "new" water. These statistics ultimately had a dramatic impact on productivity and sustainability. Perhaps even more important, the process allowed for tremendous population density increase at no additional long-term costs either financially or environmentally.

Integral to this new vision, the various landscapes outside of the structures were restored to their natural wetland, woodland, desert, forest, or other pristine state. There was no reason to further ravage the land in the name of progress. Over the next hundred years crystal structures were erected on sites where the natural landscape had been previously destroyed, such as locations of cities then gone or places where the natural aquifers had collapsed due to over-pumping, mining, or other man-made disasters.

The new cities provided agriculture, industry, government, education, and leisure activity. There was, of course, no restriction of movement between cities, nor was there any reason to remain confined within a crystal structure. The physical face of civilization on planet Earth was dramatically and positively altered. The waters of the Earth flowed freely as the water molecule itself encompassed Earth's vision and became the first step in reality creating. The planetary cell-matrix for Earth was strengthening as boundaries and personal ownership were weakening in the face of the new communities directed by the Law of One.

In future centuries, the light of Eyespell and the water of Earth might create yet another mystic paradigm. Someday extraterrestrial brothers might retrieve the golden sphere in the meadow. Today as Christian Hansen stood at the apex of his pyramid abode, watching the sun slowly rise over the desert, a brilliant water-clear crystal on its rope of light manifested around his neck. The Eldereight became Nine in a definitive cosmic gesture of planets joined.

About The Author

John Cicero lives in Northern California with his wife Christina. He is on the faculty of the business department at the local community college. He has forty-plus years of blended work experience including: faculty at community college and university levels, middle manager for a Fortune 500 company, and private practitioner as a psychotherapist. His PhD and MBA degrees are from Syracuse University and his AB is from the University of Rochester. You can find additional information at http://www.mysticmangement.com.

28099302R00173

Made in the USA
Lexington, KY
07 December 2013